COMMUNICATING PROFESSIONALLY

A How-To-Do-It Manual
for Library Applications

CATHERINE SHELDRICK ROSS
PATRICIA DEWDNEY

HOW-TO-DO-IT MANUALS
FOR LIBRARIES
Number 3

Series Editor: Bill Katz

NEAL-SCHUMAN PUBLISHERS, INC.
New York, London   1989

Published by Neal-Schuman Publishers, Inc.
100 Varick Street
New York, NY 10013

Printed and bound in the United States of America

Library of Congress Cataloging-in-Publication Data

Ross, Catherine Sheldrick.
    Communicating professionally : a how-to-do-it manual for
librarians / Catherine Sheldrick Ross, Patricia Dewdney.
        p.   cm.—(How to do it manuals for libraries ; no. 3)
    Bibliography: p.
    Includes index.
    ISBN 1-55570-031-4
    1. Communication in library administration.   2. Communication in
library science.   3. Library employees—Training of.   4. Library
science—Authorship.   5. Librarians.   I. Dewdney, Patricia.
II. Title.   III. Series.
Z678.R65   1989
023′.9—dc19   88-35713

CONTENTS

SERIES EDITOR'S PREFACE

Necessity may be the mother of invention. It is also the progenitor of Neal-Schuman's series of How-To-Do-It Manuals for Libraries. The necessity is the pressure on today's librarians to master an ever-widening universe of responsibilities. One librarian is often expected to possess a working knowledge of budgeting, computer applications, space planning and fund-raising. The list goes on and on.

The books in the How-To-Do-It series are designed to help library professionals keep pace with the varied, increasing demands on our time and talents. Each volume in the series covers a specific area, offering practical advice and information.

The initial two books in the series—*Managing Change* and *Using Lotus 1-2-3*—explained, respectively, how to plan, implement, and evaluate change in libraries and how to utilize the spreadsheet program Lotus 1-2-3 for library applications. This, the third book, is devoted to a facet of our professional lives that is increasingly important in our complex environment—communication. The main business of librarians, after all, is sharing information.

Catherine Ross and Patricia Dewdney—masters of the communication art themselves—offer verbal and nonverbal communications techniques along with specific, library-oriented applications. They include solid advice on speaking in public, leading group discussion, and communicating one on one. And they make concrete suggestions on writing reports and proposals and on teaching communications skills to library support staff.

This book will give us the tools we need to fulfill our basic mission as sharers of information.

Bill Katz

PREFACE

We've written this book in response to the many librarians, educators, and students who have asked us, "Where can we read about these communication skills?" or "How can we get copies of your transparencies?" or "Can we use your handouts to develop our own staff training?" Indeed, much of this book is based on the handouts and discussion guides that we use in our own courses and workshops. Some material was developed in teaching Reference and Interpersonal Communication courses at the School of Library and Information Science, University of Western Ontario. Other material was developed for our continuing education workshop, "How To Find Out What People Really Want To Know," which we initiated in 1982 as a way of taking our classes on the reference interview out to libraries and community information centers. But this book has become more than a collection of teaching materials. It reflects a particular way of thinking about information service and the communication skills that are needed in our field. And it incorporates two major influences: microtraining and sense-making.

Microtraining or microcounseling is a model developed by Allen E. Ivey and his colleagues at Stanford University in the 1960s for teaching interview skills to counselors. Trying to answer the question, "What makes a good interviewer?" Ivey discovered that what distinguished effective interviewers from ineffective ones, regardless of their theoretical orientation, was the use of certain skills. Furthermore, he discovered that these skills could be taught. The training method developed by Ivey for teaching interviewing skills is called microtraining because it breaks down a complex activity into its constituent parts or small (micro) skills. The trainee learns each skill, one at a time, in a systematic way that involves the following steps:

1. Getting a brief introduction to the skill
2. Observing the skill modeled
3. Reading about the skill and the concepts behind it
4. Practice of the skill in a context that provides feedback (e.g., audiotaping or videotaping).

Originally developed to train novice counselors, the microtraining model has been adapted to other fields, including librarianship. Elaine Z. Jennerich was the first person to use microtraining to teach interview skills to library school students. Intrigued by her positive results, we began to experiment with microtraining as a way of teaching basic listening skills for the reference interview—restatement, open questions, minimal encouragers, and the skill clusters of closure and avoiding premature diagnosis. We some-times added nonverbal skills such as eye contact, gesturing, and posture in a section on cross-cultural communication. Following the essential steps in the microtraining method, we focused on one skill at a time, defining the skill, modeling it, and involving students in role playing interviews. Students went through the stages of first being able to define the skill; second being able to identify it when they saw other people performing the skill; third being able to perform the skill themselves; and finally knowing under what circumstances it is suitable to use the skill. It ap-peared that the most effective method for teaching the skills involves the learner in a combination of activities: hearing short presentations in lecture format; doing independent reading; get-ting actual experience practicing the skill (and receiving feed-back); and discussing the experience afterwards in a small group setting.

This process of adapting microtraining to teaching communi-cation skills to librarians wasn't, of course, as smooth as it sounds in this account. Students reported problems. "If you teach us to nod and smile and ask open questions," they objected, "how is this different from what a store clerk learns when she's required to say to every customer, 'Have a nice day. Thank you for shopping at X.'" Or they said, "When I have to concentrate on how I formulate questions, I find that I can't think of anything to say." (Ivey calls this "the millipede effect": when a millipede stops to think about how it manages to walk, it becomes paralyzed.) One person said, "You said we should practice the skills in our everyday life, so I tried out acknowledgment on my job in the doughnut shop, and this guy looked at me like I was crazy."

Thinking about these problems, we found that we needed to emphasize two things: the concept of intentionality or choice; and the difference between learning the skill in the first place and using it with mastery later. Once articulated, these ideas, which are interconnected, seem familiar, even self-evident. They have been pointed out in a variety of fields. The first edition of *The Chicago Manual of Style*, for example, introduces its rules by saying that there is no rule that can't be broken, if the writer's purpose requires it. E.H. Gombrich in *The Sense of Order: A study in the psychology of decorative art* (Ithaca, NY: Cornell University Press, 1979—p.11) says, "Whether we use a typewriter, ride a bicycle or play the piano, we first learn to 'master' the basic movements without attending to them all the time, so that our conscious mind is left free to plan and direct the over-arching structures. . . . There is no craft which does not demand this breakdown of the skill into elements which are steered by the larger movement; mastery of plaiting, weaving, stitching or carving demands this structure of routines collectively guided by the conscious mind." The early stages of learning require concentrated attention on the small units until those units become automatic. At this point the units become part of our repertoire of responses, to be used when appropriate, and the mind is free to concentrate on the larger purpose. The problem with the store clerk who says, "Have a nice day" is that the response is automatic (too automatic) but it is not used with intentionality: the response has become mechanical because it is divorced from genuine feeling or purpose.

Through all this, we found it useful to keep reminding ourselves of Ivey's concept of intentionality (further described in Chapter 5). Intentionality has to do with choice: once the trainee has acquired the ability to use individual skills and to integrate them, he or she needs to be able to judge when these skills are appropriate, what effect they are likely to have, and what is the range of potentially helpful responses to a particular situation. As Ivey says:

> The intentional individual has more than one action, thought or behavior to choose from in responding to changing life situations. The intentional individual can generate alternatives in a given situation and approach a problem from different vantage points, using a variety of skills and personal qualities, adapting styles to suit different cultural groups. The intentional interviewer remembers a basic rule of helping: if something you try doesn't work, don't try more of the same . . . try something different!. . . Intentionality demands the ability to be flexible at the moment and try new approaches (Allen E. Ivey. *Intentional Interviewing and Counseling.* Monterey, CA: Brooks/Cole Publishing Company, 1983, pp. 3-4).

The microtraining model provided a helpful approach to teaching, but the problem remained of what to teach. Ivey had identified the set of microskills necessary to counselors, but do librarians need the same skills? We still did not feel that we had an underlying theory of information service from which we could identify the skills most appropriate to the job of linking people to our information systems. And we still needed more empirically based research to determine if, in fact, the reference interview—that microcosm of information service, that fleeting encounter with a stranger who asks for "the law section" or "The Lamplighter's Serenade"— differed fundamentally from the counseling interview in its goal, environment, and process. If it differed, would the skills suitable for the counseling interview still be appropriate? We read the literature looking for a structure that would pull it all together and justify the use of microtraining in the context of information services. But the prevailing paradigms of communication, including the "source/channel/receiver" model, did not seem to be any more helpful than the "warmth/empathy/genuineness" model of counseling psychology. Books on interpersonal communication for librarians either seemed too general ("Establish a good communication climate with the user") or else seemed not applicable to the vast number of situations in which people seek information. Clearly, we needed a different theoretical basis.

Enter Brenda Dervin, a communications researcher then at the University of Washington in Seattle. In 1977, Dervin and her colleagues had completed an extensive study of the ways in which citizens go about resolving their everyday information needs. They found that information providers could be more helpful when they changed the way they thought about information. Typically, information is thought of as an objectively existing and self-contained construct, some kind of commodity to be bought, stored, and transferred. From this perspective, the evaluation of information service would involve counting how many units of information were being bought, stored, and transferred in the system. Dervin argued that information providers needed to think of information, not in the context of the system but in the context of people's lives. She urged information providers to ask: "How does information help individuals deal with particular problems or situations that arise in their lives?"

That is, we must focus on the situations that generate information needs, the questions people have about these situations ("gaps"), and the ways in which people hope to use the information as a way of responding to these situations ("uses"). Further, these "situations," "gaps," and "uses" are not only important dimensions to the individual user but also universal dimensions that structure all information-seeking behavior. From this research, Dervin had developed "Turning Public Libraries Around," a series of workshops for California librarians, in which she introduced the theory she calls "sense-making" and the technique of neutral questioning. Here at last was a systematic basis for developing dynamic interviewing strategies, a framework that was consistent with the microtraining model but took into account the nature of information service. "Information," in Dervin's terms, is the process of making new sense or getting a new picture of the world in order to move ahead. (If this brief description is not intelligible to you now, read Chapter 5.2 for a more detailed explanation of sense-making theory.)

Our teaching began to change. We introduced the concept of sense-making, somewhat tentatively, into our training sessions, and developed a method of teaching neutral questions as a special form of open questions. An important point about the sense-making approach is its emphasis on the active nature of the sense-maker. Some theories reduce the people on the receiving end of information to passive, receptive individuals who consume the fixed meanings that already are contained in texts. Sense-making, in contrast, postulates that people are actively involved in making sense out of texts, constructing their own meanings in order to construct their own reality. Therefore sense-making is compatible with theories of reading and writing (like reader-response criticism) that are reader-centered rather than writer-centered or text-centered. Sense-making as a framework suggested new ways of thinking about and teaching writing skills. Writers are helped, for example, if they think of a piece of writing not as a self-contained object but as part of a transaction with a reader. To write a useful report, the writer should consider the situation that has made the report necessary, the questions that readers might have in their minds, and the ways in which readers might expect to use the report.

We found at the same time that we could extend the microtraining method to written communication and to group work. For written communication, the components that make for effectiveness can be identified (unity, coherence, clarity, brevity, variety, force, correctness, etc.), modeled, practiced, and taught. Many of the microskills that contribute to an effective interview are identifiable in group work, as psychologist Douglas Bales demonstrated many years ago in his work on group interaction. There is no reason, then, why group skills cannot be taught as part of a microtraining program. Accordingly, we tried out some of these ideas on our graduate students with some success.

In 1982, deciding that we needed to take some of these ideas out to the front lines, we developed the first version of our workshop on the reference interview, "How to Find Out What People Really Want to Know." This workshop used a microtraining approach to teach not only basic listening skills but also neutral questioning. Participants have told us that the workshop has helped them feel more in control of their work and more able to carry it out effectively. As one person put it, "Now there are options and choices that can be made. What a sense of control it gives to know what these skills can do." And some reported that the training improved their ability to communicate in their personal lives—with family and friends. In order to investigate the effects of this training more systematically, we began an ambitious field experiment to observe reference interviews in public libraries. Analysis of actual reference interviews conducted after training revealed that librarians could demonstrate their new skills on the job.

In 1987, our graduate school established a compulsory half-course in Professional Communication, which we welcomed as an explicit recognition of the importance of communication skills for people in our field. However, we had no textbook. The problem was not a shortage of books and articles on communication. If anything, there was an embarrassment of riches. But the information was scattered, and there were never enough exercises or examples drawn from a library context. We used Ivey's excellent book *Intentional Interviewing and Counseling* as the basis for teaching microskills, but students said they found the social work context distracting (especially when the interviewer in the modeled interviews asked about drinking problems and the interviewee's fear of going out of the house.) Students kept reminding us that "librarianship is not social work" and they demanded library examples.

In the meantime, people who had participated in our workshops or heard about them were writing to us for "the course materials," which, we confess, existed in two battered briefcases and consisted of a one-page outline with cryptic notes such as "CSR: NQ exercise: Alzheimer's 20 min.," 63 index cards for role-playing, some 900 brief accounts of reference interviews gone wrong collected from previous workshop participants, 20 handsome (and some not so handsome) transparencies in a pizza box, several modeling tapes, the "kits" or handouts, and an overworked tape recorder. Clearly, we could not expect anyone else to make sense of these items for their own training purposes. We decided to write this book.

Our colleagues in this enterprise have been the students who advised us by telling us what sort of help they needed to learn communication skills, students of the Professional Communication course who provided feedback on early drafts of this book, the workshop participants who shared with us their examples of interviews gone wrong, and the librarians who participated in a field experiment that involved the audiotaping and transcribing of over 330 reference transactions. In addition, we would like to thank very much the following people for reading drafts of the manuscript and offering ideas and suggestions which we have used freely: Bryce Allen, John Fracasso, Marti Grof-Iannelli, Roma

Harris, Mark Kinnucan, Louise Tamblyn, Gillian Michell, Paul Nicholls, Tom Rush, Betty Turock, and Don Vincent. For getting the manuscript into its final form, we thank Ellen Mangin and Susan Holt, editors, Casey Roberts, typesetter, and Alice Puddephatt, indexer. We also thank the Ontario Ministry of Culture and Communications and the Social Sciences and Humanities Research Council of Canada for their financial support of research involving observing librarians in their daily work with library users. And special thanks to three people who have influenced our philosophy of human communication—Mary Barber, Brenda Dervin, and Allen Ivey.

INTRODUCTION

HOW THIS BOOK IS ORGANIZED

In arranging *Communicating Professionally,* we've followed the basic microtraining approach. First, we present single communication skills with instructions for learning one skill at a time (Chapters 1 to 4). We show different approaches to learning each skill: each skill is defined, examples are provided, exercises are included for demonstration and practice, and the functions or effects of the skill are discussed. In keeping with the idea that theory presentation is not essential to the initial stages of learning a skill, we have delayed our discussion of the sense-making theory until Chapter 5, where we also elaborate the concept of intentionality, discuss the skills of integration, and provide some practical tips for practicing the skills. However, we've used a modular format so that you can begin anywhere.

You may prefer to begin with the theoretical aspects presented in Chapter 5 and then work through Chapters 1 to 4. The second main section, Chapters 6 to 9, consists of applications of the skills. Here we have chosen to discuss what we consider to be the most common situations in libraries that require the use of listening, speaking, or writing skills. Since any particular application usually requires the use of a combination of skills, we will refer you to relevant parts of the Skills Chapters. Therefore, if you want to begin with any particular application, you can read about the application first and then move back to the skills sections to find specific ways of responding to the situations described. Finally, Chapter 10 provides guidelines for educators or staff trainers who want to use this book to teach others.

Since learning is an active process centered in the learner, we want to involve you as much as possible in the process of discovery. Therefore, in many ways, this book presents a series of starting points for your own further exploration. Throughout the book, we've included units labelled *Did you know?* as a way of briefly introducing research results and interesting facts or examples. Most sections also include *Quick tips*—a selective list of practical hints that we've found useful—or at least worth trying. *Exercises* are included because it is not sufficient to read about a skill: to learn it you have to do it yourself. We stress this because learners have repeatedly told us that something that seemed simpleminded and easy when they read about it proved unexpectedly rich, complex, and tricky when they tried it. Every section includes suggestions *For further help* consisting of books, articles, and nonbook sources that you might want to look up. These references are by no means exhaustive; they are the publications, audiovisual aids, and people that we have found most helpful, but there are undoubtedly many more. In some cases, we have substituted references for discussion or tips because someone else has already done a much better job than we could ever do on a particular topic.

WHO CAN USE THIS BOOK?

Anybody. We subscribe to the philosophy expressed by Dale Larson in *Teaching Psychological Skills: Models for Giving Psychology Away* (Monterey, CA: Brooks/Cole, 1984) that people are weary of professional mystification. Anyone (professional or not) who has been taught helping skills can be a helper; anyone who is in need of skills can be helped. We see this book as useful not only to librarians, but to library volunteers, staff trainers, clerical assistants, board members, and information and referral counselors. (The term "librarian" throughout refers to anyone involved directly or indirectly in library and/or information service.) In short, the book is for anyone who wants to improve communication skills in the library context or help others do so. An experienced trainer can pass on the skills not only to staff but also to library users—for example, through teaching the skills needed for good book discussion groups, as the Great Books Foundation has been doing for many years.

Having said that anyone can use this book, we must add a few cautionary notes. Individuals who use this book for independent study may initially feel awkward or frustrated in practicing the individual skills or in trying to integrate the skills into their everyday behavior. This is normal! When you have a communication accident, try the tips for recovering in Chapter 5. Get support and help from others if you can. In a group training situation, the best results will come with an experienced, supportive leader (which you can all become, eventually—but begin training on a small scale first.) Use the ideas and materials in this book, but develop your own style. If something doesn't work, try it again. Examine what happens carefully. If you try again and it still doesn't work, quit, as the old saying goes, before you make a fool of yourself. Try something different. Take from this book what works for you in your situation. Perhaps you'll just copy a page for a transparency; maybe you'll use this book to develop a course outline; or you might find one or two tips that help you improve the way you handle a problem situation.

More important, you'll probably get better results from this book if you happen to share some of our fundamental beliefs that are not explicitly expressed elsewhere:

First, the primary mission of a library or information center is to serve its community by linking users (or potential users) with resources that meet their diverse and ever-changing information needs. (This may seem self-evident, but it's the premise on which all our other assumptions are based.)

Second, communication skills are important. Anyone in any kind of helping profession needs to be able to listen effectively, to ask productive questions, to write clearly, and to help groups function efficiently. The success of our mission and the survival of our institutions depend on our individual abilities to communicate.

Third (and less generally believed), communication skills are learned, rather than innate. Even those people who seem to be naturally good at interpersonal communication have learned these skills in their early lives, often from modeling others. And we know from research studies that those people who do not seem to be very good at interpersonal communication show the most immediate and lasting improvement in their behavior after training.

Finally, the training tools exist. It *is* possible for us to train our own people. The methodology and resources for successfully identifying, teaching, learning, applying, and evaluating human communication skills have existed for many years in other helping professions—social work, teaching, counseling, and health services. Now, with the sense-making approach, we have the framework for teaching those skills within librarianship and information service.

In other words, this book takes a people-oriented rather than a system-oriented approach to information service. If you believe that people can change, and that they really do want to learn how to give better service, then this book will provide you with some of the tools for helping yourself and others. Through systematic observation of behavioral changes and through feedback from our trainees, we know that these skills *can* be learned and *do* work in actual on-the-job situations.

LEARN, DO, TEACH . . . AND FEEDBACK

Allen Ivey advises his microcounseling trainees to "learn, do, and teach." The first stage of learning a skill is demonstrating the skill, not just reading about it. Learning involves practicing the skill immediately, right in the training group. The second stage is practicing or using the skill in real-life, on-the-job situations, as a way of integrating the skill into everyday behavior and experimenting with specific behavioral contexts or situations. The final stage of skill mastery is teaching another person. When you are able to teach someone else, you have truly mastered the skill. Make a commitment to the process by contracting with yourself to "learn, do, and teach" as you work through this book, whether you use it as an individual self-study manual or as a guide to group training. And we would like to hear from you. Let us know what works for you, how you adapt the material, and what new ideas or exercises you develop. We hope that you will not only make a "learn, do, and teach" contract but will also provide us with feedback so that we too can go through that cycle again.

PART I

SKILLS

1 NONVERBAL BEHAVIOR

1.1 INTRODUCTION TO NONVERBAL BEHAVIOR

Nonverbal messages are conveyed by such things as eye contact, tone of voice, facial expression, posture, gestures, positioning of arms and legs, styles of dress, or your distance from another person. Researchers have distinguished various dimensions of nonverbal behavior:

kinesics—the way we use our bodies, head, arms, legs, etc.

proxemics—the way we use interpersonal space; the distance we stand from another person

paralanguage—how we say something: the pitch, rate, loudness, and inflection of our speech

chronemics—the way we time our verbal exchanges

These nonverbal cues convey nuances of meaning and emotion that reinforce or contradict the verbal message.

When interpreting the meaning of any communication, people rely on both verbal and nonverbal cues. But if there is a discrepancy between the verbal and the nonverbal message, people believe the nonverbal message. Nonverbal communication speaks louder than words. Compare:

That's interesting. [Said in an appreciative tone, as the speaker smiles and looks at the other person.]

That's interesting. [Said in a bored tone, as the speaker looks away from the other person.]

In the second example, the verbal message, or *what* was said is contradicted by the paralanguage, the *way* it was said.

The following nonverbal behaviors all work together and reinforce each other. Notice your own use of nonverbal communication. Which skills are you already using? Which ones need practice?

Exercise

SOUNDLESS TV
Develop your awareness of body language. Watch a television program with the sound turned off. Try to interpret what the characters are doing and feeling, using no cues but the actions. If you have a VCR, tape the program so that later you can check your interpretations by replaying the sequence a second time, this time with the sound turned on.

1.2 EYE CONTACT

Making eye contact is one of a cluster of skills that are known as attending skills. You communicate that you are listening by looking at the other person. Mainstream North Americans feel that without eye contact no communication is occurring. Which students do teachers usually call upon in class? The ones who are looking at the teacher, not the ones who are avoiding eye contact. What do you do when you want service in a store? You walk up to a salesperson and look at him or her. The appropriate use of eye contact is one of the most powerful cues we have for opening and maintaining communication.

Looking at the person who is talking to you indicates warmth, interest, and a desire to communicate. We can powerfully influence how much another person talks by our use of eye contact. Frequent breaks in eye contact are interpreted as inattention, lack of interest, embarrassment, or even dislike. Therefore, looking down at the floor, up at the ceiling, over at a file, etc. will get the other person to stop talking. Maintaining appropriate eye contact indicates interest and encourages the other person to continue talking.

But what is appropriate eye contact? Too much can be as bad as too little. An unwavering stare can seem hostile, rude, or intrusive and prolonged eye contact can seem threatening. Appropriate eye contact involves neither staring nor avoiding. The time spent looking directly into the other person's eyes, however, is actually very brief. Your eyes will move from eyes to chin, hairline, mouth, and back to the eyes.

Listeners and speakers tend to adopt an alternate pattern of looking and looking away. But the looking times of speaker and listener are not symmetrical: in mainstream North American culture, listeners spend twice as much time looking as do speakers.

HOW PEOPLE PERCEIVE EYE CONTACT THAT SEEMS:	
Too long	Too short
pushy	shifty
aggressive	uninterested
trying to dominate	unconfident

DID YOU KNOW?

In the Orient, pearl buyers wear sunglasses so that sellers can't see their eyes. (The pupils in the eye get bigger when we look at something we like; they contract when we feel dislike or disgust.)

CULTURAL DIFFERENCES

It is important to be aware that body language is culture-specific. At an early age, we begin to learn how far away to stand from another person, how much physical touching is acceptable, what kind of eye contact is appropriate, and how long to look. These lessons are never formally taught, but they are learned. For example, a scolding parent or teacher might say to a child, "Stand up straight and look at me when I'm talking to you." In mainstream North American culture, this looking is understood as an appropriate listening pose. We think that children who won't look us in the eye are shifty, guilty, or otherwise lacking in openness and integrity. Chinese children, however, are taught not to look their elders in the eye: lowering the eyes is a sign of respect.

The right amount of eye contact varies from culture to culture. However, we learn what is appropriate within our own culture and interpret variations.

Exercise

ATTENDING SKILLS

Find a partner with whom you can role-play a conversation. Ask your partner to talk about a topic in which he or she is personally interested. Your role is to listen and to encourage your partner to say more by using the attending skills of eye contact, smiling, and nodding. Which of these skills do you feel comfortable doing? Which ones need more practice?

Change roles. How does your partner's use of attending skills affect your role as speaker?

DID YOU KNOW?

From one culture to another, there are startling differences in the way people think about time and space. For example, in mainstream North American culture being three minutes late for an appointment between equals might not require an apology but forty-five minutes is an insult. In some countries, however, being forty-five minutes late is considered on time and not requiring an apology. For a fascinating and accessible discussion of these and other cultural differences, see Edward T. Hall, *The Silent Language*. Garden City, NY: Doubleday, 1959.

1.3 SMILING, NODDING

Smiling and occasional nodding function as encouragers in a conversation, reassuring the other person that you are friendly, interested, and listening. If you usually listen impassively, try nodding occasionally. Don't overdo it. An occasional single nod of the head encourages people to say more; successive nods get them to stop.

1.4 POSTURE

Your posture or the way you hold your body is a clue to your mood and attitude. Slumping signals fatigue, boredom, or discouragement. Rigidity suggests nervousness or disagreement. Closed postures such as crossed arms often convey detachment or disagreement.

To convey relaxed attentiveness during a conversation, stand or sit so that you are leaning slightly toward the other person.

1.5 VOCAL QUALITIES

Vocal qualities, sometimes called *paralanguage*, are what get lost between the tape recording of a voice and the transcript of the words. These vocal cues include volume (loud or soft), pitch (high or low), rate of speech (fast or slow), rhythm, emphasis, and fluency.

After you have become accustomed to hearing your own voice played back on a tape recorder, evaluate your speaking style, using the following checklist of questions. Be objective as you listen to your voice. Ask yourself whether there are any features of your speaking style that prevent you from sounding as effective as you would like.

VOCAL QUALITIES: A CHECKLIST

Does every word and every sentence sound like every other? Or do you vary the pitch and emphasis depending on the sense?

Do you sound tired and bored? Or energetic and interested?

Is your tone tight? Nasal? Breathy?

Do you mumble? Or can your consonants be distinctly heard?

Do you speak so softly that people often can't hear you?

Do you have a machine-gun delivery—so rapid that people sometimes miss what you say?

Do you speak so slowly that people have trouble waiting for you to finish your sentences?

Do all your sentences, even declarative ones, have an upward intonation as if you are asking a question? Do you sound hesitant and unsure? Or do you sound confident in what you are saying?

The way you speak sends a message to your audience. Is it the message you intend? If not, you may want to work on correcting problems that you have identified. Following are exercises related to six aspects of voice: emphasis, variety, voice quality, articulation, projection, and inflection.

Exercise

EVALUATE YOUR VOICE
Tape record yourself in an informal conversation. Then tape record yourself reading aloud. Your first thought, as you review the tape, may be, "But that doesn't sound like me." However the voice that you hear recorded on tape by a good tape recorder is the voice that other people hear.

Exercise

ON EMPHASIS
Say each of these sentences in as many different ways as you can. In each case, how does the change in emphasis affect the meaning of the sentence?

Mary told that story to John.

Who do you think you are?

I didn't say that I think he is lazy.

EMPHASIS
Dull speakers tend to give equal emphasis to every word, overlooking the importance of emphasis to reinforce meaning. See the difference it makes to the meaning when you vary the emphasis. Read aloud the following sentence putting the emphasis on a different word each time:

Would you like me to help you?
Would *you* like me to help you?
Would you *like* me to help you?
Would you like *me* to help you?
Would you like me to *help* you?
Would you like me to help *you?*

VARIETY

There are four main ways to achieve variety: change the pitch and inflection; change the pace; change the volume; and use pauses. Read aloud the first passage, making it sound as flat and inexpressive as you can. To increase the monotony, you can use a sing-song rhythm in which the predictable pattern of rising and falling tone bears no relation to the sense of the passage. Then read it with great variety, using pauses, and exaggerating the variations in pitch, pacing, and loudness to emphasize the meaning of the passage.

A fearful man, all in coarse grey, with a great iron on his leg. A man with no hat, and with broken shoes, and with an old rag tied around his head. A man who had been soaked in water, and smothered in mud, and lamed by stones, and cut by flints, and stung by nettles, and torn by briars; who limped, and shivered, and glared and growled; and whose teeth chattered in his head as he seized me by the chin.

"Oh! Don't cut my throat, sir," I pleaded in terror. "Pray don't do it, sir."

"Tell us your name!" said the man. "Quick."

—From Charles Dickens's *Great Expectations*.

Now try the same exercise, using this passage:

"Sir, she had read the old romances, and had got into her head the fantastical notion that a woman of spirit should use her lover like a dog. So, Sir, at first she told me that I rode too fast, and she could not keep up with me; and when I rode a little slower, she passed me, and complained that I lagged behind. I was not to be made the slave of caprice; and I resolved to begin as I meant to end. I therefore pushed on briskly, till I was fairly out of her sight. The road lay between two hedges, so I was sure she could not miss it; and I contrived that she should soon come up with me. When she did, I observed her to be in tears."

—Dr. Johnson's account of his nuptial journey to church with Mrs. Porter, 1735 from James Boswell's *The Life of Samuel Johnson, LL.D.*

VOICE QUALITY

The quality of your voice depends on the way you form vowel sounds and use the resonators of your upper throat, mouth, and nose. Since the vowel carries the weight of the tone, the way to improve tonal quality is to work on vowels. The muscles in the jaw

DID YOU KNOW?

You can make your voice sound more positive and alive by using its full range. Discover the vitality of your voice.

and throat play an important role here: if the jaw and throat are tense and closed, the vowel cannot be open and the tone will sound tight or harsh.

Say, with exaggerated lip action, ee-ah-oo. Repeat 5 times.

The sound should come entirely from your mouth, not through your nose.

Read aloud the following passages, prolonging and exaggerating the vowel sounds. Repeat, paying attention to lip action.

The Rainbow comes and goes
And lovely is the Rose
—From Wordsworth's "Ode: Intimations of
Immortality"

The curfew tolls the knell of parting day,
The lowing herd winds slowly o'er the lea,
The plowman homeward plods his weary way,
And leaves the world to darkness and to me.
—From Thomas Grey's "Elegy Written in a
Country Churchyard"

Far and few, far and few,
Are the lands where the Jumblies live;
Their heads are green, and their hands are blue,
And they went to sea in a Sieve.
—From Edward Lear's "The Jumblies"

Heard a carol, mournful, holy,
Chanted loudly, chanted lowly,
Till her blood was frozen slowly
And her eyes were darkened wholly,
Turned to towered Camelot;
—From Tennyson's "The Lady of Shalott"

ARTICULATION

While the vowels carry the tone of the voice, the consonants are what distinguish one word from another. Read the following words: hit, bit, mitt, hill, his, big. The vowel is the same; only the consonants differ. Distinct pronunciation of the consonants requires the energetic use of the articulators—the lips, tongue, and palate. Mumblers are lazy pronouncers of consonants.

Read aloud the following passages. Tape-record yourself as you emphasize the consonants, especially the ones at the ends

Exercise

TEST YOUR VOICE FOR NASAL TWANG
Hold your nose as you say ee-ah-oo. Your nose shouldn't vibrate. If it does, then you have some nasality. The only sounds in English that should be nasal are m, n and ng.

DID YOU KNOW?
When talking to people who are hard of hearing, you shouldn't yell the vowels more loudly; you should articulate the consonants more clearly.

of the words. Pay attention to lip movement and tongue action. You will be surprised that what felt to you like overexaggeration of consonants comes through on the tape as good clear articulation.

> Andrew Airpump asked his aunt her ailment;
> Did Andrew Airpump ask his aunt her ailment?
> If Andrew Airpump asked his aunt her ailment,
> Where was the ailment of Andrew Airpump's aunt.
> —From "Peter Piper's Practical Principles of
> Plain and Perfect Pronunciation"

> Fillet of a fenny snake,
> In the caldron boil and bake;
> Eye of newt, and toe of frog,
> Wool of bat, and tongue of dog,
> Adder's fork, and blind-worm's sting,
> Lizard's leg, and howlet's wing—
> For a charm of powerful trouble,
> Fire burn; and, caldron, bubble.
> —From Shakespeare's *Macbeth* (IV, 1)

As you practice this next selection, emphasize the consonants. You should be able to feel the muscles of your tongue and lips working energetically. Since this is a patter song from Gilbert and Sullivan's *The Pirates of Penzance*, you might want to emphasize the rhythm too.

I am the very model of a modern Major-General,
I've information vegetable, animal, and mineral,
I know the kings of England, and I quote the fights historical,
From Marathon to Waterloo, in order categorical;
I'm very well acquainted too with matters mathematical,
I understand equations, both the simple and quadratical,
About binomial theorem I'm teeming with a lot o' news—
With many cheerful facts about the square of the hypotenuse.

PROJECTION

Children have no trouble with projection; babies can cry for hours. It's all a question of proper breathing. Breathing is what supports the voice. If your breath is shallow and irregular, your voice will be thin and weak. What is needed is an efficient and regular use of breath: not breathiness for the first few words and running out of breath by the end.

The way to increase loudness is to increase the pressure of breath below the larynx, not to tense up the muscles of the upper chest and throat. Tensing the throat raises the pitch and produces a harsh strident tone. Keep the throat relaxed.

Good projection depends on an adequate breath supply, resonance, and some prolongation of the vowel sounds. Of course, since you want to be understood as well as heard, you also have to articulate the consonants distinctly. Practice outside or in a large room by reading a prose passage (pick any paragraph from this book), using three different levels of projection:

—as if in conversation with several other people
—as if in a staff meeting with 20 other people
—as if in a large auditorium (imagine yourself bouncing your voice off the back wall.)

INFLECTION

English speakers indicate questions by ending sentences with a rising inflection: "You do?" However, some speakers use this same pattern of rising inflection when they intend to make a declarative statement. This sounds unsure, as if they don't have much confidence in what they say.

Try reading the following sentences. First read them with a rising inflection. Then read them as if you really believed them.

I think that this is a good project.

It gives me great pleasure to introduce you to this afternoon's speaker: Mary Entwhistle.

The library will be closing in fifteen minutes.

I don't agree that the plan would be too difficult.

This is a very interesting book.

No. I don't think I would like to become involved in that program.

FOR FURTHER HELP

Birdwhistle, R. *Kinesics and Context*. Philadelphia: University of Pennsylvania Press, 1940. A classic work on body language.

Evans, David R. et al. *Essential Interviewing: A Programmed Approach to Effective Communication*. 2nd ed. Monterey, CA: Brooks/Cole Publishing Co, 1983.

Hunt, Gary T. *Effective Communication*. Englewood Cliffs, NJ: Prentice-Hall, 1985. Chapter 5 on Nonverbal Communication includes exercises and questions for discussion.

These books contain exercises on voice.

Anderson, Virgil A. *Training the Speaking Voice*. 3rd ed. New York: Oxford University Press, 1977.

Berry, Cicely. *Your Voice and How to Use it Successfully*. London: Harrap, 1975.

Fisher, Hilda B. *Improving Voice and Articulation*. 2nd ed. Boston: Houghton Mifflin, 1975.

Uris, Dorothy. *To Sing in English: A Guide to Improved Diction*. New York: Boosey and Hawkes, 1971.

LISTENING

2.1 GOALS OF EFFECTIVE LISTENING

Good listening is the foundation of all face-to-face communication between people. This is so because communication is not a one-way process of a speaker's sending a message to a passive receiver. Communication is a two-way transaction in which the listener as well as the speaker is actively involved. A good listener is always engaged in selecting, interpreting, remembering, making guesses and trying to confirm them, coming to conclusions, and checking out the conclusions by playing them back to the speaker.

Listening is hard work. Some authorities on listening imply that you have to be actively listening and remembering all the time. On the contrary, this goal of full-time active listening is not only impossible; it is undesirable. There may be times when it is sensible and energy-conserving to choose not to listen. However, in this section, we are talking about those other times when it is your job to listen. In libraries, the duties of supervisors, and of reference librarians in particular, require excellent listening skills.

A good listener, who is actually listening (as opposed to just pretending to listen), has the goal of understanding the other person's point of view. Here are some possible reasons why you might want to listen more effectively on the job:

—To find out what someone wants so that you can satisfy needs. (Reference librarians do this, as do salespeople and lawyers.)
—To understand someone's point of view, attitude, feelings, or concerns so that, as a supervisor, you have the information you need to plan effectively, anticipate problems, and resolve conflicts.
—To receive information so as to form an opinion or reach a decision.
—To get feedback about your own performance so that you can correct problems before they become crises.

2.2 BARRIERS TO LISTENING

At the outset, we must recognize that there are strong reasons why so few of us listen well, even when we think we are listening. The following are five barriers to good listening.

Perceiving selectively: We may hear only those messages that fit into our model of the world and filter out other contradictory messages.

Making assumptions: Instead of listening, people often assume. But it's dangerous to assume to know what other people feel or may mean in a given situation. One person may feel quite differently than another would feel in the same situation. Instead of assuming, ask.

Giving unsolicited advice: Advice given before we have listened carefully to the problem is usually inappropriate. Moreover, people are unprepared to accept advice that they have not asked for.

Being judgmental or critical: When we are judgmental, we are not trying to understand another person's point of view; we are distancing ourselves from that point of view, often to repudiate it. We are saying, in effect: You are wrong (silly, selfish, shortsighted) to think or feel that way.

Being defensive or arguing: If we feel threatened by the other person's point of view, we tend to defend our own positions instead of listening to understand.

Be aware of these barriers to listening. Monitor your own listening style. Which of these barriers are problems in your own listening?

2.3 IMPROVING LISTENING SKILLS

There are some specific things that you can do to improve your listening skills. The first cluster has to do with really paying attention to what the other person is saying.

Don't interrupt: Be patient. Let people (even painfully slow talkers) finish their own sentences. In a conversation between people of different status, the person with the higher status is much more likely to interrupt than vice versa. Interrupting is a way of exercising power. Monitor your own responses and see how often you interrupt, especially those of lower status.

Don't do all the talking yourself: Don't be afraid of staying silent and simply listening. Often people think that they are listening when they are really doing one of the following:

—Giving advice ("If I were you, I would. . . .")
—Providing unasked-for information ("Did you know. . .?")
—Describing their own similar experience ("That's nothing compared to what happened to me. Let me tell you. . . .")
—Moralizing ("You should really be more careful. . . .")
—Evaluating or judging ("You're wrong to pay any attention to that. . . .")
—Interpreting ("I know why you are saying that. It's because you really think. . . .")
—Arguing for a contrary position ("That's not true. It's really not X at all but Y. . . .")

Wait for an answer: If you have asked a question, wait for an answer. Don't fill in the pauses while the other person is thinking by answering your own question. Again, don't be afraid of silence (see 3.4 on pausing).

Don't change the topic: If you change the topic, you convey the message that you find it boring to hear what the other person is talking about, that you want to talk about what is important to *you* rather than to find out what is important to the other person. Changing the topic is a way of asserting power.

Listen for the whole message: Listening for cognitive content is only part of the job. You also want to listen for feelings. Perceiving feelings is essential in understanding another person's point of view.

Listen between the words. Take into account gestures, facial expression, pauses, emphasis, tone of voice, changes in pitch, etc. (See Chapter 1 on the significance of nonverbal behavior.) A library user's hidden message may be, for example, "I would like help but I don't like to ask for it."

Listen for what is *not* said as well as for what is said.

However, it is not enough to be listening: you also have to show that you are listening. Therefore, the second part of effective listening involves a cluster of skills that reassure the other person of your attention. The first two are *attending skills*; the second two are *reflective listening skills*:

Use eye contact: It conveys that you are attentive and interested (see 1.2.).

Exercise

DON'T LISTEN

With a partner, role-play a conversation in which you play the part of the *worst* listener you can be.

Now analyze what you were doing. Here are some possibilities: interrupting; changing the topic; fidgeting with your pen or drumming your fingers; looking away; remaining impassive and showing no response at all to what was said. What other characteristics of a poor listener were you demonstrating? Ask your partner how these behaviors affected him or her.

Exercise

HOW DO OTHER PEOPLE LISTEN?

Observe a conversation between two people who are doing more than exchanging small talk. What do you notice? Consider the following questions:

1. What did their body language tell you? Did they use eye contact appropriately? Did their posture suggest attentiveness?

2. Did you notice anyone interrupting? Changing the topic? Jumping to conclusions? Being judgmental?

3. Did you notice any particularly good examples of attending skills or of reflective listening skills?

Use minimal encouragers: Nodding, smiling, and making short responses like "uh-huh," "oh, yes," and "that's interesting" (see 3.3) express interest and encourage the other person to continue talking. (It should be emphasized, you are not *pretending* to be attentive; you *are* being attentive and are using eye contact and encouragers to communicate that genuine attention.)

Check your understanding: Paraphrasing or restatement of content (see 3.8) is a useful skill that allows you to check whether or not you are understanding the cognitive meaning of what has been said. Reflecting feelings (3.9) allows you to check your understanding of how the other person feels.

Ask questions: Two kinds of questions are particularly useful: *open questions* (see 3.5) that act as invitations to tell you more, such as "What are your feelings about this?" and *probes* to clarify what you don't understand, such as "Can you give me an example of what you mean?"

FOR FURTHER HELP

Atwater, Eastwood. *"I Hear You": Listening Skills to Make You a Better Manager.* Englewood Cliffs, NJ: Prentice-Hall, 1982. A comprehensive book on listening written by a psychologist who runs workshops on communication skills.

Gordon, Thomas. *P.E.T.: Parent Effectiveness Training.* New York: New American Library, 1975. The basic text for Gordon's P.E.T. course, taken by a quarter of a million people.

Nichols, Ralph G. and Leonard A. Stevens. *Are You Listening?* New York: McGraw-Hill, 1957. A pioneering book in the field of listening that still commands attention.

Rogers, Carl and Richard Farson, "Active Listening," in Richard Huseman et al. *Readings in Interpersonal and Organizational Communication.* 2nd ed. Boston: Holbrook Press, 1973. This article introduced the term active listening.

Wolff, F.I. et al. *Perceptive Listening.* New York: Holt, Rinehart and Winston, 1983.

 # SPEAKING

3.1 INTRODUCTION TO SPEAKING SKILLS

The following skills should be learned and practiced one at a time. Think of the virtuoso pianist: the music sounds so effortless because the player has practiced, over and over again, the separate exercises of scales, staccatos, chord progressions, etc. Later these elements are combined into music. Similarly, you will find it helpful to work on each skill separately although your ultimate goal is to integrate the skills. Become familiar with the function of each skill, so that you can use an appropriate one in particular situations. To use Allen Ivey's term, you will be using the skill "intentionally."

3.2 ACKNOWLEDGMENT

Acknowledgment is a skill that involves restating or "playing back" the content of what the other person has just said. You restate a key part of the previous statement, using either the same words or a paraphrase. This restatement encourages the other person to confirm, correct, or explain further.

EXAMPLES
User: I need some information on computers.
Librarian: We have quite a bit of information on computers (or simply, Computers, uh-huh).
User: Have you anything on whales?
Librarian: Wales, the place? (paraphrasing to ensure a shared understanding. This gives the user a chance to correct.)

User: I'm doing a paper on the effects of stress, and I need to find out the kinds of test that can be used with subjects with a heart condition. I'd also like articles on the Jenkins inventory.
Librarian: Uh-huh. You're doing a paper on the effects of stress. . . (With complicated statements, the librarian may catch only part of what's been said. That's OK. The procedure is to repeat what you can and ask for repetition on what you missed: "You wanted articles on—what was that again?")

Exercise

ACKNOWLEDGMENT
What could you say to acknowledge a user who asks:

1. Where is your law section?

2. Where is the *Globe?* [a newspaper]

3. I'm looking for something on China. [Check your own mastery of the skill of acknowledgment: was your response useful in clarifying what kind of china is wanted? If not, what could you say instead? Look again at the whales/Wales example.]

Restatement is an excellent quick way to indicate that you have been listening (see 2.3) and helps to establish a good climate of communication. In acknowledging, follow these guidelines:

—Be brief. A phrase or even just one word is often enough. You don't want to parrot back everything that's been said.
—Use a matter-of-fact, accepting tone. Responding with an upward intonation ("Computers?") may convey amazement or even disapproval about what has just been said.

Most people already use acknowledgment in certain situations such as repeating a phone number. So it is not a question of learning an entirely new skill but of using consciously a skill already employed in other contexts.

3.3 MINIMAL ENCOURAGERS

Examples of useful minimal encouragers are short phrases such as:

—Uh-huh.
—I see.
—Go on.
—That's interesting.
—Then?
—Tell me more.
—Anything else?
—Can you give me an example?

These phrases, which encourage the other person to say more, are nonjudgmental and free of content. There is a tacit rule in conversation that people should take turns speaking, but a very brief remark will count as a turn. You do not need to respond at length to every statement made. Let the other person describe the problem, and use encouragers, along with appropriate body language, to indicate that you are interested and are listening.

EXAMPLE
User: I'm trying to find some books for my neighbor.
Librarian: Yes, uh-huh (in an interested tone).

User: You see, she's in her seventies and can't get out much. But she does like to read.

Librarian: I see.

User: She likes mysteries, but she's read all the Agatha Christies and all the Margery Allinghams.

Librarian: Anything else?

User: Well, she likes the older style mysteries—you know, the kind set in English country houses. She's not keen on a lot of sex and violence.

Minimal encouragers are especially effective when the speaker:

—has something to say that he or she is very eager to tell.
—wants to express some intense feeling.
—has a grievance.

3.4 PAUSING

The effective use of pauses, or silence, is really a kind of nonverbal behavior but it functions in much the same way as the speaking skills of questioning, acknowledgment, and minimal encouragers. A well-placed pause can productively substitute for a conversational turn.

Pausing is defined as intentional silence in place of a statement or question. When it is the interviewer's turn to speak, she waits before speaking, or says nothing until the other person speaks again. The effect of pausing varies according to culture. In some cultures, lengthy and frequent pauses are a sign of inattention; in others, such as some native Indian cultures, they are a sign of attention and respect, an indication that the interviewer is taking the interviewee's last statement seriously and considering a worthy answer. It is important to know what effect your pauses may have in different situations. In mainstream North American culture, effective pausing is a behavior that enhances the interviewer's listening skills and conveys attentiveness to the interviewee. A pause may function as an encourager or a probe. It says to the interviewee: "I'm listening" and "Go on." Because the interviewer relinquishes her turn at the conversation, the interviewee is likely to expand on what he has previously said. For example:

Exercise

TIMING PAUSES

Using a transcript of a group discussion or interview, read the transcript aloud, pausing for varying lengths of time (two seconds, four seconds, and then eight seconds) at the end of each speaker's turn. Time the pauses carefully. What was the effect of the pauses? Which lengths seemed normal? How might the pauses be interpreted by others?

Exercise

ROLE-PLAYING PAUSES

Role-play a discussion in which you attempt to encourage others to describe a recent information need. Practice using pauses of various lengths at appropriate times. Ask an observer to note the pauses and what happens immediately after the pauses. Discuss in your group. (This exercise may be recorded on videotape or audiotape for further analysis.)

Librarian: Tell me about your research (open question).
User: Well, this is in the area of applied microbiology.
Librarian: . . . (pause).
User: I'm studying the action of lactic acid bacteria in cheese.

Pauses are also important as a listening skill when they follow the interviewer's statements or questions. A common difficulty for librarians who are learning to ask open questions (see 3.5) is remembering to pause after the question while the interviewee considers her answer.

According to experiments on behavior in the online search interview (Auster and Lawton, 1984), effective pausing is more difficult to learn than one might think. Pauses longer than ten seconds may confuse the user, who becomes unsure whether the interviewer is still listening. Very short pauses tend to be ignored. It seems that some librarians habitually pause while considering what the user has said or deciding what to do next. But pausing too often or too long is awkward.

Used correctly, pausing is a skill that helps reduce the common mistakes of talking too much, cutting the user off, and interrupting. The skills that supplement pausing are restatement, encouragers, and nonverbal skills that show attentiveness.

STEPS IN USING PAUSES EFFECTIVELY:

Observe your own behavior. Under which circumstances do you normally pause? Under which circumstances do you not pause, but perhaps should?

Consciously attempt to vary the lengths of your pauses. Pause for a longer or shorter time than usual and observe the effect. Experiment by substituting short pauses for questions or statements.

When you pause, make eye contact, and use other body language that says, "I'm listening—go on."

Train yourself to wait. When asking a question, practice stopping at the end of the question until the other person answers.

A QUICK TIP
After you have asked your question ("What do you want to know about Chaucer?") wait for the answer. Don't succumb to the common temptation to turn your open question into a closed question ("What do you want to know about Chaucer? Do you want a copy of *The Canterbury Tales?*")

3.5 OPEN QUESTIONS VS. CLOSED QUESTIONS

You can ask questions in different ways. The form in which you ask the question determines the sort of answer you will get. When you have finished reading this section, you will be able to do the following: distinguish between open and closed questions when you hear them; formulate your own open questions; understand how open and closed questions function in conversations and in interviews; and recognize when it is appropriate, for your purposes, to ask an open question or to ask a closed question.

A closed question requires a Yes/No, This/That response. The question itself specifies several possible answers and requires the other person to choose from the options provided. "Which do you want on this topic—an article or a book?" is an example of a closed question.

An open question allows people to respond in their own terms. A handy way of recognizing whether a question is open or not is to look at the way it begins. If it begins with Who, What, Why, Where, When, or How, the question is probably open. "In what format do you want the information?" is an example of an open question.

Open and closed questions differ in both function and effect. Asking closed questions can be a way of assuming control because the questioner takes the initiative in selecting the aspects of the topic to be considered and what can be said about it. For this reason, closed questions are among the tools of legal cross-examination ("Did you or did you not hear the defendent say X at 8:00 p.m., Friday, May 15?"). For librarians, closed questions can be useful to confirm a fact ("You wanted to know just the name of the archaeologist who discovered the Crystal Skull?") Closed questions invite brief factual answers and may be useful when only brief answers are wanted.

The less restrictive structure of open questions invites elaboration and longer answers. When you ask open questions, you give up some control over what gets talked about. Instead of specifying the aspect of the topic to be discussed, you ask the other person what aspect of the topic concerns him or her ("What did you want to know about the Crystal Skull?"). Closed questions involve making assumptions. Open questions make no assumptions.

Exercise

PLAYING 20 QUESTIONS

This next exercise can be done with a group. Get a 30-sided die used in games like Dungeons and Dragons. Throw the die, note the number, and ask group members to find out from you what the number was by asking you *closed* questions ("Is it 30? is it less than 15?"). Note how many questions it takes for the group to discover the number. Then throw the die again and ask the group to find out from you what the number was this time by asking you *open* questions ("What is the number?").

EXAMPLE
Closed question

"I've noticed that you have come late three times this week. Are you having a problem getting your car started?"
[This closed question will probably be answered by, "Well, no, not really."]

Open question

"I've noticed that you have come late three times this week. What is the problem that is keeping you from getting here on time?"
[This open question invites the staff member to describe the problem but makes no assumptions about what the problem is. Guessing "Is it this? Is it that?" can be risky and sometimes offensive. Moreover it's not very efficient in situations like this one when the problem may be any number of things: an unreliable car, a sick child, a health problem, a concern about the job situation, etc.]

Use open questions when you want:
—to hear in the other person's own words the nature of a problem or situation.
—to encourage the other person to talk.
—to avoid guessing or making assumptions.

SOME USEFUL OPEN QUESTIONS

To find out what a person wants in order to supply the need:
—What sort of thing are you looking for?
—What information would you like on this?
—What sort of X do you have in mind?
—If you could have the perfect article (book, solution, help etc.), what would it be?
—What help would you like?
—How would you expect this to help you?
—What requirements do you have (for the project, design etc.)?

To get a description of a problem or event:
—What was the first thing that happened?
—And then what happened?
—Who have you talked to about this?
—What have you done about this so far?
—What do you think should be done?

Exercise

ASKING OPEN QUESTIONS

Library user: There are so many books on Shakespeare here that I can't find what I want.

Write down three possible closed questions that you could ask.

1 _____

2 _____

3 _____

Write down three possible open questions that you could ask.

1 _____

2 _____

3 _____

When you have finished writing down your open and closed questions, examine them to see that your closed questions are really closed and your open questions are really open. Remember: a closed question limits the response to a Yes/No/I don't know or a This/That answer.

Which of your six questions do you think would work best?

To encourage the person to elaborate:
—What aspect of X concerns you?
—What else can you tell me about X?
—Perhaps if you tell me more about this problem [project], I could make some suggestions.

To get clarification:
—What do you mean by X?
—What would be an example of that? (Can you give me an example? Please give me an example.
—Can you help me to understand X?

3.6 AVOIDING PREMATURE DIAGNOSIS

Premature diagnosis is another term for jumping to conclusions. Some examples of premature diagnosis:

A young adult, who is wearing running shoes, jeans and a polo shirt, asks for some material on bees. The librarian asks, "Is this for a school project?"

A woman in her thirties asks for pictures of Scandinavian costumes. The librarian asks, "Is this for your child—a costume to make for your child?"

An Indian woman wearing a sari asks for books on art. The librarian asks, "Do you want the art of India?"

An elderly man asks for books on entomology. The librarian asks, "Are you trying to get rid of ants?"

In each case, the librarian assumed something about the user's situation and asked a closed question that made the assumption explicit to the user. Sometimes the librarian is right (the elderly man did want to get rid of carpenter ants), but that's just good luck. When the librarian is wrong, the user may find the explicit assumptions offensive (the woman who was asked if the Scandinavian costume was for her child thrust out her ringless left hand indignantly and said, "Does this look like I had a child?")

Premature diagnosis is one of the commonest causes of communication accidents in libraries; try to avoid it. You can't help making assumptions, but you can avoid making these assumptions explicit to the user. Instead of guessing and asking a closed question based on your guess, ask an open question that makes no assumptions.

Compare the following ways of handling the same question:

User: Do you have an elementary math book?
Librarian: Is this book for a child?
User: No, I want it for myself.
Librarian: You must be teaching in the adult basic education program then.
User: No, I'm not a teacher.
Librarian: Oh, I thought you were. A lot of teachers come in asking for basic books for their courses.

User: Do you have an elementary math book?
Librarian: We have books of that sort in both the children's and the adult's sections. How do you plan to use this book?
User: It's for myself. To brush up.
Librarian: What sort of thing are you wanting to brush up in?
User: Pie charts. You see, I have to write a report for my work and need to be able to use pie charts and graphs.

3.7 NEUTRAL QUESTIONS

Open questions are effective at getting people talking. But when someone needs help and it's your job to provide that help, you may want to use a form of question called a neutral question. Neutral questions provide more structure than open questions. The concept of neutral questioning was developed by Dr. Brenda Dervin. It grew out of more than a decade of research on how people seek and use information.

Dervin uses the term "sense-making" to refer to her model of information seeking. According to this model, information needs grow out of specific situations in a person's life. Individuals go through their everyday lives, trying to make sense out of what is happening, seeking certain outcomes, and trying to avoid others. Sometimes, people can't achieve particular goals by themselves and so they turn to others for help. For example, they have to fill out their income tax form, but don't understand the difference between an expense and a capital cost. So they go to an accountant. They are looking for a job and need tips on how to write a resume. So they go to the public library for a book on writing a resume.

In general, then, people often have some gap in understanding that must be filled in before they can achieve a goal. If it is your job to provide help, you need to know three things: 1) the *situation* the person is in, 2) the *gaps* in his or her understanding, and 3) the *uses* or helps—what the person would like to do as a result of filling in this gap. How do you find out these three things? Ask neutral questions. A neutral question is a special kind of open question that asks specifically about situations, or gaps, or helps.

SOME NEUTRAL QUESTIONS

Here are some examples of good neutral questions to ask when you want to help someone but must first determine the precise nature of what would help:

To find out how the person sees his/her situation:
—What aspect of this situation concerns you?
—What problem are you having in this situation?
—Where would you like to begin?
—Where do you see yourself going with this?
—What happened?

To assess the gaps:
—What seems to be missing?
—What are you trying to understand?
—What would you like to know about x?
—What happened that got you stopped?

To assess the kind of help wanted (uses):
—If you could have exactly the help you want, what would it be?
—What would help you?
—How would this help you?
—How do you plan to use this information?
—What would you like to see happen in this situation?
—What are you trying to do in this situation?

EXERCISE
Finding out

Try this exercise in pairs. One person plays the role of the user. The other person is a librarian who asks neutral questions to find out what the user really wants to know. The librarian should keep asking neutral questions until the "user" is satisfied that the question is really understood.

User is a student who has to write an English essay, which is to be "a close analysis of the text" of some American colonial poem. He doesn't have a fixed topic in mind, and his first problem is that he doesn't know what is meant by "a close analysis of the text." He asks: "Where is the section on American poetry?"

User is worried that the green light on the photocopier at work may be harmful to her health. She wants to find articles that will tell her if this light can ever be harmful. She asks: "I'm having trouble with this index."

User has a neighbor who is building an addition to his house right up to the property line. She wants to find out whether there are any building codes that would prevent this building from going up. She asks: "Where is your law section?"

3.8 REFLECTING CONTENT

Reflecting content is a way of communicating that you have been really listening and have understood. Moreover, like acknowledgment, this skill gives you a chance to check that your understanding is accurate. When you reflect content, you focus on the cognitive aspects of what has been said. Use this skill in situations when it really matters that you have heard and understood correctly.

When you reflect content, you are not supplying any new information of your own. You are mirroring back to the speaker what you have understood from his or her verbal and nonverbal behavior. If you have misunderstood, the other person will be able to correct you.

Evans et al. point out in their book *Essential Interviewing* that the two ways to reflect content are paraphrasing and summarizing.

Paraphrasing feeds back what has just been said in the previous comment. A common structure to use for paraphrasing is an introductory clause such as:

—It sounds like . . .
—So you think . . .

—You're saying. . .
—You mean. . .
—As you see it. . .
—As I understand you. . .

plus a concise summary giving the essence of what you think was meant.

Summarizing covers a larger span of conversation. It may be used as a summary of a complex discussion, as a transition to a new topic, or as a good conclusion to an interview.

When paraphrasing:

—Be concise. Usually a short, pithy sentence is enough.
—Feed back the essence by restating what you understand to be the main idea of what was just said.
—Don't add to or change the meaning of what you have heard.
—Avoid sounding like a parrot. Use your own words as well as some of the key words you have heard.
—You may want to use a checkout such as, "Is that how you see it?" or "Did I get that right?"

EXAMPLE OF REFLECTION OF CONTENT
Librarian 1: Mary has applied for the senior position in the children's library, but I don't think she'd be a good choice.
Librarian 2: You don't think we should choose her?
Librarian 1: No. She's excellent with children and knows a lot about children's books, but she doesn't have the management skills to keep things running.
Librarian 2: So the only problem is with her management ability?
Librarian 1: Right. I've never seen anyone less organized. She can't organize her own desk. So you can see what would happen if she was responsible for a whole branch.

When summarizing:

—Synthesize the gist of what was said in the course of a number of previous statements.
—Condense.
—Go for the big picture.

A warning: don't use this skill of reflection for small-talk, or the exchange will go something like this:

User: Looks like we're in for a spell of hot weather.
Librarian: Sounds like you think it's going to be hot?
User: Yes, that's just what I just said.

3.9 REFLECTING FEELING

A statement may have cognitive content or emotional content or both. If the content is primarily cognitive, then an appropriate response is to reflect content. But if the content is primarily emotional, then it is important to acknowledge that you have heard and understood the feelings that have been expressed. An appropriate response is to use the skill of reflecting feeling. Reflecting feeling is like reflecting content except that you are focusing on the emotions expressed rather than on the informational content. In assessing the emotional content, take into account not only the other person's words but also the body language (see Chapter 1).

The skill of reflecting feeling can be a suitable response to all types of emotion: positive, negative, or ambivalent (including emotion directed toward yourself). Trying to ignore negative emotions or denying them simply doesn't work.

A common structure useful to reflect feeling is an introductory clause such as:

—It sounds as if you feel. . .
—Maybe you feel. . .
—I sense that you are feeling a bit. . .

followed by an adjective that captures the emotion such as:

—discouraged
—hopeful
—pleased
—concerned
—frustrated
—undecided
—angry
—excited

followed by "about" or "that" and a key word or clause.

Or use an introductory clause such as "It sounds as if you"

QUICK TIPS FOR REFLECTING FEELING

Take body language into account when you are assessing the feeling being expressed.

Use your own words to sum up the key emotion(s) rather than simply repeating the words you have heard.

Be tentative. Instead of saying, "You must be. . ." you could say, "You seem to be. . . ." Give the other person a chance to correct you, if you got the feeling wrong. You may want to use a checkout such as, "Is that how you see it?" or "Did I get that right?"

Avoid making statements that seem to imply judgments or evaluations of the person's ability, such as "You sound like you had a lot of trouble handling that."

Exercise

ROLE-PLAYING REFLECTING FEELING

Imagine you are talking to a colleague in the staff room who is telling you about her supervisor. She says:

"This morning I was ready to quit. You remember all that fuss that Jane made about doing a needs assessment. She made me drop everything and work on it. I spent hours on it. Now she says she doesn't think we need one after all and that we'll let the whole thing drop."

Consider the following responses:

You shouldn't let Jane get to you this way. [Giving advice]

Something worse happened to me when I was working with Jane. You wouldn't believe what she did. [Sympathy seeking]

Doing a needs assessment is very important. I have a good book on how to do one, if you'd like to borrow it. [Providing unasked for information]

What could you say instead that would reflect feeling?

You can do this exercise in a group. Write on a card the situation outlined above. A volunteer plays the role of the colleague by reading her lines, "This morning I was ready, etc." The rest of the group responds by reflecting feeling. Make up more situations to be role-played.

followed by a verb: resent, fear, mistrust, hope for, appreciate—followed by a key word or clause. You can vary this structure to get a form you feel comfortable using.

EXAMPLE

It sounds like these budget cuts have left you feeling pretty frustrated.

I get the feeling you're sorry we ever started this project.

Perhaps you feel that you are left doing all the work and you resent it.

EXAMPLE

Library user: I want to talk to somebody about this book [Norma Klein's *Love Is One of the Choices*]. My daughter is only 12. She got this disgusting book from your library. No wonder so many young people have poor values when librarians are giving this kind of book to children.

Librarian: You sound upset that your daughter got this book here.

User: Of course I'm upset! Who wouldn't be upset? Look at this passage here about abortion.

Librarian: This situation has really caused you concern.

This is not the time to explain the library's collection policy or to get into a discussion of the literary merits of Young Adult fiction. The user needs a chance to express her feelings and have them recognized and acknowledged. The librarian, in acknowledging and reflecting these feelings, is not evaluating the feelings or sharing them or saying that the user is right or wrong to feel this way.

3.10 CLOSURE

Closure is a skill that allows you tactfully to return the discussion to relevant matters. When it is apparent that the conversation is wandering, you shouldn't cut the other person off mid-sentence or change the subject abruptly. The other person may, despite appearances, be telling you something that is important to your understanding of the problem. However, when it is apparent that the conversation is off-track, you can get back to the point tactfully. You might say, "Yes, it sounds like your daughter's graduation

Exercise

REFLECTING FEELING

In a conversation in which someone is expressing emotion, listen carefully for the exact emotion expressed. Try to reflect the feeling that you think you hear.

Remember that there are two aspects to accurate reflection of feeling. You have to capture the right feeling and you have to get the intensity of the feeling right.

Consider these possibilities to convey different degrees of intensity: exasperated, irritated, nettled, sore, mad, angry, fuming, furious, infuriated. You would have to decide, in a given situation, which, if any, of these accurately reflected the feeling. Another way to suit your response to the intensity of the emotion expressed is to use an appropriate qualifying adverb:

somewhat angry
very angry
extremely angry.

Exercise

GIVING INSTRUCTIONS

Practice making instructions and directions more explicit by rewording or expanding on the following:

Look for articles about free trade in the index.

You can request back issues from the page.

Try the university library.

You'll need to get a card from the circulation department.

The fiction section is on the third floor.

dress will be very suitable. But tell me, now, about . . . " or "Yes, it's a shame what the garage did to your exhaust system. But, to get back to these pathfinders, what do you think we should do for the graphics?"

Knowing the effect of the questions you ask enables you to choose an appropriate questioning style—using open questions to encourage the reticent person to talk about what concerns her but practicing closure to focus digressors.

3.11 GIVING INSTRUCTIONS AND DIRECTIONS

People who work in libraries are frequently called on to give instructions or directions. For example, you may need to instruct a library user in the use of an index or teach someone how to operate a microfilm reader. You may need to give someone directions for finding a book or for going to another library. Bibliographic instruction programs involve complex sequences of instructions. Instructions and directions are basically descriptions of procedures or steps that another person must take. Yet giving instructions and directions effectively is a skill that must be learned and that can always be improved. Instructions and directions are often misinterpreted or ignored because they are too complicated or detailed or because they are not understood. The steps for giving good instructions or directions are:

1. Use appropriate body language. Show that you are attentive through eye contact, posture, gestures, and voice. To ensure that the person is ready to hear your instructions, be assertive: use more eye contact, make your voice stronger (but not louder), and lean forward (see Chapter 1).
2. Be clear and specific. Give explicit directions. Avoid general statements or requests. For example, "Ask the fiction librarian" is too vague. Instead, say "Go over to that desk (gesturing) where the sign says Fiction. Tell the person sitting there that you want help in finding books by George Orwell."
3. Check to make sure your instructions were heard and understood. Remember that cultural differences may affect the response. Oriental students tend to say "Yes, I understand" out of politeness, when in fact they may *not* understand. Observe

the user's reaction—a puzzled look may tell you that your directions were not clear, even though they seemed clear enough to you. Verify that the user has in fact seen the sign you pointed to or knows where the stairs are. For example: "Go over to that desk where the sign says fiction. Do you see it?"

4. Observe to ensure that the person can carry out the directions. For example, watch where the user goes and intervene if necessary. In the case of using a tool or machine, watch while the user carries out each step. It is not enough for the user to watch the librarian demonstrate—what looks simple often turns out to be hard for a first-time user. You could say:

—Now, you look for the first article while I watch.
—Show me how you are going to thread the film.
—Find an example of a subject card for Shakespeare.

3.12 INCLUSION: TELLING PEOPLE WHAT YOU ARE DOING

Many communication accidents can be avoided simply by telling the other person what you are doing. For example, you could explain to a user that you are going to look for an index, that you are checking your records, or that you are looking for other subject headings. Inclusion is an explanation or description of your behavior that you can give when the reasons for what you are doing may not be apparent.

Inclusion is an attending skill: it maintains the communication process between two people when one person must perform a task that does not, in itself, require interpersonal communication or when one person must do something that might otherwise signal an interruption or termination of the conversation. Inclusion helps to answer unspoken questions: Are you still there? Are you still working on my problem? Why are you doing something that doesn't seem related to my problem? Inclusion reassures the person you are helping, for example: "I'm going to check the stacks for you and will return in a minute." In addition, inclusion often has an instructive function. Describing and explaining your behavior helps the observer learn how to replicate that behavior. For example, when the librarian says, "What I am doing now is looking for other headings we could use," the user learns that an index may have synonymous or alternate terms.

Inclusion is a skill that is particularly useful in these situations:

—When the other person cannot see what you are doing. On the telephone, always describe behavior that interrupts normal conversation. For example, "I'm going to put you on hold. Please wait a moment" or "I'm writing this down as you speak" or "I'm looking at my calendar." Use inclusion with blind people: "I'm looking in an index now."

—When the relationship between your behavior and the problem is not immediately apparent to a layperson. For example, a library user may expect you to answer his question off the top of your head, but you need to check a reference book to be sure. Say, "I want to be sure so I'm verifying this in the current directory."

—When you want to instruct the user (and the user wants to be instructed.) Explaining precisely what you are doing helps the user learn the procedure. "I'm going to look in the latest issue of *Reader's Guide*. Here it is. . . and I'm looking under the heading Alzheimer's Disease. . . I see two items. . . one called 'Researchers study causes of Alzheimer's Disease.'"

—When you ask a question or make a request that may seem unrelated or inappropriate to a library user. Users sometimes do not understand that it is necessary for you to determine the scope of their query and may think you are prying. For example, instead of asking "Why do you need this information?" you can use inclusion to introduce your question: "The library has a great deal of material on this topic, and we'll have a better chance of finding the best sources if you can tell me something about how you plan to use the information."

—When you want to draw attention to something that could easily be overlooked. For example, although you wouldn't explain to a regular user that you're charging out the books for 21 days (the normal borrowing period), you might point out that the records are due back in one week, not three.

—When the other person will have to wait, because the task takes a few minutes, or you need to concentrate on the task without talking, or you are going to be out of sight. People usually do not mind waiting so long as they know what to expect. If there's a line-up, people become less impatient when you acknowledge them, even if you can't immediately help them. For example, "I'm going to help this man, and I have a telephone call waiting, and then I will be right with you" or "I'm going to the stacks and will be back in about three minutes" or "This will take me some time to check because I have to call the university library. Would you like to wait while I do that?"

Inclusion involves four basic steps:

1. Acknowledge. Restate the problem or otherwise indicate that you are listening so that your next action will be seen to be related. "So you want to see if we have anything on salamanders."
2. Describe briefly what you are doing (or have done or are just about to do). "I'm looking under Salamanders in this catalog, to see if we have books." If you want to instruct the user, provide more detail.
3. Explain briefly why you are doing it. State the reason for your behavior, or summarize the advantages. For example: "This could be in the biology section or it could be in the pet books. The catalog will tell us all the places we should look and it might also tell us what else to look under."
4. If appropriate, indicate how much time the task will take. Be specific. Say "It may be this afternoon before I can call you back" rather than "I won't be able to call back right away" or "This may take a while."

3.13 CONFRONTATION: DESC

When a situation arises that needs to be changed, don't ignore it. Use the skill of confrontation. The acronym DESC will help you remember four steps: Describing the situation; Expressing feelings; Specifying changes; and pointing out Consequences. In situations in which expressing feelings may not be appropriate or useful, substitute Explaining for the second step. That is, instead of expressing how the behavior makes you feel, explain why the behavior is unsuitable or unacceptable. See 6.4.1 for examples of situations in which you might use DESC.

This skill is not guaranteed to work every time. The other person is always free to listen to your explanation about how the unacceptable behavior makes you feel and then say, "So what? That's your problem." But it works a lot better than some other styles of dealing with conflict, such as:

SOME QUICK TIPS

Listen to other people when they tell you about a problem they would like you to change. DESC depends on good will and trust.

Describe clearly what the behavior is and why it is a problem. Being indirect and general usually doesn't work because the message won't get through. For example, when you want Mary to start coming to meetings on time, it is not effective to say, "Mary, we hope that next week our committee can be more efficient." Mary may heartily agree, interpreting this comment as a criticism of certain digressors who sidetrack the committee's discussions.

Involve the other person in the solution. People are more apt to make changes if they feel that they have participated in the decision.

Practice the DESC script in your own mind before you use it.

Exercise

USING DESC

You are a librarian in charge of an information center in the head office of a large petrochemical company. Your clientele are the 200 scientists and researchers who work for the company.

The company has decided to expand the space available for offices. When you look at the plans, you see no provision to expand the space for the library. This is disheartening to you, especially since you have long been pointing out to your management committee that overcrowding limits your ability to provide information. Furthermore, you see that space is being wasted: the large hallway that bisects the library space is unnecessary and takes up space that you need.

What do you say?

D _____

_____

_____

E _____

_____

S _____

_____

C _____

_____

_____

—saying nothing about the problem and bottling up your feelings until one day you can't stand it any more and you explode. The other party may not have realized that her behavior bothered you. Let her know how you feel and why, so that she has the option of changing.

—attacking the other person's character and motives. An approach that makes other people feel guilty, put down, or maligned doesn't motivate them to change; it makes them defensive so that they stop listening and start arguing ("No, I'm not; no, I didn't; what about last week when you did such-and-such?").

DESC

Describe the unacceptable behavior in factual and unemotional terms. Simply describe the behavior. Do not attribute blame. Do not suggest reasons why the situation has occurred (such as that the other person has been selfish, thoughtless, careless, malicious, etc.)

"Mary, we have noticed that for the past three meetings of our committee, you have been fifteen minutes late."

Express how this makes you feel and why (or **Explain** why the behavior is unsuitable). If you can't explain why, the other person is not likely to feel motivated to change.

"When we have to wait for you, we *feel* frustrated *because* we are wasting our time when all of us are very busy."

Specify what changes you would like to see happen. Often it is best not to specify exactly how to implement the change, but to involve the other person in thinking through how best to achieve the desired outcome.

"We would like to schedule the next meeting at a time when everyone can be on time." (This gives Mary a chance to say, "I can't seem to get to 3:30 meetings on time because that's when I'm busiest. But if we could reschedule the meeting for 9:00 a.m., I could be on time.")

Consequences. Explain the good consequences of the proposed change or the bad consequences that the change will prevent.

"If you could come promptly, our committee could be more efficient."

3.14 GIVING FEEDBACK

You may be called upon to provide feedback in many situations that arise in libraries. For example:

—you are a supervisor doing a performance appraisal
—you are teaching a skill in a staff training session and have to evaluate a learner's performance
—your colleague has asked you to read over his report and offer suggestions for improvement
—your friend has asked you to listen to her booktalk and offer suggestions.

Here are some some guidelines for giving feedback. Start with one or two positive comments, even when the performance is not generally very good. Find something good that you can praise. You could say to the booktalker, "You chose an excellent book to talk about" or "I liked the way your own enthusiasm for the book came across" or "You kept very good eye contact throughout." Feedback that is entirely negative undermines the receiver's self-respect and discourages further effort. The person getting the entirely negative feedback is apt to think, "So-and-so is out to get me/isn't fair/doesn't appreciate how much work I've done on this." Conversely, suggestions for improvement offered in a generally encouraging and supportive climate are more likely to be accepted.

If you are a supervisor doing a performance appraisal, it is your job to provide feedback, both positive and negative. But if a friend or colleague asks you for feedback, leave that person in control of the kind and amount of feedback wanted. Feedback is more likely to be useful when it is solicited rather than imposed. For example, someone who says, "Please read my research proposal and point out places where it seems unclear or inadequate" probably will act on suggestions given.

Be specific. Don't say, "Your transparencies need improvement." Better to say, "I can't read your transparencies from the back of the room. Perhaps you might want to cut some of the text and use a larger size of type." Focus on concrete examples.

Be descriptive rather than simply evaluative. Don't say, "You kept the discussion going well" but "When you lead the group discussion, you asked five open questions that generated a lot of response." When you give negative feedback, it is especially important to stick to observable facts and behaviors. Not "You didn't do very well with that last reference interview" or even "When you were negotiating that interview, you seemed bored." It is better to say "When the user was talking to you, you were looking away and tapping your pencil."

Be realistic. Suggest improvements that you think the person is actually capable of making.

Limit your suggestions to two or three. If you ask for ten changes all at once, your suggestions will be discouraging rather than helpful.

Suggest rather than prescribe. In most situations, it works best to suggest a change tentatively as something the other person may want to consider, accept, modify, or set aside.

Consider the needs of the receiver of your feedback. Provide the amount of information that the receiver can use, rather than everything that can be said.

Seek out opportunities to offer sincere praise (people will recognize and resent insincerity). People work and learn better when their value is recognized and acknowledged.

Remember the key to giving feedback: create a climate that is positive and encouraging.

3.15 OFFERING OPINIONS AND SUGGESTIONS

Librarians are often asked to offer their opinions and suggestions: recommendations for reference sources or search procedures, feelings about an issue, opinions about preferred options. Even when opinions or suggestions are not requested, the librarian may find it helpful to bring new facts, skills, or points of view to the discussion. Offering opinions and suggestions involves many of the same skills as giving directions (see 3.11): using appropriate attending behavior, making clear and specific statements, and asking for feedback. However, unlike directions, opinions involve evaluative statements, judgments based on experience, personal perspectives, or individual attitudes and beliefs that may not be shared by the other person. Suggestions about what to do or how to solve a problem are a matter of personal judgment.

The first step in learning to offer opinions and suggestions effectively is to assess the situation. Has your opinion been sought? Have you been asked for suggestions? If not, consider the possibility that the other person may not be receptive. A common communication accident is to offer opinions and suggestions prematurely. (The user says, "I have to do a project on high technology" and the librarian responds with some suggested topics or sources, but the user just wants to find a picture of a computer.) Avoid premature diagnosis (3.6) by delaying suggestions until it is clear what kind of help the person wants.

Sometimes, the other person does not ask for your opinion or suggestions, but it seems that a new point of view might help. Check out the other person's willingness and readiness to hear what you have to say: "Would it help you if I told you how I feel about this?" or "Would you like some suggestions for what to do next?" Or indicate how your opinions and suggestions could help: "It might help you to decide if I suggested some options."

Even when someone asks for your opinion, there are times when it's not appropriate to offer either opinions or suggestions. In some cases, the other person is looking for support or reassurance rather than a true opinion ("How do you like my new office furniture?"). In other cases, it's unwise to offer an opinion that may be interpreted as expert advice or fact, especially when the topic is not within your expertise—when, for example, a library user wants to know if you think he should sue someone, or eat magic mushrooms. Or someone may ask whether you personally agree with the library's book selection policy when he really wants to find an ally for his crusade to remove certain books. In these cases, exercise intentionality by deciding the consequences of an opinion or suggestion. If you're not sure when or if you should offer an opinion, ask yourself "How would my opinion help (or harm) this person? What might the consequences be? What is this person trying to do?"

Offer suggestions or opinions in cases where they will help to solve a problem, but only when the other person is receptive. Follow these three steps:

1. Make sure that the other person is ready to hear your suggestions or opinions. Use your active listening skills. Make eye contact and use appropriate body language (see Chapter 1).
2. Be brief and specific, as in giving directions (3.11). State the suggestions clearly, and be specific without giving unnecessary detail. Do not let your opinions become a vehicle for excessive self-disclosure or long stories justifying the opinion.
3. Ask for feedback. Make sure the suggestions have been understood (or that the opinions have been correctly interpreted). For example, "Do any of these suggestions seem useful?" "Does

this seem reasonable to you?" "Does this give you any new ideas?"

SOME QUICK TIPS
Offering suggestions and opinions

Identify your opinions as opinions: "My personal feeling is. . ." "I think that. . ." "This is my opinion of this book, and it may not be shared by others."

Avoid saying "You should. . ." "You must. . ." "What you ought to do is. . . ." Most people don't like to be told what they *ought* to do. Say: "Let's think about some alternatives—one might be to change your topic" rather than "You ought to change your topic." Do not make suggestions in the form "If I were you, I would. . ." because, of course, you're not the other person and you can't really know what they would do. "If I were you" is the form in which a great deal of unsolicited and not very useful advice begins.

Express suggestions as options: "You can go three ways with this. You can place a reserve, and we will call you when the book comes in—this may take about three weeks. Or you could try the music library. Or perhaps we could look for a similar book that would help you."

Try using acknowledgment or reflection of feeling instead of giving unsolicited, irrelevant opinions or suggestions: For example, "It's certainly a problem when you're not sure what the teacher wants" may work better than "Oh, those teachers never explain the assignment. It drives us crazy trying to figure out these assignments. You ought to complain."

Distinguish between professional and personal opinions. Know when to express your professional opinion and when to express your personal opinion. "Some people have told us that they didn't like the violence in this book" is better than "Oh, don't read that— it's full of violence. You won't like it. I hated it." In this example, it is better when the librarian offers information rather than a personal opinion that may not be shared.

FOR FURTHER HELP

Ivey, Allen E. and Jerry Authier. *Microcounseling: Innovations in Interviewing, Counseling, Psychotherapy and Psychoeducation.* 2nd ed. Springfield, IL: C. C. Thomas, 1978.

Ivey, Allen E. *Intentional Interviewing and Counseling.* Monterey, CA: Brooks/Cole, 1983. This textbook provides a structured approach for learning the hierarchy of microskills. It includes a section for trainers.

3.4 Pausing

Ethel Auster and Stephen B. Lawton. "Search interview techniques and information gain as antecedents of user satisfaction with online bibliographic retrieval," *JASIS*, 35, 2 (1984): 90-103.

3.7 Neutral questions

Dervin, Brenda and Patricia Dewdney. "Neutral Questioning: A New Approach to the Reference Interview," *RQ*, 25, 4 (1986): 506-513.

Ross, Catherine Sheldrick. "How to Find Out What People Really Want to Know," *Reference Librarian*, 16 (Winter 1986): 19-30.

3.8 and 3.9 Reflecting content and feeling

Evans, David R. et al. *Essential Interviewing: A Programmed Approach to Effective Communication.* 2nd ed. Monterey, CA: Brooks/Cole, 1983. Chapter 4 deals with reflecting feeling and chapter 5 deals with reflecting content.

Hunt, Gary T. *Effective Communication.* Englewood Cliffs, NJ: Prentice-Hall, 1985.

3.11 Giving instructions

Ivey, Allen E. "Directives" in *Intentional Interviewing and Counseling.* Monterey, CA: Brooks/Cole, 1983, pp. 174-179.

3.12 Inclusion

Michell, Gillian and Roma M. Harris. "Evaluating the Competence of Information Providers," *RQ,* (Fall 1987): 95-105. A report of experimental research in which librarians who demonstrated the skill of inclusion in the reference interview were judged to be more effective information providers under certain conditions. This study suggests that males and females may perceive the use of inclusion differently.

White, Marilyn Domas. "The Dimensions of the Reference Interview," *RQ* (Summer 1981): 373-381. This article describes how the librarian can increase the coherence of the reference interview by explaining to the user what is happening.

3.13 Confrontation: DESC

Bower, Gorden and Sharon Bower. *Asserting Yourself: A Practical Guide for Positive Change*. Reading, MA: Addison-Wesley, 1976. Explains the technique of DESC and how to use it.

Caputo, Janette S. *The Assertive Librarian*. Phoenix, AZ: Oryx Press, 1984. Chapter 5 on "Verbal Assertion" includes a discussion of DESC.

Gordon, Thomas with Ruth Gordon Sands. *P.E.T. in Action*. New York: Bantam Books, 1976. Chapters 6, 7, 8 on I-Messages deal with managing confrontation.

3.15 Offering opinions and suggestions

Ivey, Allen E. *Intentional Interviewing and Counseling*. Monterey, CA: Brooks/Cole, 1983. Chapter 9 introduces the influencing skills of directives, logical consequences, interpretation, self-disclosure, advice, information, explanation, instruction, feedback and influencing, all of which are useful for learning how to offer suggestions and opinions.

4 WRITING

4.1 ANALYZING THE AUDIENCE

A written text is an intermediary in the process of communication between two active parties: the writer and the reader. As a writer, you expect to spend a lot of energy thinking about how to express your message in words. But you should also spend some time thinking about what your readers will do with the words you have written. Your readers will have to interpret your text, and their interpretation will be colored by many factors:

—their relationship to you
—their roles
—their skill at reading
—their knowledge of the topic
—their previous experiences, expectations, and biases.

Some of these constraints may be barriers preventing certain readers from interpreting your words as you intended. Unfortunately you won't hear from your readers about the difficulties they are having. They can't provide you with the sort of feedback that is posssible in a face-to-face conversation. Therefore, you should try to anticipate problems. Before starting to write, ask yourself these questions about your readers:

What is your *purpose?* What effect do you hope to have on your readers? Here are some common reasons for writing: to amuse; instruct; explain; generate interest; foster goodwill; ask for or give information; persuade to act; make a request; turn down a request; recommend; thank or congratulate someone; report some activity. Write with your effect in mind. Use a style suited to your purpose.

What do your readers *want to know* about this topic? Don't let your own need to inform take precedence over your readers' need to know. Use the "Who cares?" or the "So what?" test. If the answer is "Nobody cares" or "It makes no difference," than leave out the information, no matter how factual and accurate it may be. Consider the needs, interests, and experiences of your readers, and slant your writing to take these needs, etc. into account.

What *gaps* are there in your readers' understanding of your topic? What do your readers not know that you must tell them?

What do your readers *already know* that you won't need to tell them?

What sort of *format, organization*, and style of *presentation* will best help your readers understand your text?

What *biases* of your readers should you take into account?

Are your readers a *homogeneous group* who will understand a specialized vocabulary and professional jargon? If not, you will have to translate the jargon into understandable language.

Is your intended audience *internal or external* to your organization?

Will your writing have *more than one audience?* If it will go up a chain of approval through the hierarchy of the library, library board, or university senate, you need to take into account all of your audiences and not just the first one.

4.2 CHOOSING A STYLE

A good writer doesn't use the same style all the time but suits the style to the occasion. As Cicero put it in *De Oratore*, "no single kind of style can be adapted to every cause, or every audience, or every person, or every occasion." Here are some elements to consider when choosing a style:

FORMALITY

Choose an appropriate degree of formality. The range goes from slang to a style that is very formal. Avoid the extremes: slangy familiarity is unsuitable for business writing; equally unsuitable these days is the formal legalistic style that used to be recommended. Avoid phrases like *pursuant of, incumbent upon, aforementioned, heretofore, herewith, the said matter, letter of the 14th inst., please be advised, deem it advisable, the subject of your request, in accordance with your instructions,* and the like.

Views on writing style are embedded in their historical period and change through time. Thus Almonte C. Howell advised readers in *Military Correspondence and Reports* (New York: McGraw-Hill, 1943) "The writer should . . . not use the first person pronoun . . . not even the second should be used." These days such formality is out of fashion. A moderately informal style is best for most kinds of writing done in a library setting. For letters, memos, and internal reports, aim for a conversational style. Make your memo sound as if a real person has written it, not a machine. Use contractions like *it's* and *can't* rather than *it is* and *cannot*. Use personal pronouns like *we, you,* or *I think* rather than the impersonal *one thinks* or *it is thought* or *this writer thinks*.

For formal reports, you may want to achieve a more formal style by avoiding contractions and personal pronouns. But even here a plain style is best; there is no excuse for sounding stuffy, pompous, or bureaucratic.

EXAMPLE

Stilted and overly formal: This is to advise you that your request of the 18th inst. has been approved.

Conversational: You will be pleased to know that you may use the materials that you asked about in your May 18 letter.

TONE

Tone is the emotion or attitude that is conveyed by your writing. The basic rule of good professional writing is to adopt a courteous tone that respects the feelings of your readers. You may want to convey other tones as well: enthusiasm for a particular book in a book review; pride in institutional accomplishments in a report; regret in a letter that turns down a request; pleasure in a letter of congratulation. The following tones, however, are never appropriate: tones that are sarcastic; contemptuous; belittling; indifferent to the reader; or threatening. After you have written something, ask yourself how the reader will experience this memo, letter, report, etc. If in doubt, revise. Often you can improve the tone by recasting a negative message into a positive form.

EXAMPLES

Negative: Unless you pay these fines within two weeks, the library will cancel borrowing privileges and turn your account over to a collection agency.
Positive: Please pay these fines within two weeks so that we can settle your account promptly.

Negative: No exceptions can be made to this policy.
Positive: This policy applies equally to everyone.

Negative: We don't allow reference books to circulate.
Positive: We keep the reference books always available on the reference shelves to answer your questions.

READABILITY

Some writing is harder to read than others. The harder the text, the fewer the readers who will be able to understand what you have written. If you want your writing to be intelligible to the general population, don't write something requiring a college reading level

Exercise

STUDY READABILITY

Select a paragraph or two from something that you have written recently as part of your work.

Examine the passage in terms of the six factors that affect readability.

How readable is the passage?

Is its level of difficulty appropriate for the intended audience?

If not, revise the passage to make it easier to read.

or specialized background knowledge. The following are some of the factors that affect the readability of a text:

Vocabulary. Long abstract uncommon words are harder to understand than short concrete familar ones. Specialized jargon and acronyms are often unintelligible to the nonspecialist. Consider the following: OCLC, ALA, Sears, ILL, CIP, LC, CD-ROM, NUC. Unless you are sure that your readers will understand the shortened form, spell it out when you mention it first: ILL [Interlibrary Loan] or CIP [Cataloging in Publication].

Sentence structure. Long complex sentences with several subordinate clauses are harder to understand than short simple ones. Inverted word order is harder to understand than the normal order of Subject/ Verb/ Object. To make the text easier for readers, use short simple sentences written in normal order. On the other hand, using too many short regular sentences is deadly. Remember "See Sally jump. See Spot run"?

Conceptual difficulty. Some texts may be hard to read because the concepts being discussed are unavoidably complex and difficult. You won't be able to to simplify the concepts, but you can help the reader out by making your text as readable as possible in other respects: vocabulary, sentence structure, word order, organization, etc.

Background knowledge required. Sometimes readers need certain background knowledge before they can make sense of a text. You can help them by putting this necessary background information first or by referring them to some other source where they can find out the necessary background.

Organization of the text. Texts are easier to read when they are organized with the needs and expectations of the reader in mind. A method of organization that works well for many kinds of writing is: order of importance to the reader. Consider: what is the one thing that the reader most wants to know? and put this first. For other patterns of organization, see 4.5.

Motivation of the reader. If you can motivate your readers by showing that your text can help them, they will be more willing to cope with its difficulties.

A reminder: people commonly talk about readability as if it were a property of the text alone; it's not. Readability depends upon the interaction of the reader with the text. Simple texts are readable by almost all readers. The more complex the text, the fewer people will find it readable.

4.3 WRITING WITH IMPACT

Here are some suggestions for giving your writing more punch.

Try reading your sentence or paragraph out loud
If you can't read it without stumbling, there is probably something wrong with the rhythm. Usually it helps to revise it so as to make its rhythm closer to the cadences of the spoken language.

Use personal pronouns
If you want to involve your audience, don't be afraid to address the reader directly or to say *you, we,* and *I.*

Change: When the report was read, it was considered convincing.
To: When I read your report, I found it convincing.

Be concrete and specific
Use concrete words. You will convey a more precise image to the reader if, for example, you change *for some time* to a specific time period such as *for three years.*

Change: The event did not take place due to poor conditions.
To: The literacy program was called off because of the blizzard.

Prefer verbs to noun phrases
Verbs convey more energy than nouns. Compare:

He had the expectation of	He expected
She had knowledge about	She knew about
He made arrangements for	He arranged for

Watch for nouns formed from verb stems that end in -ation and

Exercise

WRITING WITH IMPACT
Rewrite the following sentences using verbs instead of noun phrases to convey the action:

1. She brought to a conclusion her examination of the problem.
2. Vincent undertook an evaluation of the system software.
3. The teacher was in a questioning mode.
4. The witness gave her testimony to the effect that. . .

Exercise

ACTIVE VERBS

Rewrite the following sentences to make the verb active.

1. In this book, step-by-step directions are provided on how to build a sauna.

2. An initiative was taken by the committee to survey the YA community.

In the following case, does it make any difference to the meaning which variant you use? Explain.

1. The children were taught long division by their teacher.

2. The teacher taught the children long division.

3. Long division was taught to the children by their teacher.

-ization. Using too many will bloat your sentences and spoil their rhythm.

Use the passive voice sparingly

Some styles of writing, such as certain kinds of research papers, require the passive voice. However, you can improve most writing and give it more energy by systematically replacing passive verbs with active ones. Using the passive voice is usually undesirable because:

—it wastes words
—it is often vague and impersonal, leaving the actor unidentified
—it leads to dangling constructions and misplaced modifiers (see 4.7).

Passive verbs are appropriate in the following instances:

—when you want to avoid shifting gears in mid-sentence: When the water started dripping through the ceiling onto the books, it was first noticed by the security guard.
—when you want to emphasize the object of the sentence rather than the actors: The card catalog was replaced in June by an online catalog.
—when the actors in the sentence are unknown: The elderly woman was run over on the street.
—when you know the actors but, for reasons of tact, don't want to identify them: The file was misplaced.

If your sentence is not among these exceptions, use the active voice. (You may find that it takes a conscious effort on your part to fight the passive construction syndrome. The problem is that so many people suffer from this syndrome that passive constructions may seem to be the norm.)

Change: After discussing options, the policy was developed by the committee. [Note the dangling construction here. See 4.7]
To: After discussing options, the committee developed the policy.

Change: It was noted by the Director. . .
To: The Director noted. . .

Change: The method of making a piñata was demonstrated by Carol to the children.
To: Carol showed the children how to make a piñata.

4.4 WRITING BRIEFLY

Here are two relatively easy ways to make your writing tighter and more economical.

OMIT UNNECESSARY WORDS

If you can leave out a word or phrase without changing the meaning, then cut out the unnecessary words. Go through your text after you have written it, looking for clutter. Replace wordy constructions.

Change:	To:
due to the fact that	because
in the event that	if
at this point in time	now
it is clear that	clearly
there are some librarians who	some librarians
twenty in number	twenty
in the majority of cases	usually
it is interesting to note that books	books
it is probable that	probably

PREFER SHORT, SIMPLE, AND CONCRETE WORDS

Change:	To:
discontinue	stop
utilize	use
commence	start
terminate	end
optimum	best
remuneration	pay

EXAMPLE

Wordy: Due to the fact that Mary lacks the necessary expertise to utilize word processing software to the required extent at this point in time, she is ineligible to obtain a promotion to a position with higher remuneration. [37 words]

Better: Because Mary doesn't yet know how to do word processing, she can't be promoted. [14 words]

Wordy: It is interesting to note that in the majority of cases where the introduction of new technology is initiated in an organizational setting, there is an increase in anxiety on the part of workers with respect to the continuence of their employment. [42 words]

Better: When new technology is brought into the workplace, workers often feel that their jobs are threatened. [16 words]

4.5 ORGANIZING

There is no "one best way" to organize. Everything depends on the subject matter, your purpose, and the reader. Choose the style of organization that will *save your reader's time.*

BE CLEAR ABOUT YOUR PURPOSE FOR WRITING

Don't leave your readers guessing what your main point is. Tell them right away unless there is some good reason not to. Subtle indirection and obliqueness, which are often virtues in literary writing, are usually faults in business writing. Here are four things you can do to clarify your purpose:

1. State your purpose clearly at the beginning. Tell your readers: a) why you are writing; and b) what, if anything, you want them to do.

[A report] This report summarizes the results of a six-month study of staff training programs for reference librarians.

[A memo] Please look at the attached proposal for reorganizing the Children's Department and let me know if you agree with the recommendations.

2. Write a first sentence for each paragraph that indicates what the paragraph is about and how the paragraph is related to your purpose overall. This *topic sentence* provides a generalized state-

ment, which the rest of the paragraph supports by specific details, examples, etc.

[Topic sentence] Last year, in planning our conference, we paid too little attention to timing.

[Supporting details] Three of the talks didn't start on time and several speakers went over their allotted time. . .

Participants had no time to ask questions. . .

Presenters giving talks at the end of the day ran out of time.

3. Summarize complex arguments at the end, repeating the key ideas.

In summary, the three reasons to oppose Sunday openings of the library are. . . .

4. Use formatting to help your reader see the overall structure of long or complex passages. Break up a long block of text into coherent units. Use titles, headings, and subheadings to draw attention to the content of the units. Commonly used headings for various kinds of reports and memos include: Statement of the problem, Background information, Scope, What happened, Findings, Results of the study, Recommendations, Further considerations, Points for further study, Possible problems, Implications, Current status, Action requested, and Implementation.

INCLUDE ONLY NECESSARY DETAILS
If one of your examples, statistics, and quotations fails the "So what" test, cut it out. Be selective and discriminating. Don't overwhelm your readers with facts they don't need to know.

CHOOSE AN APPROPRIATE ORDER
The following are common methods of organization:

Order of importance: With this form of organization, you start with the most important points first and proceed in decreasing order of importance. Information and arguments presented early in a piece of writing have more impact than information and arguments presented later. The details at the end are least important and can be cut by an editor who is short of space. (When in doubt, arrange the points in order of importance to the reader, not in the order of importance to the writer.)

Topical: This method is useful when a topic has some obvious subdivisions (management and union; writers, publishers, and distributers; three ways to improve reference service).

Chronological: Use this method when the time sequence is important, as when giving instructions (first do this, second do this, and so on), explaining a process, narrating an event, reporting information about trends, or describing historical development (beginnings; expansion; flowering; decay).

Spatial: Use this method to indicate spatial relationships, as when presenting information on geographical regions or when describing the physical layout of a building (the east wing of the library; the west wing; the regional room on the second floor). Pick one spatial sequence and stick to it: left to right; top to bottom; north to south; the first room reached on the tour to the last room.

Comparison: When you want to compare two or more items, you may find it best to select relevant attributes and discuss each of the items with respect to these attributes. For example, if you were evaluating which jobber to use, you might organize your findings like this:

Turnaround time	Jobber A
	Jobber B
Cost	Jobber A
	Jobber B
Completeness in filling orders	Jobber A
	Jobber B

Pro and Con: When you are evaluating something, you can cluster into two sets all the arguments *for* a proposal and all the arguments *against* a proposal.

Logical sequence: Two kinds of logical arrangements are problem/solution and cause/effect (or effect/cause).

4.6 USING TABLES, CHARTS, AND GRAPHS

A writing task often involves the summarizing of quantitative data. You may present quantitative data in words, in tables, or in graphics, and each method has its own advantages. A presentation in words can explain, interpret, and evaluate. But a sentence is a poor way to show the relationships among a lot of numbers. Consider this sentence: "Nearly 61% of Group A did such-and-such, as compared with 29% of Group B and 35% of Group C." The comparison is much clearer when the data is presented in a table (see at left.)

Charts and graphs can present a mass of numeric data in a visual form that readers can take in at a glance. Appropriately used, charts and graphs:

—show the data in a way that clarifies relationships
—present many numbers in a small space
—make the data easier to understand
—provide visual impact
—save the reader's time.

PERCENTAGE WHO DID SUCH-AND-SUCH	
Group A	61%
Group C	35%
Group B	29%

The most commonly used charts are pie charts, bar graphs, and line charts.

DID YOU KNOW?
You can easily calculate the proper angle to use to draw a pie segment if you keep in mind the following formula for conversion.

Think of a circle as divided into 100 equal parts to represent 100 percent. Since a circle is 360 degrees, each of the 100 parts is equal to 3.6 degrees. To get the proper angle for a pie segment, multiply the percentage by 3.6. For example, a segment representing 25% of the whole is drawn with an angle of 90 degrees (25 x 3.6).

Pie charts show how the whole of something is divided into its parts. The circle or pie always represents 100 percent. Pie segments are drawn in proportion to the size of the parts making up the whole. Proportions are therefore very easy to see at a glance, which is why pie charts are so popular for showing how a sum of money is spent.

Pie charts work best with six or fewer segments. With more segments, they become confusing and lose their effectiveness. However, if the data you are reporting has more than six categories, you can reduce the number of segments in your pie chart by collapsing some of the categories. For example, suppose that you wanted to show the percentage of English book readers who lived in various provinces. Instead of using ten segments for the ten provinces of Canada, you could use five segments: Atlantic provinces 10%, Quebec 5%, Ontario 47%, Prairie provinces 21%,

1987 Library Budget

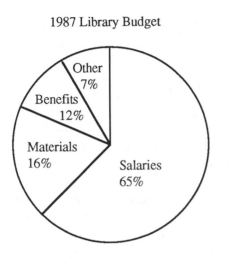

British Columbia 17% (From James Lorimer's *Book Reading in Canada*, Toronto: ACP, 1983).

The illustration (left) shows how a pie chart can be used to summarize how the library budget was spent in 1987.

The problem with pie charts (apart from the trickiness of drawing the pie segments accurately) is that it can be hard for the reader to compare small variations in the size of the segments. This is why pie charts are not highly esteemed by statisticians. However, pie charts can be a very effective way of illustrating the relative size of the parts to the whole, e.g., market share held by individual computer manufacturers, the breakdown of the total cost of manufacturing a book.

Label the pie chart clearly (all lettering should be horizontal so that the reader won't have to turn the page sideways to read the label). You need a title over the chart that explains the factor being analyzed (expenditures, age, ethnic origin), the time period referred to, and the unit of measurement (number, percent). And you need a label for each segment, children x% , young adults y% , adults z%.

Two or more pie charts can be used to illustrate comparisons—one pie chart to represent the sources of income and another pie chart to represent expenditures. But make sure that you make the circles the same size.

Bar graphs use the length of bars to represent values such as frequency, amount, weight, cost, participation rate, etc. Since each bar is separate from its neighbor, the bar graph is suited to representing information about separate units, as in the illustration showing the percentage of readers who read different genres of fiction books. Bar charts can be used to show percentages or to show absolute numbers.

The length of the bar is determined by the value or amount of each variable, measured on a scale that should begin at zero. The bars should be arranged systematically in a form appropriate to the chart's purpose. An arrangement by size from largest to smallest is common, but other possibilities include an arrangement by time, by alphabetical order, or by geographical location.

Bar and column graphs differ only in the placement of the oblong boxes: when the box is placed horizontally, it is called a bar graph; when it is placed vertically, it is called a column graph. Deciding which way the bars should run is a matter of convenience and common sense. Horizontal bars are easier to label, but vertical

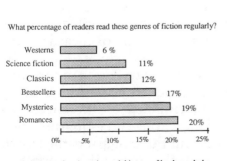

What percentage of readers read these genres of fiction regularly?

Percentage of readers who read this type of book regularly

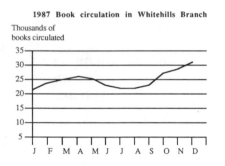

1987 Book circulation in Whitehills Branch

columns seem to some people a more appropriate representation of growth factors such as weight or height or units produced.

Line charts are made by plotting a series of values along two scales (the line is the result of connecting the dots that represent the plotted values). Line charts show how changes in one factor are related to changes in another. Familiar examples include patients' temperature graphs, graphs showing fluctuation in share prices or increases in government debt, and graphs showing the distribution of students' marks. Whereas bar graphs present information in a limited number of discrete steps, line charts present continuous information spread over a lot of data points.

The most commonly used line chart is the time-series, which plots the occurrence of something over time, measured in seconds, hours, months, years, decades, centuries, etc. The time-series is a succinct way of showing trends, patterns, or changes over time, such as the number of books circulated each month or the number of Masters of Library Science degrees granted each year. Line charts can also be used to link two variables that are not in a time-series, such as the relationship between the number of school years completed and the amount of income earned.

The essential elements in a line chart are the horizontal or X-axis, the vertical or Y-axis, the plotted line, the scale or grid lines, and the plotted points. In a time chart, you should use the horizontal axis to represent time, expressed in units such as days, months, years, decades, etc. Use the vertical axis to represent the amount of the variable being measured such as temperature, price, circulation figures. When your line chart is not a time-series, use the horizontal axis to represent the variable that changes regularly in a series of equal divisions, such as the number of school years completed (often the independent variable, i.e., the variable treated as the cause). Use the vertical axis to represent the variable that changes irregularly, such as amount of income earned (often dependent variable, i.e., the variable treated as the effect).

Sometimes line graphs can convey a distorted impression of the data. The distances you select to represent units of measurement are crucial. If you compress the vertical axis by reducing the distance between the grid markings, you tend to flatten out the line and minimize differences. If you lengthen the vertical axis by spacing out the grid markings, you emphasize differences. To avoid these distortions in scale, follow the three-quarter rule: make the height of the vertical axis about three quarters the length of the horizontal axis. Distortion can also occur if quantitative scales are not made to start at zero. If a large part of the scale is left out, small changes appear exaggerated and are hard for the reader to keep in proportion.

SOME QUICK TIPS
Using charts and graphs

Before you decide on the form of visual display to use, ask yourself, "What am I trying to show?" Choose the form that will best convey your intended point.

Make the data stand out clearly.

Eliminate clutter. Too much detail can be confusing. Limit the number of curves on a line chart to three if the lines cross, four if they don't.

Avoid what Tufte calls "chartjunk"—all that ink that doesn't convey information such as "overbusy grid lines and excess ticks, redundant representations of the simplest data, the debris of computer plotting, and many of the devices generating design variation".

On line charts, don't use grid marks that interfere with the presentation of the data. Small tick marks are usually preferable.

Label all the parts of the graphic clearly. Whenever possible, put labels on the graphic itself to eliminate for the reader the extra step of consulting a legend. Give your chart a descriptive label so that the reader can easily tell what the graphic is supposed to demonstrate.

Design the graphic with the reader's convenience in mind. Don't use cryptic abbreviations or coding involving crosshatching that make reading the graph into an exercise in code-breaking. Avoid using all capitals for labels. Keep the lettering horizontal: vertical lettering is hard to read, and words running in several different directions look cluttered.

Proofread. Doublecheck the accuracy of the numeric data.

4.7 AVOIDING COMMON GRAMMATICAL ERRORS

Hundreds of excellent books are available on grammar and correct usage. Use them by all means. However, since 20% of writing errors account for 80% of actual problems, you should pay most attention to the 20%. Eliminate from your writing the following most common errors.

Exercise

DANGLING CONSTRUCTIONS

How would you correct the following dangling constructions?

1. Being in a damaged condition, I was able to buy the book very cheap. (What was in a damaged condition? the buyer or the book?)

2. As a mother of three teenagers, my telephone is always busy.

3. To find something quickly, the book must be indexed.

4. Lifting the heavy stack of encyclopedias, her face turned quite red from exertion.

5. As the Project Director, several of Bill's initiatives for getting funding were successful.

6. Being open on Sunday, the circulation staff was very busy.

DANGLING CONSTRUCTIONS

A participial phrase, infinitive, or modifier at the beginning of a sentence must refer to the grammatical subject. A rule of thumb is to look at the word directly after the comma; is this word the one that the modifier is really intended to refer to? If not, revise the sentence. Consider this sentence:

Worried about the coming examinations, even the houses on the street seemed threatening to Sally. [Who was worried—the houses?]

It should be revised as follows:

Worried about the coming examinations, Sally found even the houses on the street threatening.

AMBIGUOUS OR FAULTY PRONOUN REFERENCES

Make sure that your pronouns agree with their antecedents and that each pronoun has a clear antecedent. Consider:

Anne had hoped to go with Carol to the theater but she couldn't afford the ticket. (Who couldn't afford the ticket? Anne or Carol?)

The advisory group recommended a national survey of libraries to assess bibliographic control of official publications, but the committee thought it unsuitable. (What does the *it* refer to—the use of a national survey? or the entire recommendation?)

A writer must first analyze their audience. (This construction avoids the problem of deciding whether to use *his* or the inclusive but awkward *his or her*. However the sentence is still wrong because the plural pronoun *they* does not agree with the singular antecedent *writer*. It would be better to use the plural for both the noun and the pronoun: Writers must first analyze their audiences.)

COMMA ERRORS

Do not use a comma to separate two independent clauses.

Change: Carol was on time, however, many others were late.
To: Carol was on time. However many others were late.
or, Although Carol was on time, many others were late.

Enclose a parenthetic expression between commas.

Change: Many people however, like spy stories.
To: Many people, however, like spy stories.

FAULTY PARALLELISM

Present parallel ideas in a parallel form.

Change: She has the necessary writing skills, background knowledge, and can organize well.
To: She has the necessary writing skills, background knowledge, and ability to organize.

When you use the construction *not only X but also Y*, remember that X and Y should be grammatically equivalent. If X is an infinitive, then Y must be an infinitive; if X is a clause, then Y should be a clause.

Mary was not only *late* but also *unrepentent.*
Mary not only *came late* but also *left early.*

PROBLEMS WITH POSSESSIVES

Add an apostrophe and s to form the possessive of all nouns, both plural and singular, unless the plural already ends in an s. If the plural already ends in an s, add an apostrophe only. Hence: a year's work; three years' experience; Dickens's book; this library's staff; all the libraries' staff; woman's work; women's work; *Morris's Disappearing Bag.*

With regard to pronouns, only indefinite pronouns use an apostrophe to form the possessive. Hence: anybody's guess; someone's mistake. But note that there is no apostrophe used to form the possessive of definite pronouns: hers; theirs; its. [*It's* is not the proper form of the possessive but a contraction for *It is.*]

4.8 FORMATTING THE PAGE

Printed materials convey nonverbal messages too. Consider the messages that are conveyed by the following: spelling mistakes; strikeovers in typing; a letter crowded onto the top half of the page; poor quality paper; inconsistency from page to page in the width of the margins, the placement of the page numbers, or the capitalization of headings.

Appearance counts. At worst, a cramped, unattractive page design may discourage readers from reading the text at all (this is especially true of publicity materials, where the reader has no obligation to look at what you have written). At best, a good design can enhance, reinforce, or clarify the text's significance. Design elements should not be simply decorative; they should be functional, helping to make the text intelligible or to draw attention to something of importance.

SOME QUICK TIPS
Keep the design simple

Get help from professional designers. The ALA Public Information Office has published *ALA Library Clip Art* (Chicago: American Library Association, 1983). The introduction tells you how to do a basic pasteup, while the body of the book contains professional designs on "crack and peel" backing that you can peel off and use in your own layouts. The designs are grouped by the topics Services, Programs, People, Occasions, and Ready To Go.

To see what other librarians have done, write the ALA Heaquarters Library for materials from its PR Info Bank. Use interlibrary loan to borrow a packet of library publicity material (packets available are: annual reports, booklists, calendars, information brochures, newsletters, programming flyers, and promotion of information and referral).

Be consistent. Decide on the width of margins, the size, style and placement of headlines, and stick to the same design throughout.

Break up long chunks of text into smaller units. People find shorter passages of text more inviting and less intimidating to read.

Use white space. Think of the blank page as space to be organized into an intelligible design of black and white. Remember that the white space is not the accidental area left over, but an an active part of the design of the page. Use white space to frame the text and highlight important divisions. For letters and reports, leave generous margins of at least 1.25 inches (3 cm.). Break up long blocks of text by leaving space between the sections. For newsletters, flyers, and publicity materials, use empty spaces boldly as a deliberate contrast to the full spaces.

When the text is to be printed, take legibility into account in the selection and arrangement of type. For most printed materials, it is best to pick one family of type and stick to it throughout. Mixing typefaces can produce a cluttered appearance. Sans serif typefaces like Helvetica are spare and modern-looking. (Serifs are the small counterstrokes at the ends of the main strokes.) But readability studies support the view that serif typefaces are easier to read

48 point Times

48 point Helvetica

than sans serif for long blocks of text. Most readers like serif type better too (when the old *New York World Journal Tribune* switched from sans serif to serif type, circulation went up).

Most of this book is set in twelve point type, but readers that are either under ten or over sixty-five often prefer something larger (and no one likes to read anything as small as six point type).

Other factors that affect legibility of type include: the number of characters per line; the amount of space between the letters and between the words (called letter spacing and word spacing); and the amount of space between the lines (called leading and pronounced to rhyme with sledding). For an excellent discussion of these matters, see Miles Tinker, *The Legibility of Print.*

Give emphasis to a heading, phrase, or word by using one or more of the following methods: **Boldface**, <u>underlining</u>, size, *italic*, CAPITALS, **different typefaces**, borders, or typographic devices. If you are using a typewriter, but want larger type for headlines, you can use dry-transfer or press-down lettering such as Letraset. Available in art stores, it comes in a variety of type styles and sizes. But, again, use restraint. Remember that combining more than two or three different styles or typefaces makes the page look cluttered.

Use charts and graphs to summarize numeric information (see 4.6).

Use graphics to catch the reader's interest. If you yourself aren't skilled at drawing, you can use clip art of noncopyrighted materials to paste into your page layout (clip art is already prepared artwork that you can cut out and paste onto your page). Line drawings in black and white reproduce better on photocopy machines than does art that uses shades of gray, which is why 19th century line engravings are so plentiful in books of clip art. A convenient source of clip art is the above-mentioned *ALA Library Clip Art*, compiled by the American Library Association in 1983. In addition, Dover Publications Inc. publishes paperback books containing noncopyrighted clip art illustrations, motifs, emblems, costumes, designs, patterns, symbols, borders, alphabets, and typographic devices like arrows, flourishes, florets, and hands. "Up to ten illustrations may be used on any one project or in any single publication, free and without special permission." For a list of titles, write Dover Publications, 31 East Second St., Mineola, NY, 11501. Some titles available are: Carol Belanger Grafton, *1,001 Floral Motifs and Ornaments for Artists and Craftspeople* (New York: Dover Publications, 1987); Blanche Cirker, *1800 Woodcuts by Thomas Bewick and His School* (New York: Dover Publications, 1962); Jim Harter, *Hands:*

A Pictorial Archive from Nineteenth-Century Sources (New York: Dover Publications, 1985); Jim Harter, *Food and Drink: A Pictorial Archive from Nineteenth-Century Sources*. 2nd rev. ed. (New York: Dover Publications, 1980); Jim Harter, *Animals: 1419 Copyright-Free Illustrations of Mammals, Birds, Fish, Insects, etc.* (New York: Dover Publications, 1979).

Jan White's *Editing by Design* (pp. 204-210) offers some usable ideas for making your own illustrations for publicity materials: inexpensive materials from the stationery store such as rubber stamps, mailing labels, gummed stars, and stickers saying Air Mail, Special Handling, Do Not Fold, or Confidential can all be used; ink blots printed in red ink make convincing blood stains (for your bookmark on crime stories perhaps?); electrostatic impressions of small, flattish objects like a pencil or magnifying glass can be made on a photocopier and reduced or enlarged.

4.9 USING THE COMPUTER

Computers can make you a more more productive writer and can help you produce attractive letters, forms, reports, newsletters, posters, brochures, etc. Although the better you are at typing the more efficient you'll be, you don't have to be an accurate typist to get professional-looking documents. Mistakes can be fixed on the screen before the document is printed. Here are five ways in which using computers can enhance your written product.

WORD PROCESSING

Word processing has revolutionized the task of writing. This new technology makes editing easier and gives control over the final appearance of the printed document. Used along with sophisticated printers, word processing software allows you to justify margins, combine different type faces, and integrate text and graphics.

All word processors allow you to input text, edit text, move chunks of text from one place in the document to another, and format output. Optional features provided by some word processors include the following: automatic hyphenation; outlining; spelling checker; search and replace features; the ability to create footnotes, indexes, or running heads (the same words repeated at the top of each page); the ability to sort selected text alphabetically or numerically; the ability to number lines in a document; and the

DID YOU KNOW?

You can now get the full text of reference books on CD-ROM discs to use with the word processor on personal computers. Microsoft Corp's *Microsoft Bookshelf* provides ten reference works and writing tools on a single CD-Rom disc (such as *American Heritage Dictionary*, Roget's *Thesaurus*, Bartlett's *Familiar Quotations, Chicago Manual of Style, World Almanac and Book of Facts*, etc.)

ability to integrate graphics and tables into the text. Such features can save you time: for example, if you realize that in a long report you have sometimes referred to your bibliography as a Bibliography or you have consistently misspelled a particular word, you can use the search and replace feature to find the unwanted variant and replace it with the preferred form. Since the search and replace feature looks for typed characters, it can be asked to check punctuation for inconsistencies. For example, you can search for ". and replace with ." Another useful feature of some word processors, the outliner, allows writers to print out the outline of a text to any level of heading, sub-heading, or sub-sub-heading.

Some word processors now offer features formerly the preserve of page layout programs: the ability to create running heads that get typed in once and thereafter appear automatically at the top of each page; multiple columns of variable size; and frames. (Frames are windows that can be of any size, can be placed anywhere on the page, and can be filled with either text or graphics. See below for desktop publishing.)

The widespread phenomenon of word processing has also had the effect of generally raising the standards expected of printed materials. People are getting used to seeing documents formatted using multiple typefaces and type sizes and printed on a laser printer giving almost typeset quality output. The public is therefore less tolerant of amateurish newsletters, flyers, and publicity materials manually produced on typewriters, especially if the typing isn't perfect.

Spelling checking and style checking

A document created on a word processor can be checked on a spelling checker. A spelling checker works by matching the words in your text against the words in its own dictionary. Therefore it catches misspelled words and typographical errors like *alot* or *errrors*. But be aware of what it *won't* do: it won't catch mistakes like *it's* used as a possessive or *stationery* used to mean motionless; it won't recognize that you have written *you* instead of *your*, *batch* instead of *match* or *wards* instead of *words*. A spelling checker matches patterns of letters; it doesn't analyze meanings of words to determine whether a word is correct in its context.

Other programs check stylistic features. Commonly, such programs check sentence length for overly long sentences and point out solecisms such as passive constructions, cliches *(through thick and thin)*, split infinitives *(to cheerfully serve)*, wordiness *(at this point in time)*, imprecise language *(a lot)*, polysyllabic words

This border pattern, created with a drawing program, was formed by rotating, reflecting, and duplicating the single design element shown below. (Design by Jacob Ross) For more design ideas, see Peter S. Stevens, *Handbook of Regular Patterns: An Introduction to Symmetry in Two Dimensions*. (Cambridge, MA: The MIT Press, 1980.)

(inadvertent infelicities) and faulty punctuation. Like spelling checkers, style checkers work by matching patterns and do not take into account meanings. They are useful because they highlight for your attention suspected stylistic faults that you may have overlooked. But they don't relieve you of the final responsibility of exercising your own judgment: you may still decide that a passive construction or a very long sentence like this one is appropriate to achieve your intended meaning. But if you decide to leave unchanged certain passages highlighted by your style checker, you will be making a conscious choice rather than falling into inadvertent infelicities.

Graphics

You can create your own, using one of the many graphics software packages available, or you can buy electronic clip art containing designs and illustrations that you can paste into your own document. (Electronic clip art, like ordinary clip art, consists of noncopyrighted pictures, maps, decorative borders, except that you do the cutting and pasting electronically.)

Charts and graphs

With software for making charts, you input the correct data, choose the format, and the software does the drafting work—calculating the correct size of the segments in a pie chart, creating the grid, and drawing the line(s) on a line graph, etc. However, you still have to know enough about graphic presentation to select the graphic form most appropriate for your data set (see 4.6) and for your audience. Be cautious with design: it is fatally easy to clutter up your computer pie charts and bar graphs with cross-hatchings, dots, lines, checkerboards, etc. so that your graphs have the restless, flickering moiré effect of pop art rather than the desired simplicity and functionality of a good chart.

Desktop publishing

Desktop publishing is not really publishing. It is an inexpensive way of producing high quality camera-ready copy. Desktop publishing became possible when inexpensive laser printers came on the market, providing output that most people can scarcely distinguish from typeset quality. Until the laser printer, the limiting factor was the output device. Daisy wheel printers couldn't do graphics; dot matrix printers, which could produce graphics and a variety of typefaces on the same page, didn't produce a sharp enough image. Dot matrix printers produce around 80 dots per

DID YOU KNOW?

Xerox claims that studies show that documents produced on desktop publishing systems are read 27% faster than the same documents produced on typewriters.

inch (dpi). Laser printers changed all this, giving graphics and a variety of typefaces with greater speed and a lot less noise. Laser printers now produce 300 dpi (and there are 600 dpi laser printers coming onto the market)—less than the 1200 dpi of medium quality typesetting, but acceptable for most purposes.

In addition to a laser printer, the other things necessary for desktop publishing are: a personal computer; a software package that does word processing; and a software package that does page layout. Pages produced on the laser printer can be cheaply reproduced in quantity on photocopiers or used as the camera-ready copy for offset printing. Most libraries already own a computer and word processing software. By acquiring a page layout program and a laser printer, the library can also achieve near typeset quality for its newsletters, flyers, posters, ads, and handouts. (If you haven't got a laser printer, you can rent the use of one fairly inexpensively from a business that sells time on printing equipment.) Other uses of desktop publishing include making the originals for transparencies and handouts.

A common pattern for organizations acquiring desktop publishing capabilities is to start out with short jobs like transparencies, flyers, and bookmarks. The next step is longer texts: reports, procedures manuals, newsletters, books. Here's where desktop publishing offers dramatic savings in money and time over traditional publishing methods.

With traditional methods, a published text goes through many labor-intensive stages, each of which provides chances for the introduction of error. The writer types out the copy and it is sent to the typesetter. The typesetter rekeys the words (usually adding typographical errors), prints out a galley for proofreading, corrects errors that the author or editor find, and prints out the text again. Graphics, which must be handled separately, require camera work if halftones are used or if the pictures need to be enlarged or reduced to fit the available space in the layout. Meanwhile the editor designs the preliminary layout. Next comes the pasteup. The corrected text, the photos, and the artwork all have to be physically cut up into pieces and pasted onto sheets to produce the camera-ready copy that goes to the printer. Errors caught at this stage have to be re-typeset and the corrected copy pasted in.

Desktop publishing eliminates many of these steps. The writer produces the text in the first place on a computer using a word processing program. The electronic text is then imported, without changes or new errors, into a page layout program. The writer (or editor as the case may be) can use the page layout program to generate very quickly alternate page layouts: What would this page look like in three columns? In two columns? With the graphic centered in the middle of the page? With the graphic placed at the bottom? What would it look like in ten point Times roman type leaded three points? What would it look like in Palatino? Computer graphics can be imported into a page layout program and then scaled, cropped, and moved around on the page. Since all the pasting of the separate elements of the page is done electronically, the page printed by the laser printer is camera-ready. A mistake found at the last minute can be quickly fixed and the page reprinted.

With this desktop revolution in publishing, libraries can afford to give printed documents the professional, designed look that used to be the preserve of large commercial organizations.

4.10 POSTSCRIPT: KEEPING YOUR READER IN MIND

Consider the three elements that enter into any piece of writing:

WRITER   TEXT   READER

Throughout this chapter we have emphasized the importance of the reader, the invisible partner in the enterprise. Try to make your writing reader-centered rather than writer-centered. Writer-centered texts are organized in ways that are convenient for the writer and contain information that the writer wants to convey. Reader-centered texts are organized in ways that help the reader make sense of the text and that contain information that answers questions in the reader's mind.

Some quick tips for writing reader-centered texts:
—Write the first draft in whatever order is easiest for you. But organize (or reorganize) the final draft so that it serves the needs of your intended readers.
—Write from the reader's point of view. Your reader approaches the text with tacit questions in mind: How does this text help me? How does it answer my questions? Why should I care about this? So what? What does the writer want me to do? Why is it in my interest to do what the writer wants me to do? What are the

DID YOU KNOW?
When the US Federal Communications Commission issued its regulations for citizen band radios written in traditional legal language, it took five staff members all their time just to answer the public's questions. When the regulation was rewritten in plain language, all the questions stopped and all five people could be reassigned to other duties. Cited in Gail Dykstra, *Plain Language and the Law.* (Toronto: Canadian Law Information Council, 1986, p. 11.)

implications of this information for me? *Your writing should answer these questions.*

—Write texts intended for the general public in plain language that ordinary people can understand. Your language should not be a barrier between the public and what the public wants to know.

FOR FURTHER HELP

Guides to technical writing

Alred, Gerald J. et al. *Business and Techical Writing: An Annotated Biblography of Books 1880-1980*. Metuchen, NJ: Scarecrow Press, 1981. Lengthy annotations on 100 years of books on technical writing put the topic into historical perspective.

Bowman, Mary Ann and Joan D. Stamas. *Written Communication in Business: A Selective Bibliography 1967 to 1977*. Champaign, IL: American Business Communication Association, 1980. Designed for teachers, writers, and librarians, this bibliography briefly annotates 800 books and articles published 1967-77 on the writing of business letters, memos, reports, employee publications, resumes, and direct mail.

Moran, Michael and Debra Journet, eds. *Research on Technical Communication: A Bibliographic Sourcebook*. Westport, CT: Greenwood Press, 1985.

These journals regularly publish articles on aspects of business writing:
IEEE Transactions on Professional Communication
The Journal of Business Communication

4.2 to 4.4 Writing clearly, concisely, and correctly

Corbett, Edward P. *Classical Rhetoric for the Modern Student*. 2nd ed. New York: Oxford University Press, 1971. For a discussion of the figures, tropes, arrangements of words, and other stylistic resources available to the writer. This book covers aspects of writing style that are not covered in *Communicating Professionally* and that are usually shortchanged in books on business and technical writing.

Gunning, Robert. "The Fog Index After Twenty Years," *The Journal of Business Communication*, 6, 2 (Winter 1968): 3-13. Discusses the development and use of the Fog Index, an index of readability presented first in Robert Gunning's *The Technique of Clear Writing*. New York: McGraw-Hill, 1952.

Laird, Dugan. *Writing for Results: Principles and Practices*. Reading, MA: Addison-Wesley, 1978. Contains assignments, discussion questions, and exercises on the general principles of business writing and organization, on letter formats, and on report writing.

Mendelson, Michael. "Business Prose and the Nature of the Plain Style," *The Journal of Business Communication,* 24, 2 (Spring 1987): 3-18. Argues that the plain style currently advocated in business communication texts is too narrow and limiting. He recommends that writers develop a repertoire of stylistic choices that includes figures of speech and rhetorical arrangements of words.

Northey, Margot. *Impact: A Guide to Business Communication.* Scarborough, ON: Prentice-Hall Canada, 1986.

Selzer, Jack. "Readability is a Four-Letter Word," *The Journal of Business Communication*, 18, 4 (Fall 1981): 22-30.

Strunk, William Jr. and E.B. White. *The Elements of Style.* 3rd. ed. New York: Macmillan, 1979. Concise and elegant—a classic.

Zinsser, William. *On Writing Well: An Informal Guide to Writing Nonfiction.* 3rd ed. New York: Harper and Row, 1988.

4.6 Using charts and graphs

Hartley, James. "Eighty Ways of Improving Instructional Text," *IEEE Transactions on Professional Communication*, PC-24, 1 (March 1981): 17-27. Part of the article summarizes research on what makes for effective tables and graphs.

Tufte, Edward R. *The Visual Display of Quantitative Information.* Cheshire, CT: Graphics Press, 1983. An elegant book that sets forth the theory and practice of designing statistical graphics, charts, maps, and tables.

4.8 Formatting the page

Dair, Carl. *Design with Type.* Toronto: University of Toronto Press, 1967. Discusses the elements of typography, considered separately and then in relationship. A model of excellent book design in itself.

Gray, Bill. *Tips on Type.* New York: Van Nostrand Reinhold, 1983. Discusses topics like picking a typeface, design of first lines of paragraphs, achieving emphasis, spacing, using dry transfer type, etc.

Munce, Howard. *Graphics Handbook: A Beginner's Guide to Design, Copy Fitting and Printing Procedures.* Cincinnati, Ohio: North Light Publishers, 1982. Intended for "people who suddenly find themselves appointed to be in charge of mailings, brochures, flyers, announcements, booklets and advertisements."

Pocket Pal: A Graphic Arts Production Handbook. New York: International Paper Company. Revised every few years and now in its 13th edition. An authoritative introduction to printing and the graphic arts for designers, artists, and students. Available from International Paper Company, International Paper Plaza, 77 West 45th St., New York, NY, 10036.

Tinker, Miles A. *The Legibility of Print.* Ames, IA: Iowa State University Press, 1963. An excellent summary of research on the factors that make print legible: the kind of type used, type size, leading, line length, color or print and background.

Turnbull, Arthur T. and Russell N. Baird. *The Graphics of Communication: Typography, Layout, Design, Production*. 4th ed. New York: Holt, Rinehart and Winston, 1980. A basic textbook.

White, Jan. *Editing by Design: A Guide to Effective Word-and-Picture Communication for Editors and Designers*. 2nd ed. New York: R.R. Bowker, 1982. An excellent how-to book that explains the why's behind the how-to's. White discusses page layout, choice of type faces, how to avoid design errors, and how to use pictures and charts.

4.9 Desktop publishing

Small Computers in Libraries runs articles on all aspects of using small computers in libaries, including using desktop publishing, page layout programs, graphics programs, etc.

Publish! A "How-to" Magazine of Desktop Publishing.

Personal Publishing: The Magazine for Desktop Publishers.

The number of books on desktop publishing has grown exponentially in the past few years. Keep watching for new titles.

Kleper, Michael L. *The Illustrated Handbook of Desktop Publishing and Typesetting*. Blue Ridge Summit, PA: Tab Books, 1987. Calls itself "the definitive sourcebook."

Seybold, John W. and Fritz Dressler. *Publishing from the Desktop*. New York: Bantam Books, 1987.

Waite Group. *Desktop Publishing Bible*. Indianapolis, IN: Howard W. Sams, 1987. A collection of essays on the various aspects of desktop publishing written by experts.

Willis, Jerry. *Desktop Publishing with your IBM PC & Compatible*. Tucson, AZ: Knight Ridder Press, 1987. A useful introduction to the intricacies of selecting and using laser printers, page composition software, and electronic graphics.

5 PUTTING IT TOGETHER

The strategy of this book so far has been to provide you with a lot of separate pieces. Moreover, we have recommended that initially you focus on these separate pieces or skills one at a time. But it is a simplification to think of these skills as separate—a fiction used to make the initial learning easier. When used in the library, the skills are combined. So you learn open questioning in a workshop setting by practicing asking open questions and nothing else. But the ultimate goal is to use the individual skill of open questioning as appropriate, along with some other appropriate skills, in the service of a larger purpose.

So, like the king's horses and the king's men, you have the job of putting Humpty together again. The real test of the skills presented in Chapters 1 to 4 is how they fit together in the applications presented in Chapters 6 to 9. In fact, one approach to using this book is to start with some application such as making a speech (8.6) and then work backwards to the skills involved (1.1 to 1.5, 4.2 to 4.6). We are giving you pieces and suggesting in the applications sections how these pieces might fit together. But we hope that you will make a lot of the connections yourself to suit your own needs.

Use this chapter to help in the process of putting things together. The organization goes from general to specific. We start with a rapid survey of some of the theoretical underpinnings of the book, go on to discuss a theory of communication that is particularly suited to information work, describe Ivey's concept of intentionality as a prerequisite for learning how to integrate skills and everyday behavior, and end with some very specific suggestions for learning and integrating new skills.

5.1 THEORY AND PARADIGMS

In writing this book we have been fairly eclectic, passing on a variety of ideas and suggestions that we have found helpful and that have worked for us. Much of the advice we pass on is absolutely standard (every book on writing will tell you to write concisely and to avoid the passive voice). However, a source of unity is our theoretical orientation (or paradigm or set of mental maps about the world).

Anyone writing about communication/reading/information has some mental model, however unexamined, of what is involved in these processes. One model, let's call it Paradigm A, is based on these assumptions:

PARADIGM A

1. Knowledge is objective. The way to know about the world is to stand outside it somehow and observe it objectively.
2. Information consists of objective observations about the world.
3. Information is a commodity, valuable in itself, regardless of its use. Information is made up of a lot of separate little bits. The more separate little bits of information one has, the better.
4. Communication is a one-way process of sources sending messages to receivers.
5. Giving information requires the creation of structures in which messages travel top-down, from expert to layperson (e.g., doctor-to-patient, or advertiser-to-television viewer).
6. The receiver of messages is passive, expected to hear or read the message accurately and in its entirety, and to incorporate its content in unaltered form.
7. Meaning is in the message itself, fixed in the text.
8. Evaluating information service consists of counting up the frequency with which the information is exchanged and measuring the extent to which people receive messages accurately and completely.
9. Information is context-free.

This book has been written within the framework of an alternative model, Paradigm B, which is based on these assumptions:

PARADIGM B

1. We are part of the reality that we study. We can't stand outside the world to view it as it really is because our instruments, experiments, culture, language, and worldview affect what we perceive. Where we stand and look from affects what we see. Knowledge depends on perspective.
2. Information consists of observations about the world that are affected by the contexts in which the observations are made.
3. Information is valuable only in relation to the context in which it is used.
4. Communication is an interactive process between speakers and listeners, writers and readers.
5. The receiver of the message participates actively in making meaning.
6. The meaning that is created depends on previously learned

cultural codes, previous life experience, the present situation, and individual perspectives.
7. The ultimate test of the value of an information service is the helpfulness of the information to the user in terms of what he or she is trying to do or know at a particular moment in space and time.
8. Information is situationally-based, and changes meaning according to context.

Arguments in support of the assumptions of Paradigm B have all been elaborated at length elsewhere (see For further help). It is enough to say here that this paradigm, along with its implications, lies behind three recurrent themes in this book:

—communication is an interactive process involving feedback.
—any good theory of communication (including teaching and reading as well as one-to-one interactions) must give a starring role to the learner/reader/message-receiver, who is an active participant in constructing the sense of what is said or written.
—to understand the meaning of something you have to know its context.

5.2 SENSE-MAKING: INFORMATION AS COMMUNICATION

Many books on communication for librarians and others begin with a theory of the communication of information derived from electrical engineering—a model developed by Claude Shannon and Warren Weaver and usually presented something like this:

CHANNEL
SOURCE → SIGNAL → RECEIVER

This model is useful for solving the problem for which it was originally developed: determining the most economical way to send and receive electronic signals along channels that are noisy with random electrical interference. The original theory was concerned not with meaning but with electronic pulses: it doesn't matter what you send over the wires, including nonsense, because information is anything that reduces uncertainty for the decoder. When we transpose this model from the engineering context to the context of human communication, we are really just using a metaphor. The metaphor highlights certain areas of similarity between decoding electronic messages and decoding human messages, but it obscures an important difference: with human communication, meaning is of primary importance. Meaning, moreover, is not so much there in the message as constructed by the receiver (listener or reader). For a discussion of models of communication, see Kevin McGarry, Chapter 1, *Communication, Knowledge and the Librarian*. London, Clive Bingley, 1975.

Dr. Brenda Dervin is a communications researcher who works from within Paradigm B. We have found her work especially fruitful for the field of librarianship because it focuses on what she calls "the human side of information." Dervin argues that most prevailing models of communication, including the Shannon-Weaver model, assume that information is a commodity that can be generated, stored, accessed, and transferred. That is, information is understood to be an autonomous object with meaning and value in itself, apart from any user. Following others who have argued for the social construction of reality, Dervin maintains that information is a construct of the user. In her constructivist theory of information, human beings are not seen as passive receptacles, but as actively involved in constructing their own reality. This theory allows us to explain some of the puzzling problems of research into information-seeking behavior: why the same message means different things to different people at different times; why people do not always follow directions or seem to understand what they are told; and why they sometimes reject so-called high quality information as useless.

Dervin and her colleagues developed their alternative theory of information in the course of extensive research, beginning in the early 1970s, that examined actual citizen information-seeking behavior: the kinds of situations that people see as problematic, the kinds of questions they have in these situations, where they go for help, the kinds of answers they get to their questions, and how the answers help them cope with their situations. Dervin called this theory "sense-making" to emphasize information-seeking as a primary human activity. It is what people are trying to do as they work through situations in their lives—going on quests, meeting barriers, facing dilemmas, running into contradictions, asking questions, and seeking happiness. When people become stymied; when, as Dervin puts it, their own knowledge or sense has run out with respect to a particular situation; when they are unable to progress without forming some kind of new sense, then they seek outside help. They ask their mother or the taxi-driver, they call up their accountant, or they visit some institutional system, including the library. This visit is a detour from their usual life path made in order to get help not otherwise available. The information need, we should note, is not context-free but has arisen from a specific situation unique to the individual.

Given this uniqueness, the problem that the sense-making approach tries to address is this:

> How can institutions meet information needs when those needs are overwhelmingly unique, having arisen from unique situations? Human individuality seems too complex to handle. How can we deal with people on their own terms and do it systematically?

The answer is that although the situations themselves are unique, there are some obvious patterns in the ways that people need, seek out, and use information. We can use these similarities to develop a systematic approach to understanding people's information needs. Three kinds of significant questions can be used as keys to understand people's sense-making journeys: questions about the *situation* and how people see it; questions about what seems to be missing—*gaps* in their understanding of the situation; and questions about *uses*—the kind of help they hope to get. These dimensions—the crucial elements in the sense-making process—form the model that has already been presented in the section on neutral questions (3.7).

The direct, practical relevance of the sense-making approach is clearest in library work involving finding out people's needs for information, especially reference service. There are others: research into community needs, program evaluation, readers' advisory work, and even collection development and organization. (Consider, for example, that we can improve public access to our collections by organizing them according to the situation/gaps/uses model. Library materials from different subject areas might be used in a display or special collection focusing on the situations that people face in job-hunting. For example, they may want to get some ideas about career options or learn resume-writing skills or decide what to wear to an interview or locate career counseling services.)

The sense-making approach also offers a vantage point from which to think about writing and working in groups. Readers receiving written texts and participants at group meetings are each sense-makers, valuing information to the extent that it helps them fill in gaps in their understanding and make progress toward their goals. Therefore, a writer drafting memos, reports, or public service announcements may do a better job by remembering that readers are in unique situations, have gaps in their understanding, and want certain kinds of help. The writing should address these situations, gaps, and sorts of help wanted.

5.3 INTENTIONALITY

In this book, we take from other approaches those skills that will help librarians most in the situations they encounter most often, and we choose the skills on the basis of what we know about human sense-making behavior. You, likewise, will choose the skills that are helpful in particular library applications. Choice is central to what Allen Ivey calls intentionality, possibly the most important concept in microtraining. Intentionality in the microtraining model goes hand-in-hand with the sense-making model: both theories are based on an image of human beings as actively pursuing goals and making choices to reach those goals.

So what is intentionality? Ivey describes intentionality as the knowledge of a range of alternative responses and the ability to use a helpful response in a given situation:

> The person who acts with intentionality has a sense of capability. He or she can generate alternative hehaviors in a given situation and "approach" a problem from different vantage points. The intentional, fully functioning individual is not bound to one course of action but can respond in the moment to changing life situations and look forward to longer term goals. (Ivey and Simek-Downing. *Counseling and Psychotherapy.* Englewood Cliffs, NJ: Prentice-Hall, 1980, p. 8).

Skills must be learned individually, but together they form a repertoire from which the helper can draw spontaneously, selecting one skill in a certain situation, adapting another skill to supplement, trying yet another skill if the first one doesn't work. Intentionality means flexibility—the ability to use a range of skills and to improvise. It means not depending on one skill or always using the same skill in similar situations. As mastery of skills increases, so does intentionality.

Intentionality is not limited to verbal skills. The intentional helper becomes adept at using nonverbal or writing skills as the need dictates. Much of the rest of this book illustrates how various skills can be used to supplement each other, how one skill can be substituted for another, and how several skills can be integrated to achieve specific purposes in the process of communication.

5.4 MANIPULATION VS. GENUINENESS

When library workers first learn new communication skills, they may react by saying that they're being taught to manipulate their own behavior in order to manipulate others. Some trainees say that they feel deceptive when they try to make the transition from practicing a skill in a training setting to using the skill in a real-life setting. Suppose, they say, that it's not natural to me to use encouragers or ask open questions to get people to talk. But I learn these skills and use them, and presto! people open up and tell me things. Isn't there something deceptive and manipulative about this?

Well, there might be, depending on motives. In the service of base motives, these skills can be abused. In the service of shared goals, these skills facilitate communication and allow you to be more helpful. To communicate more effectively with others, we may need to change our own behavior—to learn new skills such as different ways of asking questions or of organizing a report. (In fact, although the complaint of manipulativeness could be leveled at writing skills, few people feel that changing their writing style to make it clearer and more forceful makes their style less genuine.)

This issue of genuineness is not simply a matter of motivation, however. When we first learn a new skill, it may seem awkward and alien to our normal behavior—not genuine we say. However, the skill becomes more natural with practice (see 5.5). When we find that we can make the skill work for us in a variety of situations, it becomes part of our normal behavior. Then it is perceived as genuine. In the meantime, our genuineness consists of our sincere desire to help, even if helping more effectively means behaving a little awkwardly at first.

Exercise

GENUINENESS

In your group, ask each person to identify a skill or behavior that she/he feels is both "manipulative" and alien to her/his normal behavior. List the skills mentioned for discussion. To what extent does everyone share this feeling? Ask those not sharing this feeling for some suggestions on decreasing the feeling of lack of genuineness.

DID YOU KNOW?
If you don't use it, you lose it, according to studies of paraprofessionals who were trained in basic microskills. Trainees who did not practice or use their new skills during the year following training lost the skills, although retraining could rapidly bring them up to criterion levels again. (Allen E. Ivey and Jerry Authier. *Microcounseling.* 2nd ed. Springfield, IL: C.C. Thomas, 1978, p. 306.)

5.5 TIPS FOR PRACTICING

5.5.1 Practicing verbal skills

Changing your communication behavior is hard work. It's not easy to break old patterns of response. But unless you practice your new skills, you'll lose them. Here are ten tips to help you through the learning process:

1. Make a commitment. Promise yourself that for a specified period of time—the next hour or on Thursday afternoons—you will consciously use one of your new skills.
2. Start immediately. Begin practicing the skill right away. Remind yourself by taping a handout to your desk, or putting an elastic band on your wrist. At first, you may feel awkward, but practice anyway. Most library users respond positively when they see that you are trying hard to help.
3. Practice one skill at a time. Best results come from practicing one skill over and over. Don't try to use all the skills at once. A good skill to start with is acknowledgment or restatement. An easy neutral question to use is "What kind of help would you like?"
4. Use support groups. Practice with a coworker who has made the same commitment. Give each other feedback and share experiences. Or set aside time at regular staff meetings to discuss your progress.
5. Learn from missed opportunities. Each time you do *not* use one of these skills, think about the situation afterwards. Was there a neutral question you might have used? How could you have used the DESC sequence to influence the outcome of the conversation?
6. Develop your own style. There is no magic list of open questions, and no perfect sequence in which to use your skills. Adapt your behavior in a way that is comfortable for you in that situation. Use words that function in the same way as the examples, even if the exact words differ.
7. Learn from communication accidents. When you are first learning these skills, you may find that they do not always work. If the user seems puzzled, you may have had a communication accident. Recover by explaining to the user what you are trying to do. For example: "I asked you that question

because I can help you more if I know a little bit about what you plan to do with the information" or "I want to make sure I understand what you're looking for." Users hardly ever become angry in such situations, but if it happens, recover simply by saying "I'm sorry" and explaining.

8. Practice off the job. Microskills work in any situation where your help is being sought—by family, friends, even strangers asking directions. Practice these skills in your daily life—you may be surprised at how much everyday communication improves.

9. Observe others. Notice how others use microskills—the salesperson who restates your request, the talk show host who asks open questions, the physician who encourages you to describe your problem, the museum guide who gives directions well. Pay particular attention to those people you like dealing with—chances are they are using microskills.

10. Teach someone else. After you have learned a skill and practiced it, pass it on to someone else. Teach a coworker one skill that you have found to be particularly effective. Your ability to teach someone else demonstrates that you have really mastered the skill.

5.5.2 Practicing new writing skills

Improving writing skills requires a conscious choice to pay attention to the "how" as well as to the "what" of writing. Here are some tips to help you practice new writing skills:

1. Make a commitment. Be prepared to work hard.
2. Take stock. Analyze something that you have written recently when the quality of the writing mattered. Consider this written work in terms of the skills discussed in Chapter 4—choosing an appropriate style, writing with impact, writing briefly, and so on. Which writing skills did you use well? Which ones need more work?
3. Focus on one skill at a time. You can't do everything at once. Pick one area in which you feel your writing needs to be improved. In everything that you write for the next week, scrutinize each paragraph with this skill in mind. If you were focusing on writing briefly, you could ask yourself: do I need every word? Could I convey the same idea more succinctly?
4. Revise. Don't be content with your first draft. Good writers edit their work and revise and revise.

5. Leave enough time. Let an important piece of writing sit for a day or so. When you come back to it, you will see things to improve that you didn't see at the time of writing.
6. Read your piece of writing out loud. If it's hard to read out loud without stumbling over it, there is probably something wrong with the rhythm that you should fix.
7. Ask for feedback. Show an important piece of writing to someone whose opinion about writing you respect and ask for suggestions for improvement.
8. Sharpen your critical awareness. Examine other people's writing. What is there about a particular letter, memo, or report that makes it good (or not so good)?

5.6 SKILL INTEGRATION

In any communication process, the participants have certain goals. In some situations (for example, giving information to a mass public about a new service) the goals are explicit, limited, and planned in advance. In other situations, such as reference transactions, the goals may be developed right in the situation, hidden goals may become apparent, and goals may change.

Usually achieving a goal will require the use and combination of several skills. Although the process of learning a new skill requires you to focus on one skill at a time, the effective use of new skills depends on your ability to draw on a range of skills for the purpose of achieving a specific goal. You may even overlap skills. Let's say the user has asked for "information on solar energy." One of your goals is to *obtain a more complete description* of the information need. At the same time, you want to *establish a good communication climate* by showing the user that you are attentive. Two goals, and at least two possible skills: restatement and open questions. When you practiced restatement, you focused on simply repeating or paraphrasing what the user has said: "You're looking for something on solar energy?" When you practiced asking open questions, you learned to ask "What would you like to know?" A simple example of skill integration might be: "What would you like to know about solar energy?" Of course, the interview goes on—pursuing your goal of query clarification, you may find it helpful to use encouragers, more open questions, a neutral question, and a closed question to confirm your understanding. If the user gets sidetracked, you may use the skill of closure. Once you understand what's needed, your goal may change: you may need to *give directions* or *instructions* and, at the end, *elicit feedback*. Being able to use any or all of these skills appropriately to further the goals of the interview is evidence of skill integration.

On a larger scale, skill integration may mean combining different forms of communication (each of which involves several skills) to achieve a goal. Let's say your goal is to persuade your staff to attend a meeting. Related objectives involve *giving information* about the time, location, and purpose of the meeting, *getting information* about how many people are coming, *persuading* people to come, and *assessing opinions* on the value of the topic to be discussed at the meeting. To achieve your goal, you might send a written invitation, requesting confirmation of attendance. If you get 100% confirmation, you've probably achieved all your objectives. If not, perhaps there were writing skills that could have improved response, or you might supplement the invitation with a some personal telephone calls, during which you use appropriate verbal and nonverbal skills.

The subsequent sections of this book present situations in which more than one skill and perhaps more than one form of communication can be used, with examples of how skills can be integrated to achieve particular purposes.

FOR FURTHER HELP

5.1 Theory and paradigms

Bateson, Gregory. *Steps to an Ecology of Mind*. San Francisco: Chandler, 1972.

Berger, Peter L. and Thomas Luckmann. *The Social Construction of Reality: A Treatise in the Sociology of Knowledge*. New York: Doubleday, 1966.

Bernstein, Richard J. *The Restructuring of Social and Political Theory*. Oxford: Basil Blackwell, 1976.

Brown, Richard H. *A Poetic for Sociology: Toward a logic of discovery for the human sciences*. Cambridge: Cambridge University Press, 1977.

Geertz, Clifford. "Blurred Genres: The Refiguration of Social Thought" in *Local Knowledge: Further Essays in Interpretive Anthropology*. New York: Basic Books, 1983.

Ogilvy, James. *Many Dimensional Man: Decentralizing Self, Society, and the Sacred*. New York: Oxford University Press, 1977.

Tompkins, Jane P. *Reader-Response Criticism: From Formalism to Post-Structuralism*. Baltimore and London: Johns Hopkins University Press, 1986.

5.2 Sense-making

Dervin, Brenda. "Useful Theory for Librarianship: Communication, not Information," *Drexel Library Quarterly*, 13, 3 (July 1977): 16-32.

Dervin, Brenda and Kathleen Clark. *ASQ: Asking Significant Questions. Alternative Tools for Information Need and Accountability Assessments by Libraries*. A Publication of the Peninsula Library System, 25 Tower Rd. Belmont, California 94002 for California State Library, Sacramento, California, July 1987.

Dervin, Brenda and Patricia Dewdney, "Neutral Questioning: A New Approach to the Reference Interview," *RQ*, 25, 4 (Summer 1986): 506-513.

Ross, Catherine Sheldrick. "How to Find Out What People Really Want to Know," *Reference Librarian*, 16 (Winter 1986): 19-30.

Zweizig, Douglas. "The Informing Function of Adult Services in Public Libraries," *RQ*, 18, 3 (Spring 1979): 240-244.

5.6 Skill integration

Allen E. Ivey. *Intentional Interviewing and Counseling*. Monterey, CA: Brooks/ Cole, 1983. See "Intentionality as a goal for interviewing and counseling," pp. 2-4, and Chapter 11, "Skill Integration: Putting It All Together."

PART II

APPLICATIONS

6 SPEAKING ONE-TO-ONE

This section considers the application of speaking skills in commonly occurring situations involving two people: answering the telephone; conducting an interview; coping with special situations; and handling awkward customers.

6.1 ANSWERING THE TELEPHONE

Since your caller cannot see your nodding and smiling over the telephone, you should pay special attention to vocal qualities and verbal skills. For the caller at the other end, your voice represents the whole library. You are literally the front line. Here are some suggestions:

Develop a pleasant speaking voice. Monitor how you sound over the phone. Is your tone interested and courteous? Do you speak slowly and clearly enough to be easily understood? (See section 1.5 for exercises to improve variety and articulation.)

Identify yourself. When you answer the phone, your greeting should identify yourself and your library and indicate your willingness to provide service. Instead of saying Yes or Hello, try something like this:

—Hamilton Public Library, Bill Robinson speaking.
—Reference Department. How may I help you?
—Good morning. The Legal Information Center. This is Frances Lopez speaking.

Acknowledge. Be sure to acknowledge the caller's question promptly by restating at least part of it. If you didn't quite catch the question, repeat what you did understand and let the caller fill you in on the rest.

—Yes, I'd be happy to check that for you in Books in Print.
—Uh-huh, the new Margaret Atwood book.
—Beerbohm. And that's spelled B-E-E-R-B. . .?

Use minimal encouragers. Minimal encouragers like "Uh-huh," "Go on," "That's interesting," and "Anything else?" are especially important over the phone as cues that you are listening. Without these encouragers, the caller is apt to wonder if you are still there.

101

Volunteer your help. Don't force the caller to pry help out of you. If the caller asks, "Is Miss Lapointe there?" don't just say "No." Say, "Miss Lapointe will be back at 1:00. If you'd like to leave a message, I'll make sure she gets it when she returns" or "Miss Lapointe is on vacation until July 15. Can anyone else help you?" If the caller asks, "Do you have a storyhour Saturday morning?" don't say "No." Volunteer to tell the caller the times when you do have a storyhour.

Understand the question or request. Use open questions (3.5) to find out what kind of help the caller wants. For example,

—How may I help you?
—What information would you like on that?
—What aspect of X are you interested in?
—What are you working on?
—What are you trying to find?

Some librarians feel that the user's anonymity over the phone makes it easier to ask how the information is expected to help. But the guidelines for asking about intended uses remain the same as they are for an in-library user: explain that you are asking this question so that you can be more helpful; and don't make any assumptions. Sometimes, when the question cannot be answered over the phone, the user must be advised to come in person to the library. But before you can make appropriate referrals or recommendations, you must still find out what the user really wants to know. Again, open questions work well.

Explain. Since the caller cannot see what you are doing, it is often a good a idea to explain what you are doing (see 3.12). If you are going to ask people to wait, don't just say, "Hang on a minute" or "OK, I'll look" and then go away. The caller won't know what you are doing or how long to expect to wait. Studies show that people can cope better with frustrating experiences if they are told ahead of time what to expect. Therefore you should explain what you are doing. Say, "I'll check that for you in the index. It will take about three minutes. Would you like to wait or should I call you back?" If the problem turns out to be unexpectedly difficult, return to the phone to give your waiting caller a progress report. Say, "I haven't forgotten you. I'm checking that information and will have it for you in a minute." If it will take longer than a minute, offer to take the number and call back.

Refer. If you can't answer the question yourself, don't say, "No, I don't know anything about that program" or "That's not our department." Instead you could say something like this:

—If you would leave your number, I'll find out about that program and call you back.
—Let me transfer you to our reference librarian who specializes in legal questions.

Verify. If the caller has asked for some particular help, repeat and verify the key facts before you rush off to find the answer.

Record messages accurately. Restate names and telephone numbers as you write them down (see acknowledgment 3.2). This will give the caller a chance to correct errors. Standard message forms are helpful and save time.

Exercise

PRACTICE INTERVIEW

This exercise focuses on the difference between the stated and hidden purposes of interviews.

A personnel director wants to select the best applicant for a job. The applicant knows she is not as qualified as others but feels she deserves a chance.

Questions for discussion

1. If you were the interviewee, what might you want to have happen as a result of this interview? (Specify several desirable outcomes.)

2. If you were the interviewer, what might you want to have happen? (Specify some desirable outcomes.)

3. To what extent do the interviewer and interviewee share the same interview purpose? To what extent do the purposes conflict?

4. What could the interviewer do or say to achieve a mutual understanding of purposes in this interview?

6.2 INTERVIEWING

6.2.1. What is an interview?

An interview is a conversation directed intentionally to some purpose. It usually involves the asking and answering of questions. People who work in libraries and information centers participate in different kinds of interviews with different purposes. Consider personnel interviews conducted to select or terminate an employee, do a performance appraisal, hear a grievance, or counsel a troubled employee. Public service staff may conduct reference interviews with the adult independent learner, including online presearch interviews, end-user counseling interviews, readers' advisory interviews, and problem-solving interviews. Research interviews comprise another category of directed conversation: the interview is a primary way of collecting data for oral history projects, user surveys, needs assessment, and evaluation research.

Whatever the purpose of the interview, the interviewer should have a clear idea, before the interview starts, of why she is conducting the interview and what she hopes to have accomplished by the end. Two common purposes for an interview are *giving information* or *getting information*. Usually one of these purposes predominates. When the primary purpose of an interview is to give information or instruction, the interviewer is justified in doing much of the talking. However, if the primary purpose is to get information, the interviewer should spend most of her time asking questions and listening. Other purposes of the interview may include *problem-solving* and *counseling*.

An important factor in any interview is the extent to which the interviewer and interviewee share a common purpose. At one end of the scale, both parties share a common purpose and know that they do. At the other end, each party has a separate and opposed purpose. Consider the case in which a supervisor wants a staff member to realize that her work is inadequate but the employee feels she is doing the best she can under poor working conditions. Or a library user has asked for "a book about a classic novel," hoping to find a brief plot summary for a book report due today. He wants the minimum possible to get through the assignment and is not really interested in reading the book. In such cases, the interviewer must be aware that the interviewee may be working on a "hidden agenda" or the interview will be ineffective.

6.2.2. Dimensions of the interview

Interviews can differ greatly, one from another, in terms of the five dimensions discussed below. An interviewer who is aware of the range of possible variation can select the style of interview that best suits the occasion and purpose.

CONTROL
Who is in charge? At one end of the scale are interviews in which the interviewer controls everything: which topics to discuss and which aspects of the topics to consider. This style of interviewing, sometimes called the *directed* interview, relies to a large extent on closed questioning (see 3.5) and can be useful when certain, specific facts are wanted. At the other end are those interviews in which both parties are equal partners. The interviewer asks open questions, encourages the interviewee to introduce topics of importance, and allows the interviewee to ask questions of his own. This style of interviewing, sometimes called the *nondirected* interview, is effective at finding out the interviewee's attitudes and perceptions, or in exploring a problem for the first time. The dimension of control is also related to the roles assumed by the participants. For example, if the interviewer is perceived as having a much higher status or more power than the interviewee (such as in the employment interview), the interviewee is likely to expect a

directed interview; if the interviewer wants to conduct a less directed interview, she'll have to use particular skills to reduce the effect of perceived roles. Conversely, if the interviewer is perceived as having a lower status (say, a student interviewing a library director for a school project), the interviewee may attempt to direct the interview.

TRUST

How much trust is there between the interviewer and the interviewee? The range goes from the *hostile* interview, in which neither side trusts the other, to the *mutual trust* interview, in which both participants respect and trust the other. The hostile interview, exemplified in an extreme form by the police interrogation, provides the poorest possible climate for either giving or receiving information. Again, this dimension is often affected by the participants' perceptions of roles and status. When interviewers spend time at the beginning of an interview to establish rapport, they are increasing the level of trust.

DURATION

How long does the interview last? The typical reference interview lasts three minutes or less, but a reference interview with a client who wants an online search may last for twenty minutes or longer. Interviews for hiring, performance appraisal, and counseling typically last between twenty minutes to an hour. Research interviews (for example, oral history) may be even longer or may extend over a series of one or two hour sessions. The length of the interview may be within the interviewer's control or it may be constrained by other factors including the time that either the interviewer or interviewee can devote to the interview.

STRUCTURE

Unlike ordinary conversation, an interview (directed or nondirected) has a structure that must reflect its purpose. The stages of an interview usually are:

1. establishing rapport
2. general information gathering or getting the big picture
3. specific information gathering
4. intervention such as giving information, advice or instructions
5. ending, including feedback or summary.

These stages may be iterative, occurring in loops throughout the interview, as for example when the interviewer needs to reestablish

DID YOU KNOW?

About 50% of the questions presented by public library users require further clarification. However most public library reference interviews take no longer than three minutes. M.J. Lynch, "Reference interviews in public libraries," *Library Quarterly,* 48 (April 1978): 119-142.

rapport or do some more general information gathering before the interview ends. Three patterns for the structure of the interview are recognizable:

The funnel sequence. The interview begins with open conversation and moves towards closed questioning and specific information gathering or information giving at the end.

The inverse funnel sequence. The interview begins with specific information gathering and moves towards more open conversation.

The tunnel sequence. The interview proceeds through a series of the same kind of questions throughout.

ENVIRONMENT

Physical surroundings profoundly affect the nature and outcome of an interview. The environment can range from reassuring to intimidating (for an extreme example of the latter, think of the prisoner being questioned under a naked light bulb.) The employee selection interview can be conducted in a pleasant room with both participants seated in comfortable chairs with no barriers between them. Or the applicant may face a panel of interviewers seated behind a large table.

The interviewer generally has some control over the environment. The interviewer can arrange the furniture to reduce the physical barriers between participants. The reference librarian can walk with the user into the stacks to gain more privacy. And the supervisor can choose a neutral room (neither the employee's office nor the employer's office) for a counseling interview.

6.2.3. All-purpose interviewing skills

Certain basic skills are useful in every type of interview, including those conducted in settings as varied as social work, medicine, health services, management, journalism, and vocational counseling. To these settings, we can add information services. Dr. Allen Ivey has organized these basic skills as the Microskills Hierarchy. In libraries and information centers, the most useful skills for any kind of interview are those in the basic listening sequence—introduced in Chapter 2 of this book and elaborated in the sections on acknowledgment (3.2), encouragers (3.3), open questions (3.5), neutral questions (3.7), summarization (3.8) and reflection of feeling (3.9). In addition, the basic *attending skills* of culturally

DID YOU KNOW?
Body language in the interview situation often expresses perceptions of status and power. In an interview between people of different cultures, it's important to pay attention to body language. For a discussion of communication between black students and white librarians, see R. Errol Lam, "The Reference Interview: Some Intercultural Considerations," *RQ*, 27, 3 (Spring 1988): 390-393.

appropriate eye contact (1.2) and body language (1.3 to 1.5) enhance most kinds of interviews. The *influencing skills*—giving information, direction, explanation, and advice (3.11 to 3.15)—are particularly useful for the reference interview, employment interviews, and performance evaluation interviews.

Individual skills are learned one at a time. But once the individual skills have been mastered, the next step in the hierarchy is learning how to sequence and structure the interview. Finally comes the skill of integrating these behaviors. In our discussion of this synthesizing process, we will focus on interview situations unique to the information worker. The following sections use examples derived from what we call the generic reference interview. Since librarians also conduct interviews for purposes of selecting or evaluating employees, counseling, problem-solving, and conducting research, we refer you to general texts on these topics.

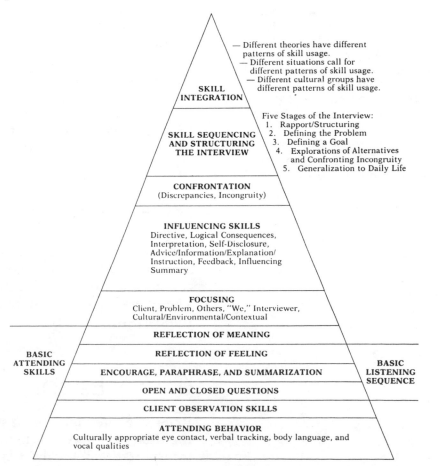

— Different theories have different patterns of skill usage.
— Different situations call for different patterns of skill usage.
— Different cultural groups have different patterns of skill usage.

SKILL INTEGRATION

Five Stages of the Interview:
1. Rapport/Structuring
2. Defining the Problem
3. Defining a Goal
4. Explorations of Alternatives and Confronting Incongruity
5. Generalization to Daily Life

SKILL SEQUENCING AND STRUCTURING THE INTERVIEW

CONFRONTATION
(Discrepancies, Incongruity)

INFLUENCING SKILLS
Directive, Logical Consequences, Interpretation, Self-Disclosure, Advice/Information/Explanation/ Instruction, Feedback, Influencing Summary

FOCUSING
Client, Problem, Others, "We," Interviewer, Cultural/Environmental/Contextual

REFLECTION OF MEANING

REFLECTION OF FEELING

ENCOURAGE, PARAPHRASE, AND SUMMARIZATION

OPEN AND CLOSED QUESTIONS

CLIENT OBSERVATION SKILLS

ATTENDING BEHAVIOR
Culturally appropriate eye contact, verbal tracking, body language, and vocal qualities

BASIC ATTENDING SKILLS

BASIC LISTENING SEQUENCE

Exercise

THE 55 PERCENT PROBLEM

Read "Unobtrusive reference testing: the 55% rule" by P. Hernon and C.R. McClure, *Library Journal,* 111 (April 15, 1986): 37-41. This article reviews many research studies that indicate that only about 55% of the answers provided by reference librarians are accurate. To what extent do you think the accuracy rate could be increased by a more effective reference interview? To find out, read Sandy Stephan et al., "Reference Breakthrough in Maryland," *Public Libraries,* 27, 4 (Winter 1988): 178-181. In Maryland, a three-day workshop given to 200 staff in fourteen public libraries raised the percentage of complete and accurate answers from 55 to 77. The Maryland consultants identified the three most important reference behaviors in order of importance as: paraphrasing or repeating the question (acknowledgment); asking a follow-up question; and using open questions.

6.2.4 The generic reference interview: definitions

The term reference interview suggests to most librarians a short interview conducted for the purpose of finding out what the user really wants to know. However librarians conduct other related kinds of interviews that we will also consider in this section. The development of online information retrieval systems has introduced variants on the reference interview: the presearch interview and the counseling session for end-users. There's what we're calling the reference interview by remote control—the interview in which you cannot communicate directly with the user but must work through some intermediary such as an interlibrary loan form. And finally there's the readers' advisory interview, where the librarian needs to find out what a user wants to read before making recommendations. All of these interviews in their various guises can be defined simply as *a conversation between the librarian and the user in which the librarian asks one or more questions in order (a) to get a clearer and more complete picture of what the user wants to know, and (b) to link the user to the system.* In addition to these purposes of query negotiation, the reference interview may include related functions—giving information, advice, or instruction; getting feedback; and following up to assess the user's satisfaction with the help provided.

6.2.5 Stages in the interview

Although all reference interviews are unique, they have common structural features and go through similar stages: establishing contact with the user, finding out the user's need, and confirming. The interview can go wrong in predictable ways, and there are standard ways of recovering from "communication accidents."

6.2.5.1 Establishing contact

Reference interviews often start out in one of two possible ways: the user asks a very general question ("What have you got on transportation?") or the user asks a very specific question ("I'd like to see the University of Wisconsin's catalog.") When these ques-

DID YOU KNOW?

A familiar example of using language to establish contact rather than to exchange information is the phrase "How are you?" "How are you?" isn't really an inquiry into your health, but a way of saying "I acknowledge your presence" and perhaps "I'm available to talk to you." (This is why, when the doctor says "How are you?" people often say, "Fine" before going on to describe life-threatening symptoms.)

Exercise

WHAT'S THE REAL QUESTION?

In your group, think back to a conversation that you had with a library user in which it was not initially clear what that person really wanted to find out. What did the user first ask? What did you think might be wanted? What did the problem turn out to be? How did you find this out? Collect several examples and write key words for each on the blackboard or flipchart:

Books on entomology

How to get rid of ants

Leader's notes: This exercise is more useful for practitioners with some experience. Give each participant a few moments to recall a situation. Then ask for volunteers to describe, briefly, the user's first question and the question as it finally turned out. When you have five or six examples, open general discussion.

tions are answered literally ("Thousands of books, articles and clippings" or "Here's the catalog"), the answers may not help the user. Suppose, for example, the users in these examples wanted the name of the company that built a local incline railway or the first name of a scientist thought to be on faculty at Wisconsin. The literal answer may not help.

But why would a person wanting a company name ask for information on transportation? Why don't people say what they want in the first place? Brenda Dervin has coined the term Bad Guy User to describe the person who won't use the system on *our* terms—the one who refuses to read signs and follow instructions or the one who asks for "books on transportation" when it's clear there are thousands of such books. All of us, from time to time, are Bad Guy Users in other people's systems, particularly when that system is unfamiliar. (Have you ever called up a government department and asked for "information on by-laws?" or asked "Is this the bus to Albuquerque?" when the sign clearly says "Albuquerque?")

Linguists have an explanation for what seems to be the perverse way in which people phrase their initial requests for help. This explanation is based on the fact that language can have several functions, including exchanging information and establishing contact. At the outset of the reference interview, the librarian expects from the user an exchange of information in the form of a clear statement of the information need. But the user's first concern is to establish contact. The user has tacit questions in mind that need answering before he can go on to clarify his need for information: Am I in the right place? Are you available and listening to me? Are you the person who's going to help me? Can you help me with a problem that falls into this general area?

You need to respond in a way that answers these unspoken questions. PACT is an acronym for remembering what the user wants to know first.

P Place is right
A Available and listening
C Contact made
T Topic (in general) understood

Communicate these responses through nonverbal skills such as eye contact, smiling, and standing up (see 1.1 to 1.4) and through verbal skills such as acknowledgment (3.2) and encouragers (3.3). When the user asks for books on transportation, look up, perhaps stand up, smile, and acknowledge the user immediately, e.g.,

Exercise

CLARIFYING THE QUESTION

If someone asked you for information on China, what kinds of materials do you think would prove most helpful? The diagram below shows some different meanings the term might have for the user. (Adapted from a transparency used for staff training by Leicestershire Libraries and Information Service and reprinted in Ray Prytherch. *Handbook of Library Training Practice.* Aldershot, Hampshire: Gower Publishing Co. 1986, p. 181)

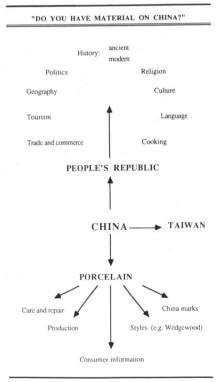

"Transportation, hmm." By using PACT, you establish the contact that will encourage the user to tell you more.

WHAT PEOPLE REALLY WANT TO KNOW

Initial question	*Negotiated question*
Where are your books on entomology?	I want to get rid of ants.
Does anyone on your staff speak German?	Will the library buy my collection of German books?
I need a book on office organization.	How can I get along better with a coworker?
Have you got *Down on Broad Street?*	I was told to ask for *Dun and Bradstreet*
I need a back issue of *Time* magazine.	What is the address of Hans Selye? I want to write to him.

6.2.5.2 Finding out what is wanted

After you establish contact, you still have to find out what the person wants to know. This next stage in the reference interview involves the integration of skills introduced in Chapter 3 (see 3.5 for open and closed questions; 3.6 for avoiding premature diagnosis; 3.7 for neutral questions; 3.11 for giving instructions; and 3.12 for inclusion). A good reference librarian uses the skills intentionally and combines them to advance the purpose of the interview. The following transcript of a reference interview (edited and annotated for instructional purposes) gives an idea of how the various microskills function in context. You'll note that the librarian in the transcript is better at using some skills than others.

THE LAMPLIGHTER'S SERENADE

User: Excuse me. . . . I'm sorry to bother you, but where are your song books?

Librarian: Do you want song books for children or for adults? [*Restatement* helps to establish contact; however the *closed question* may include an assumption.]

User: Adults, I guess.

DID YOU KNOW?

According to one Maryland study, the factors most likely to lead to a more accurate answer are communication skills within the control of the individual librarian. Factors such as the size of the reference collection, the size of the staff, or the degree of business were not factors contributing to good reference performance. Ralph Gers and Lillie J. Seward, "Improving Reference Performance: Results of a Statewide Study," *Library Journal* (November 1985): 32-35.

Librarian: They're in the 700's, over there. Is there a particular song that you wanted or did you just want a collection? [*Gives directions*; the *closed question* limits the user's response.]

User: It's a particular song called "The Lamplighter's Serenade."

Librarian: Is that an American song, do you know? [The user may not be able to answer the *closed question*; it's system oriented.]

User: I guess.

Librarian: I'm not familiar with that song. What else do you know about it? [*Open question* is not highly structured but breaks out of the 20 questions game.]

User: It's a popular song. I just need the words.

Librarian: Just the words, OK. [*Restatement* confirms.] Let me look in these song indexes and see if I can locate it [*Inclusion* tells the user what she is doing.] Hmmmm. . . . [After a few minutes:] Sorry, I can't seem to find it. However, I could take your number and give you a call later if I found it. [Offers further help.]

User: I'm in a bit of a hurry so . . . no . . . but thanks anyway.

Librarian: I'm sorry. Would anything else help you? [*Follow up question*]

User: No, I need the words to that song.

Librarian: I wish I could find the words for you—if I could find the words, how would that help you? [*Neutral question* taps intended uses more successfully.]

User: Well . . . I need to find a particular word, the name for that long pole that they used to light the gas lamps with—it's for a story I'm writing—and I think the word was in that song. [User describes query in her own words.]

Librarian: So if we could find out the correct term for that pole, would that be all the help you need? [*Summarization; Closed follow up question* to verify.]

User: Yes—that's why I need the song.

Librarian: Well, I think I can find that out and we may not need the song after all.

User: Oh, great!

(Adapted from an example provided by Brenda Dervin)

EXERCISE
Situation/gaps/uses

(You can do this exercise either on your own or in a training session as part of a small group. As a group exercise, it takes about 30 minutes.) The purpose of this exercise is to help trainees think about the situation/gaps/uses model in the reference interview.

Situations: A user asks for "information on Alzheimer's Disease." Think of as many situations as possible that might have given rise to this request. Write each down. (Make sure that you have a situation or event, not some other dimension.) Some examples of situations lying behind the user's question on Alzheimer's Disease are: the user is a nurse in a chronic care hospital; the user is a volunteer worker for United Way; the user is a student who has been assigned a term paper on any aspect of this disease. After you have generated at least ten situations, choose one.

Gaps: In the situation that you have chosen, what questions (gaps) might the user have about this situation? What does she want to know? Generate as many gaps as possible and write them down in question form. For example: How do you spell Alzheimer's? Is Alzheimer's contagious? Who is doing research in this area? Is there a local support group? Choose one gap.

Uses: Now, using the gap you have chosen, generate at least ten uses for the answer to this question. Think of a "use" as something that helps the user. For example, if the gap is "Is there a support group?" then the answer might help the user get connected to others in the same situation (if your chosen situation was illness of a relative), or it might help the user identify a guest speaker (if the chosen situation involved a teacher wanting to develop a class on this topic.)

Sources: Now, choose one of the "uses" or "helps." What sources do you have in your library that might help this user (given the situation, gap, and use)? List several, then decide which is likely to be the most helpful in this case.

General discussion: Groups reconvene for general discussion. Write on blackboard or flip chart:

—Information on Alzheimer's.

Then list the sources recommended by each group. Discuss how the groups arrived at the "best source."

Leader's notes: The complete exercise may be conducted with groups that involve experienced librarians. If participants are not experienced in use of sources, begin the general discussion after the third round and discuss how different types of sources would be useful in different cases. The rounds may also be done as general (not small group) exercises. If time is limited, the first round may be

Role Playing

TWENTY QUESTIONS IN THE REFERENCE INTERVIEW

The "user" is given a reference question on a card, with a scenario that gives some background information about the question:

The initial question is "Where is your agriculture section?" The user wants to know what makes Mexican jumping beans jump.

The initial question is "Do you have information on snow conditions?" The user wants to know what the skiing is like in Colorado in February.

The initial question is "Where can I find information on allergies?" The user wants recipes that do not contain gluten.

The initial question is "I need information on popular music." The user has just heard of a singer Rita MacNeil and wants the names of her albums and something about who she is.

The user presents the initial question and thereafter answers only closed questions, i.e., responding "yes," "no," "this," or "that." The librarian is instructed to find out as quickly as possible what this user wants to know, using only closed questions. Observers are to ensure that all questions are closed, to count the number of closed questions asked, and to call time if the librarian does not discover the true query in three minutes. If the query is not fully negotiated in three minutes, the librarian may ask open questions. This exercise may be conducted with class members who each ask one question or with one librarian who asks all the questions.

used as an exercise in itself to show how many different situations can give rise to a reference question.

6.2.5.3 Six common causes of communication accidents

Inexperienced interviewers, including librarians conducting reference interviews, tend to have predictable communication accidents that can be avoided or at least remedied through the use of basic microskills.

1. Not acknowledging the user. Establish immediate contact with the user by acknowledging her presence through eye contact (1.2) and gestures and by restating the initial question (3.2).
2. Not listening. The inexperienced interviewer talks more than the experienced interviewer, who listens more. Librarians who are talking or thinking ahead about search strategy aren't listening (2.2). Practice active listening. Pause (3.4) or use an encourager (3.3) instead of responding at length to everything the user says. To show that you are listening, use appropriate body language; reflect feeling and content (3.8 and 3.9); summarize.
3. Playing twenty questions. An open (3.5) or neutral question (3.7) such as "What would you like to know about X?" will get you further in less time than playing twenty questions in the form "Is it this? Is it that?"
4. Interrupting at inappropriate times. If you're talking or cutting the user off when the user is telling you something that's relevant to the query, you're not listening (2.3). Use closure (3.10) to direct the conversation and pauses or encouragers to signal the user that it's her turn to talk.
5. Making assumptions. Some assumptions (e.g., that the user would like some kind of help) are necessary. Assumptions based on the user's appearance or your own perception of the problem are usually inaccurate and may offend if you make them explicit. Avoid premature diagnosis (3.6). Instead, ask neutral questions.
6. Not following up. Recover from other communication accidents by following up. Ask a closed or open follow-up question: "Did that help you? What other help would you like?" Even when you're busy, invite the user to ask for further help or

give instructions ("If you don't find it, ask the person at the Information Desk.")

6.2.6 The presearch interview

The skills that work for the generic reference interview also work for the presearch interview, where the searcher needs to find out what the user wants to know before going online. However, the interviewer needs to consider some important differences:

Because the presearch interview is usually scheduled by appointment, there is more time and privacy; these conditions allow the interviewer to plan the structure of the interview, to probe more, and to encourage the user to talk more.

The user's expectations tend to be greater because "computers can do anything" and because there's usually some charge ("you get what you pay for").

The searcher's anxieties about developing a good search strategy, choosing databases, and formulating commands may interfere with her ability to listen or she may tend to rush the interview.

The searcher must usually do more initial information giving—what an online search can (or can't) do, costs, time, etc.

System constraints make certain closed questions necessary: do you want abstracts or not? Just English or other languages? Ask these after the interview, but before you search.

New technology begets new jargon, from which many communication accidents can arise.

If the user is not present during the actual search, renegotiation of the query is difficult (see 6.2.8 on the interview by remote control and 9.10 on the presearch interview form).

QUESTIONS FOR THE PRESEARCH INTERVIEW
Defining the problem:
—Please tell me about the problem you're working on.
—What would you like to find out about X?
—What are some other things that X might be called?
—If you could find the perfect journal article, what would its title be?

Helps and uses:
—What do you hope to find out as a result of this search?
—How will the search results help you?
—What will the search results help you do?
—How are you going to use this information?

Identifying barriers:
—What have you done so far?
—What happened when you did that?
—What has helped you the most so far?
—What got you stuck?

6.2.7 The end-user interview

This is a conversation between the librarian or search consultant and the person who is going to do his own searching online or on CD-ROM. Consequently, much of the interview will focus on what the user knows or doesn't know about the system, what help is needed, and how the user can get the best results. But it should also include some element of query negotiation since the consultant needs to know enough about the query to give useful instructions or advice. The end-user interview therefore has two levels and purposes:

—the query level, where the consultant's purpose is to find out about the problem that initiated the search
—the system level, where the consultant's purpose is to help the user with the searching procedures.

At the query level, one of the most useful things the consultant can do is to teach the end-user how to interview himself. First, explain that a clearly formulated information need produces more effective search results. Ask the user to think about what he'd like to find out, how that would help him, and how he plans to use the information. Or make up a handout or poster listing such questions:

GOING ONLINE? ASK YOURSELF THESE QUESTIONS

—What do I know already about this topic?
—What do I want to know?
—How do I plan to use this information?
—How will the search results help me? What will they help me do?

—What aspect of this topic concerns me most?
—What results are *not* likely to help me? What do I not want to know?
—If I could have any help at all, what would it be?

At the system level of the interview, the consultant needs to find out how much the user already knows about the system, what's missing in the user's understanding of the system, what might get the user stopped, and what kind of help is needed. Avoid assumptions (3.6) about the user's experience and abilities. Leave the user in control by asking neutral questions:

NEUTRAL QUESTIONS TO ASK THE END-USER
—Tell me what you know about searching on this system.
—What happened the last time you did a search? How did that help you (or hinder you?)
—What parts of this procedure concern you?
—What would help you most right now?
—What kind of results are going to help you most? How are these results going to help you? What aren't they going to do for you?
—What other help would you like?

Other skills for helping the end-user include giving instructions (3.11), giving advice (3.15), and inclusion (3.12). Remember to be specific, follow up, and ask for feedback. Don't overload the user with too much information at once.

6.2.8 The reference interview by remote control

In some situations you cannot communicate directly with the user. You may be expected to do an online search from information on a presearch questionnaire. Or you have received an interlibrary loan request by mail or telephone through an intermediary. Or you have just a second-hand account ("Marge, I'm leaving now. Would you get some stuff on transportation for Mr. Schmidt? He'll pick it up at six.")

If you feel you don't have a complete picture of what the user wants, try to contact the person who spoke to the user ("Hold it, Jim, tell me more about what Mr. Schmidt said he needed") or contact the user directly before you put in a lot of searching time, request an interlibrary loan, or mail out a lot of material. When there's no way of contacting the user, the best you can do is to find one or two examples of what you think may be wanted (as a gesture of good intentions) and invite feedback through a note asking the user to call or write again if this material doesn't help.

A better way to solve this problem is to prevent it. Make sure that everyone who is in a position to receive requests knows the importance of the reference interview and knows how to ask at least one or two basic questions. "What would you like to find out about X?" is a good all-purpose question to teach your colleagues to ask. Another good question is "If we can't find X for you, what else might help you?" Then, ask everyone who might receive a request to write down everything the user says—this reduces the chance of premature diagnosis or incorrect interpretation. You can also avoid some communication accidents and save a lot of time by routinely asking the user, "If we have any trouble finding this, do you mind if we call you to get more information?" and take a number. These should be routine procedures for accepting requests, no matter how clear the requests seem to be. You might supplement (but not replace) these procedures with a brief form that is filled out by the user or with the user present (see suggestions for the presearch interview form in section 9.10).

6.2.9 The readers' advisory interview

First a clarification and a definition. When we talk about readers' advisory in this section, we do not mean the readers' advisory service practiced in public libraries in the '20s and '30s. The idea behind that service was "reading with a purpose"—systematic reading on socially significant topics for purposes of self-improvement and adult education, what is now called Adult Independent Learning (see, for example, Jennie Flexner, *A Readers' Advisory Service*. New York: American Association for Adult Education, 1934). Rather, we are talking here about reading for pleasure and about the interview that occurs when someone asks, "Can you recommend a good book?"

The problem for readers' advisors is that the term "good book" is a relative term. Readers mean: a good book *for me*; a book that

Exercise

A COSTLY MISUNDERSTANDING

The user of a rural branch library asked for "a book on bats." "Bats as in animal? not baseball bats?" asked the librarian, mindful of premature diagnosis. "Bats that fly, yes," confirmed the user. So the librarian sent to headquarters and within a week proudly presented the user with a new natural history book that had a hundred color plates and everything you could possibly want to know about bats. But not quite everything: the user was very disappointed. "I wanted to know how to get rid of them," he said.

1. What could the librarian have asked the user to avoid this misunderstanding?

2. What could be the economic consequences of this misunderstanding? Might there be other consequences? How serious are they from the viewpoint of the user? from the viewpoint of the branch librarian? from the viewpoint of headquarters?

3. If you were the headquarters librarian and had received this request for a book on bats, what would you have done? What training or procedures would help to avoid this problem in future?

Thanks to Ron Baker, formerly of Lambton (Ontario) County Library for providing this example.

suits my level of reading ability; a book that matches my mood right now; a book that satisfies my particular needs and interests. Therefore it doesn't work to have on hand a list of "Good Books" (masterpieces of Western Civilization perhaps?) and recommend these same books to everyone. It's necessary to find out what each individual reader considers to be a good book—hence the need for the readers' advisory interview.

The readers' advisory interview has the characteristics of the generic reference interview, to which are added some further characteristics related to the activity of reading. Recent research has uncovered the variables that are important to readers as they search for "a good book."

FACTORS THAT AFFECT READERS' BOOK CHOICES

The following list, adapted from Annelese Pejtersen, shows what factors readers take into account when they look for a fiction book to read:

Subject:

What kind of *action* occurs in this book?

What sorts of *relationships* take place between characters? (If it's a love story, how "spicy" is it?)

What is the *theme*?

Setting:

When does the story happen? (past? present? future?)

Where does the story happen? (another planet? an archaeological dig? a village in Kashmir? Manhattan?)

Kind of experience:

Does the reader *learn something* from this book? ("I learned so much about the training of Olympic athletes or the early settlement of Australia from this book.")

Does the reader *feel something* as a result of reading this book? ("It made me feel happy/sad/hopeful about human goodness/terrified to death.") Does it have a happy ending? Or is it an unrelenting look at the bleakness of the modern Waste Land?

Accessibility:

What *reading skills* are demanded by this book? Does this book use literary conventions that may be unfamiliar: stream of consciousness narrative method, an ironic first person narrator, flashbacks, literary parody?

How *predictable* is it? The more conventional it is and the more it follows a formula, the more the reader already knows what to expect.

How *accessible* is it *physically* in terms of size and heaviness? In terms of the point size of the type?

Not all of these factors will be salient for all readers. A reader with strong arms and good eyesight may find the physical characteristics of the book irrelevant. A reader may not care where the book is set so long as it depicts strong, independent-minded female characters. On the other hand, a reader may refuse to read anything with too much sex and violence in it, or anything with confusing Russian names in it, or anything set in historical times. To find out which factors matter to an individual reader, ask open questions (3.5). The list "Some questions for readers' advisors" suggests some questions from which to choose the next time someone says, "Can you recommend a good book?"

EXAMPLE

User: Can you recommend a good book?

Librarian: You're looking for a good book to read *(acknowledgment)*. Which types of books have you enjoyed before? *(open question)*

User: I like a book I can get my teeth into. Something with two or three generations in it.

Librarian: Can you give me an example? (closed question that functions as an *open question*; the user could have answered this question with a simple "Yes," but most people would interpret the question to mean the same as the open question, "What would be an example of that?")

User: I loved *The Thorn Birds*.

Librarian: OK. And is there something that you would not like? (literally a closed question—the user could just say "yes"—but it usually functions in the same way as the *open question* "What would you not like?")

User: Nothing depressing. There's enough of that in life without having to read about it.

SOME QUICK TIPS

Remember that you are trying to understand what the reader thinks is a good book. Don't fall into the trap of recommending the last book that you enjoyed unless you have reason to think that the reader shares your reading tastes.

If you are in a library small enough for you to get to know readers, talk to them about their reading. Ask them what they liked or didn't like about the books they are returning. Show an active interest.

SOME QUESTIONS FOR READERS' ADVISORS

To get a picture of previous reading patterns:
—What have you enjoyed before? (which authors? what types of book?)
—What did you enjoy about that book (author/type of book)?
—What other books have you liked?
—What do you *not* like?

To determine current reading preferences:
—What do you think you might like to read today?
—What have you looked at so far? [to a person who has been looking unsuccessfully for reading material]
—What did you not like about the books you looked at?
—If we could find the perfect book for you today, what would it be like? (What would it be about? What would you like best about it?)

To understand the function of the book:
—What would you like this book to do for you?
—What do you want to get from this book? What do you find satisfying?
—What kind of reading experience do you want from this book?

To follow up on a recommendation:
—What do you think you might like/not like about this book?
—What else can I help you with?

6.2.10 Integrating reference interview skills

When librarians first attempt to apply new interviewing skills in an intentional, integrated way, they often wonder about the appropriateness of some skills, about the effect of the skill on the user, or whether they will ever be able to use the skill without awkwardness. Here are some questions that trainees commonly ask about reference interview skills.

1. When someone asks for something specific, do I still need to conduct a reference interview? A common type of request is for a particular title or reference tool such as Charles Dickens's *A Christmas Carol* or the *Encyclopedia Britannica*. A reference interview might seem redundant because the user obviously

knows what's wanted. But are you sure? It often turns out that the user, who is not familiar with the whole range of sources available, asks by name for the one he happens to know about, not necessarily for the one that will actually answer the question. A recommended approach is to acknowledge the request and fulfill it whenever it is possible to do so quickly. But follow up by checking to see if the requested item is really going to help. When the requested item is unavailable and you are about to suggest an interlibrary loan or reserve or refer the user to another library, try this instead: "Perhaps there's something else that would help you. What sort of information are you looking for?" In the case of *A Christmas Carol,* for example, it turned out that all copies were out. But the librarian was able to determine that the user wanted to put on a play with her grade seven class and was thinking of making a play out of Dickens's Christmas story. The librarian was then able to provide a book of Christmas plays that included a dramatic version of *A Christmas Carol.*

2. Doesn't it seem like prying to ask how someone plans to use the help they have asked for? Most people are quite willing to tell you if you ask the question appropriately. There are four guidelines for asking this neutral question:

   —Never ask "Why" directly, because it often sounds abrupt and judgmental, the kind of question a parent asks ("Why didn't you wear your boots? Why were you late for supper?") Moreover, "why" questions aren't necessarily efficient at eliciting answers about situations or uses; users may answer by saying "Because this library is closest," "Because the teacher told me to ask," or "Because I can't find what I want."

   —Make it clear that you are asking this question because you can be more helpful if you know intended uses, and not simply because you are curious. Say, for example, "We have a lot of material on Alzheimer's and some might serve your purpose better than others. Please tell me a bit more about what you are trying to find out." (see 3.12)

   —Avoid assumptions. A user who looks like a student may be asking the question for personal reasons while an older, harried-looking person may be trying to get a few statistics for an assignment due tomorrow for a night course. Let users tell you themselves what they are trying to do. Don't guess. Guessing is often inefficient and sometimes, when you guess wrong, can be offensive. It is much safer to ask questions that encourage users to describe the need in their own words. (See 3.6)

—Leave the other person in control. When you ask a neutral question like "How do you plan to use this information?" users can say as much or as little they want. They may tell you everything, which will help you suggest the most appropriate material. But if they choose to, they can say, "Oh, I'm just interested," a response that lets you know they don't want to say anything further.

3. Won't it take too long to ask open questions and use all these other skills? You may find that the reference interview takes a little longer. But extra time spent at the beginning to clarify what the user really wants often saves far more time later—time that would otherwise be wasted searching for the wrong thing. Inefficient use of time is especially apparent in online searching, where somebody's paying for connect time, printing, and perhaps document delivery. You can conduct short interviews by simply answering the user's initial question literally ("Sorry, all our copies are out"), but is that real service? Furthermore, a well-placed neutral question often yields a better query description faster than twenty closed questions.

4. Won't I sound awkward to the user? When librarians first start practicing their new skills, they do sound awkward, but more awkward to themselves than to the user. There's no substitute for real practice, however, and the message that most users are getting is that you're trying hard to help. Use the general practicing tips in Section 5.4 and the five easy questions for the reference interview.

5 EASY QUESTIONS FOR REFERENCE INTERVIEWS

Ask	*Instead of asking*
What can I help you do today?	Can I help you?
What have you done so far?	Have you looked in the catalog?
What would you like to know about X?	Do you want to know A or B?
What kind of help would you like?	Do you want me to do C?
What else can you tell me about X?	Is it this? Is it that?

6.3 COPING WITH SPECIAL SITUATIONS

In public service, special communication problems are often due to a barrier between you and the user. Such barriers may involve a physical disability, where the user is unable to speak, hear, or move normally, or they may involve differences in language, speech, or culture. Special communication problems also arise when there is a conflict between the user's expectations and yours, as in situations where the user has a complaint that seems reasonable to him but unreasonable to you. And then there is the problem patron, whose behavior not only seems unreasonable but may also be disruptive or even dangerous. These various situations should be distinguished and correctly identified because each type of situation requires different skills and attitudes. It is inappropriate, ineffective, and sometimes offensive to try to solve all special communication problems the same way. Most important, learn to judge when a problem situation is developing into more than a communication problem.

6.3.1 Helping the disabled user

An individual is disabled when he has any condition that prevents him from functioning normally in society—the inability to walk, see, speak, hear, or learn at full capacity. People disabled in some way are often apprehensive both about their own abilities and about how they are perceived in public places, including the library. Nondisabled people sometimes fear and avoid situations where they need to communicate with people with disabilities. We can reduce this apprehension by learning more about specific disabilities and by learning skills for getting around the communication barriers that some disabilities pose. Here are some suggestions:

1. Leave the user in control. Ask if he would like help or what kind of help is wanted.
2. Don't make assumptions about the user's abilities or needs. One physical disability doesn't necessarily mean other disabilities. For example, a speech disability may or may not affect a user's ability to hear or understand you.

3. Treat the user as an individual. Speak directly to him as you would to any other user. Don't ever talk about him in the third person to his companion ("Would *he* like help getting upstairs?")

4. Maintain eye contact, a relaxed posture, and other appropriate nonverbal behavior. Even if the user cannot see you, your physical attitude is conveyed in your voice.

5. Don't underestimate the disabled user. Like all users, disabled people have a broad range of interests and mental abilities. Don't stereotype disabled users as unable to cope with challenging materials but suit the material to the individual needs of the particular user.

6. Don't assume that the user wants special materials. You may have a fine collection of talking books, but these may not be what the user wants and it is offensive to recommend them when the user has said nothing about being unable to read regular print.

7. Know the facts about specific disabilities—needs and abilities vary with the kind and degree of disability.

8. Know the limitations of your library—the high shelves, narrow aisles, stairs. Be watchful—as you would with any library user—and be ready to give help as required or requested.

9. Don't pretend the disability doesn't exist—users with a visible disability know they are different. But don't be supersensitive or try to change your normal behavior. For example, visually disabled users understand the word *see* and are not offended by it.

10. Encourage the user's independence. Be patient and don't interfere with the user who wants to do something himself, even though you could do it for him better or faster. Offering an orientation tour of the library often provides greater freedom and encourages future independence.

11. Encourage feedback. Disabled users can often make excellent suggestions about how your facilities and services could be improved for disabled people. Comments about difficulties encountered in the library are important—pass them on to the library decision-makers. Let disabled users know that you are concerned about the negative aspects of the library's environment.

Quick tips: communicating with the hearing-impaired user
Know the facts about the kinds and degrees of hearing disabilities. Some people have had normal hearing ability and are gradually losing it through age or disease. Such people often feel isolated.

Some have lost significant amounts of hearing as adolescents or working-age adults and are learning new communication strategies. Others who were deaf before they learned to speak may vary widely in their ability to receive and express communication.

Don't exaggerate your speech but speak more slowly and distinctly. Make sure the light is on your face and not behind you. Keep your lips flexible, not rigid.

Face the user when you speak. Look into his eyes and use any gestures that you feel will help. Use all the nonverbal language available through your face, eyes, and hands.

Write on paper if you do not understand the user. Do this matter-of-factly, not apologetically.

Adopt the form of communication indicated by the user. If the user makes his request in writing, don't ask if he can read your lips.

Knowing sign language or finger spelling is an advantage—or know which staff members can communicate this way and call on them if necessary.

Quick tips: communicating with wheelchair users

Know the facts. People may be confined to wheelchairs by particular disabilities such as paraplegia, amputation, stroke paralysis, multiple sclerosis, and cardiovascular disease. The disability may be chronic, progressive, or temporary. Some users may just be learning to use wheelchairs; others have remarkable mobility and dexterity through long experience. Wheelchair users are usually able to use any kind of library material or service so long as it is physically accessible.

Know your library's physical barriers and how to help the user overcome them. Using drinking fountains, microfilm readers, high shelves, and narrow aisles may require your assistance.

If you do get involved in a conversation with the user, *sit down.* It is tiring for a wheelchair user to look up for any length of time.

Quick tips: communicating with the blind user

Know the facts. The ability to see and read varies greatly. People who use seeing-eye animals or white canes are legally blind (less than 20/200 visual acuity) but may still be able to see contrasts.

Listen carefully. The blind user depends more on speech as a means of communication than the fully sighted person.

Some of your nonverbal behavior is communicated through your voice, so *don't stop smiling and nodding.* However, remember that the user cannot read many of the messages that you routinely send through your body language, so be careful to acknowledge the user verbally with restatement and verbal encouragers. Use the skill of inclusion (see 3.12) to describe what you are doing or where you are going.

To guide a blind person, allow her to take your arm; don't grab hers.

Don't treat seeing-eye dogs as pets. They are trained working animals. Don't allow other library users to distract them. "Please don't pet him; he's busy working!" will usually get the message across.

6.3.2 Language and speech barriers

Since the basis of communication is a common language, communication accidents may occur when you and the user do not share the same first language or dialect, or when the user has a speech disability. If you cannot understand what the user is saying, try these four steps:

1. Restate what you *do* understand (see acknowledgment 3.2). If you catch the word "book" or "information," respond with some acknowledgment such as: "You're looking for a book on. . .?" or "You need some information. . .?" This establishes your willingness to help, encourages the user to repeat or fill in the part you missed, and gives you a second chance to listen.
2. Take ownership of the problem. Say, "I'm sorry, I seem to be having trouble understanding people today. Could you tell me again?"
3. If you still do not understand what the user wants, ask him to write it down. Again, take ownership: "It would help me if you could just write the name (or topic) down on this paper."
4. If all else fails, ask someone else to help. Sometimes another librarian will be able to hear immediately what the person is saying. Do this gracefully: "Maybe Mrs. Jones will be able to help. Let's just go over there and ask her." Often just moving with the user to another, less public, area, will lessen tension or frustration for both of you and encourage the user to express the request in another way.

Always show the user respect. Remember, it may be more difficult for him to ask the question than for you to understand it.

DID YOU KNOW?

In some cultures, such as some North American Indians, people deliberately leave a silence between a statement or question and the response, as a sign that they are considering the answer very carefully. Mainstream North Americans feel uneasy with this silence and tend to react by repeating or talking louder.

Exercise

HANDLING COMPLAINTS

In pairs, role-play these situations. Take turns being the user and the librarian. Practice one skill at a time: acknowledgment or restatement, encouragers, open questions, reflection of feeling, and broken record.

1. The user has not been able to find a parking space and had to circle the library lot for 15 minutes. He is now double-parked. He says to the circulation clerk: "You'd better do something about that parking lot."

2. A woman whose daughter brought home a Harold Robbins novel wants to speak to "the head librarian" about pornography.

3. A professor has just discovered that the library has cancelled its subscription to his favorite (rather esoteric) journal. He demands its reinstatement.

Never speak about the user in the third person ("Marge, I can't understand a word this man is saying.")

Pay attention to cultural differences as well as to language differences. In your effort to understand what the user is saying, you may be sending other, negative messages (such as asking too many questions or infringing on personal space) that hamper communication.

Don't raise your voice—the user's difficulty in speaking doesn't necessarily have anything to do with his ability to hear you. A person who isn't fluent in English (or in your dialect of English) is not deaf.

Above all, stay calm and be patient. Don't say to yourself: "I didn't understand a word of what he said—and I never will." Work through the strategies of acknowledgment, taking ownership, asking the user to write the question down, and finally, referral. One of these will work.

6.3.3 Handling complaints

Everyone in an organization—from the custodian to the chief executive officer—needs to know how to handle complaints efficiently, effectively, and tactfully. The most common complaints from library users involve circulation procedures: overdue fines, charges for lost books, and loan periods. Users may also complain about selection decisions such as holdings that they consider unsuitable for the library or material that the library doesn't have. Other types of complaints may involve parking availability, hours of opening, noise, or staff behavior. Helpful hints for handling complaints are provided in many publications about problem patrons or awkward customers. However, it's important to remember that the largest proportion of unpleasant encounters originate not from unreasonable demands or deviant behavior but from legitimate complaints or misunderstandings. Techniques for dealing with emergency situations serve a different function. Treating the user as the bad guy, even if the complaint initially seems unreasonable, is an invitation to confrontation.

To prevent a complaint from escalating into a full-blown display of anger or a similar scene, follow these steps:

To understand the problem

1. Listen to the complaint. Show that you are giving your full attention: use eye contact, appropriate posture, and all those nonverbal skills that say "I'm paying attention."

QUICK TIPS FOR HANDLING COMPLAINTS

Remain calm. Never argue or negotiate. Speak quietly. Be pleasant, no matter what the user says.

Listen. Let the user blow off steam.

Don't take complaints personally. Complaints are directed at the system. Taking them personally leads to burnout.

Don't give your own opinion or tell a story about something similar that happened to you. Self-disclosure is a skill that is often inappropriate for handling complaints: either the user will become impatient or will feel encouraged to describe more complaints.

Know when a complaint is beyond your control; refer quickly and accurately.

When you receive repeated complaints about something outside of your control and for which there seems to be no appropriate procedure or referral, it's time to discuss the problem at a staff meeting.

2. Acknowledge the user's concern and the user's right to question or criticize library regulations. Use restatement (3.2) to assure the user that you are listening ("You have just received this notice, hmm") and reflection of feeling (3.9) to communicate empathy ("I can see that this has really upset you.")

3. Allow the user to describe the complaint fully. Use encouragers (3.3) such as "Hmm," "I see," "Tell me more about this." Ask the user to be specific ("Can you give me an example?") and to describe what has happened to cause this complaint. For example, the user may say that he is very angry about the way this library is run and especially about the way books are chosen. Rather than responding at this stage with an explanation of the book selection policy, find out what initiated the complaint. Ask an open or neutral question (3.5 and 3.7) such as "What is it about our policy that upsets you?" "What aspect of this concerns you?" or "What has happened?"

4. Let the user do the talking at first. Don't be too quick to explain or defend. In nine cases out of ten, the user just wants to blow off steam and let someone know what has happened. The user isn't going to listen to you until he gets a chance to do this.

5. If it's not clear what the user expects, ask. "What would help you?" "What would you like us to do about this?" "What can I do that would help resolve this situation?"

6. If it's clear what the user expects you to do, restate (3.8) to confirm that you understand the proposed action: "You'd like us to remove this book from the collection" or "If I understand you correctly, you received a bill for a book that you already returned, and you want us to cancel the bill."

These six steps are necessary before you make a decision or take action. Often, by the time you've worked through these steps, the user will no longer be angry or will at least be ready to listen to you. To decide what you are going to do about the complaint, consider:

—Is this a situation over which you have control?
—Is it a common situation for which you have a standard procedure?
—Is it an unusual situation that you may be able to solve?
—Is it a situation that you must or should refer to someone else?

To take action towards resolving the complaint

7. Indicate that you are prepared to take some action—any action. Examples:

—I'm going to report this immediately.

—I'll check our files.

—Usually our records are accurate but occasionally they are not. What we do in these cases is to file a report and then check the shelves over the next two weeks until we find the book.

—This is a serious problem and the director would certainly want to know about it. I'll call him.

If you need to refer, tell the user what you are doing: "I'm not sure what to do about this, but Mrs. Harris, who is head of circulation, will know. If you will wait for a moment, I'll call her." Be prepared to make quick and accurate referrals.

8. Explain what the user should expect as a result of your action. "You will not receive another notice unless we definitely cannot locate the book. If you don't hear from us within two weeks, you'll know we found it."

9. Suggest what the user can do to help resolve the situation. Make specific suggestions without implying that the problem is the user's fault. Example: "While we're checking here, you might have another look at home and ask your family when they last saw this book."

10. Finally, thank the user for reporting the problem: "I'm glad that you brought this to our attention. It's only when people tell us that we can check into these records." Again, acknowledge the concern: "I'm very sorry that this happened to you. It was upsetting, I know" or "It never hurts to ask about the rules. I'm sorry that I couldn't let you take this magazine home."

These ten steps resolve most complaints. However, sometimes the user becomes emotional or abusive, even when you have listened carefully and acted appropriately. In such cases, do not argue, bargain, or be drawn into unnecessary justification of library policy. Use the *broken record* technique to emphasize your point:

User: That's ridiculous. What's the point of having magazines that don't circulate?

Librarian: We don't allow the latest issue to circulate because we need to be sure it's here when someone wants to consult it in the library.

User: Nobody ever reads this magazine but me.

Librarian: Still, we need to have it here in case someone does.

User: How about letting me have it overnight?

Librarian: I'm sorry. We don't circulate the latest issue.
User: That's a stupid rule.
Librarian: That is our rule.

If the user is still not satisfied, refer to a supervisor who is immediately available. This referral provides an opportunity to remove the discussion from a public area and to allow someone else to try to solve the problem. Sometimes people feel their complaint has been taken more seriously if they are referred to a supervisor. If the supervisor is not immediately available, however, the user may feel that she is being given the runaround. A simple way of making this decision is to ask the user: "There are many people waiting to charge out their books, so I am wondering if you would like to talk to my supervisor about this. I can show you to her office."

6.4. AWKWARD CUSTOMERS AND PROBLEM PATRONS

Before you can respond effectively to problem behavior, you must correctly identify the type of behavior. Is the person's behavior dangerous? disruptive? merely annoying or eccentric? annoying to you, but not to other staff or users? Much written about the problem patron fails to distinguish between the kinds of behavior that pose problems. If a person's behavior is dangerous or unlawful, it is probably also disruptive and inappropriate. But often a person's behavior is not dangerous— only inappropriate or mildly disruptive. Distinguishing between dangerous behavior and inappropriate behavior is important because these two problems require different responses at both the personal level (the staff member who experiences or observes the problem) and the institutional level (through policy statements and written procedures). Section 6.4.1 discusses the difference between routine problems that any public service worker can adequately handle with good communication skills (provided there is the support of written policies if required) and more difficult situations involving deviant or socially unacceptable behavior. Some situations require only an understanding of the behavior and do not require intervention until the behavior is disruptive or generally offensive in some way.

Exercise

PROBLEMS AND SOLUTIONS

(This exercise may be done individually or in small groups.) Suggest three ways in which a library staff member might respond to each of the following situations. Choose the best solution and justify your choice.

1. A group of five or six boys (around eleven years old) have been sitting at a table, getting increasingly louder—laughing, calling out to other students, using offensive language. One has now knocked over a chair. Other library users ask you to do something about the noise.

2. An elderly man in poor clothes has come in out of the rain. He seats himself in the corner of the reading lounge and produces a brown paper bag from which he takes a drink.

Section 6.4.2 describes appropriate responses to behavior that may be unlawful or dangerous or both.

6.4.1 Disruptive behavior

This section considers behavior that includes the following: the eccentic; the disruptive; and the both eccentric and disruptive. The man who sleeps away the afternoon in the library may be eccentric but he is nevertheless harmless and not disruptive. This sort of behavior can usually be ignored. The behavior of the irate user may seem disruptive to the library staff, but perfectly reasonable and completely justifiable to the user. This is usually a one-shot situation—behavior that is not habitual but arises from a user's reaction to a specific situation. So long as the irate user doesn't start throwing books or punching out the circulation clerk, library staff can usually resolve the problem with the communication skills described in the section on handling complaints (6.3).

The most common source of disruptive and inappropriate behavior is the rowdy student. But there are others: the regular user with strong and offensive body odor; the woman who wants to use two reading tables to spread out her Christmas cards on a busy day; and the sleeper when he begins to snore loudly. These people are all behaving in a way that impairs other people's ability to use the library. To this category we might add behavior that is both disruptive and eccentric, but not dangerous: the man who talks to himself constantly or the woman who approaches other users or staff with peculiar stories or requests. This is deviant behavior, but usually not a sign of dangerous behavior. It helps to understand the reasons why people act this way and to develop communication skills that can modify the unsuitable behavior.

The communication skills that are most useful in problem situations are listening (Chapter 2); nonverbal skills including tone of voice and gestures (Chapter 1); confrontation (3.13); and giving directions—to both users and staff (3.11). First, listen carefully and assess the situation before you act. Active listening will help you pick up on cues to the user's behavior and intentions. Use a calm tone of voice; do not speak loudly or too quickly. Use gestures that communicate calmness and control. Never use sudden gestures. Confrontation is a skill that works well for changing behavior that is unacceptable or disruptive but not dangerous. The DESC sequence is useful as a means of dealing with the rowdy student:

Exercise

THE PROBLEM PATRON

For each of the following situations, role-play the problem patron and the librarian's response. Experiment with different responses by having several people play the librarian's role, in turn.

1. A man has left a large pile of overdue books on the circulation desk and is walking away. Some books appear to be damaged. The man refuses to pay any fine. He gives the circulation clerk a hard time and is making a scene. You are the circulation supervisor and have been summoned to handle the situation.

2. A well-dressed professor is leaving the library, apparently empty-handed, when the security alarm goes off. When asked if she has forgotten to check out a book, she refuses to let you look in her briefcase and becomes abusive. She threatens to call the chairman of the Board of Regents.

3. A library user asks you to make photocopies of an article for him because he is in a hurry. You explain that staff members do not provide this service and that he must use the coin-operated copier himself. He orders you to make the copies and begins to shout at you about poor service.

Describe: You are making a lot of noise.
Explain: This is preventing other people from working.
Specify: I would like you to stop talking.
Consequences: If you are quiet, you can stay. If you continue talking loudly, I will ask you to leave.

This will work better than: "You'll have to stop that noise, or else." If the DESC sequence doesn't work the first time, repeat the cycle:

Describe: A few minutes ago I asked you to stop talking loudly but you didn't stop.
Explain: Your talking is still bothering other people.
Specify: Pick up your books and walk out that door. Please don't come back tonight.
Consequences: If you don't do as I ask, I will call the security guard (or inform your school, mother, etc.)

Use the *broken record* technique to keep the conversation on track and to focus on the way you want the problem resolved:

User: But I have to photocopy my hands.
Librarian: I'm asking you to leave now.
User: I put my quarter in. I can do what I want.
Librarian: I'm asking you to leave.
User: I won't go.
Librarian: Please leave now.
User: You're an old bag. [But she leaves.]

Finally, you may need to give instructions to either the person who is creating the problem or to other staff. Instructions should be clear and concrete with an opportunity, in this case, for feedback. For example:

Take your hand out of the photocopier. Pick up your books and leave the library. Please don't come back today. Do you understand?

Marge, please use the phone in the back room. Ask Mrs. Newton to come to the front desk immediately.

Exercise

DANGEROUS CUSTOMERS

Discuss the appropriate procedures for dealing with these situations.

1. You are working in the stacks when a man asks you for more than information. You recognize him as a local masher.

2. You have repeatedly asked two teenaged boys to leave the library. One of them says, "Make me!" and pulls out a knife.

QUICK TIPS FOR POTENTIALLY DANGEROUS SITUATIONS

Be alert. Initial signs of a problem situation include: users moving away from another user; users staring at someone; and users looking at staff as a form of complaint.

Stay calm. You may be able to defuse the situation or at least prevent it from escalating.

Do not speak loudly, use patronizing phrases, or make sudden gestures.

Act immediately.

Know the appropriate agency to call. If possible, use a signal system so that an assistant can call the police quickly and quietly.

Ask other users and staff to move away from the disturbed person for their safety.

Do not attempt to prevent the person from leaving the library.

File an incident report (see 9. 5.2. 2).

6.4.2 Unlawful and dangerous behavior

Unlawful behavior includes contravention of library regulations and possibly the law. In this section, we are talking about the person who cuts up library books, defaces library signage, steals, threatens, or assaults. Unlawful behavior may or may not be overtly disruptive or dangerous, and the person who engages in it may or may not be mentally ill. The best advice we can give is to use caution: such behavior may escalate and is unpredictable. *These are not situations in which to practice your new communication skills. Do not attempt to do the work of the police or mental health professionals.*

However, the fact remains that it is the front-line staff who first encounter these situations, often in the absence of a supervisor. There should be specific procedures to follow, and these procedures must be supported by institutional policies. Some libraries have written their own manuals for dealing with these problems, and if your library doesn't have such a manual, it should. The tips (left) for dealing with dangerous situations have been derived from Brian Ingram's *Survival Manual*, prepared for the Sault Ste. Marie (Ontario) Public Library.

FOR FURTHER HELP

6.1 Answering the telephone

Baeckler, Virginia. *Sparkle! PR for Library Staff.* Hopewell, NJ: Sources, 1980, pp. 31-9. Chapter 4 deals with telephone answering skills.

6.2 Interviewing

Conroy, Barbara and Barbara Schindler-Jones. *Improving Communication in the Library.* Phoenix, AZ: Oryx Press, 1986.

Eichman, T.L. "The Complex Nature of Opening Reference Questions," *RQ,* 17 (1978): 212-222. Explains that the initial question asked by the user functions more as a greeting than as a fully elaborated question.

Goodale, James G. *The Fine Art of Interviewing.* Englewood Cliffs, NJ: Prentice-Hall, 1980. An excellent general text, particularly useful for the employment interview. Goodale has also written a booklet, "Recruiter's

Guide to Successful Interviewing," available from the University and College Placement Association, Toronto, Ontario, Canada.

Ivey, Allen E. *Intentional Interviewing and Counseling.* Monterey, CA: Brooks/ Cole, 1983. The best text on microcounseling and the individual skills approach.

Lindsey, Jonathan A., ed. *Performance Evaluation: A Management Basic for Librarians.* Phoenix, AZ: Oryx Press, 1986. Includes "The Ten Commandments for Performance Appraisal Interviews" and "How to Give Feedback."

Spradley, James P. *The Ethnographic Interview.* New York: Holt, Rinehart and Winston, 1979. Written for the student of ethnography, this book contains advice on asking questions and structuring the interview useful to anyone doing oral history interviewing.

Stewart, Charles J. and William B. Cash. *Interviewing: Principles and Practices.* 5th ed. Dubuque, IA: William C. Brown, 1987. This little book remains one of the best general guides to interviewing. Based on sound theory and extensive research, it is both practical and easy to read. Each chapter includes training exercises.

6.2.6 *The presearch interview*

Somerville, Aileen N. "The Presearch Reference Interview: A Step-by-step Guide," *Database,* 33 (February 1982): 32-38. An excellent guide.

6.2.9 *The readers' advisory interview*

Pejtersen, Annelise and Jutta Austin, "Fiction Retrieval: Experimental Design and Evaluation of a search system based on users' value criteria," *Journal of Documentation,* 39, 4 (December 1983): 230-246; part 2, 40, 1 (March 1984): 25-35. As a preliminary to designing their classification system for fiction retrieval, the authors analyzed 300 user/librarian conversations as the basis for identifying the dimensions of fiction books that are important to readers.

There's not much written on conducting the readers' advisory interview itself. But after you have found out the kind of book the reader wants to read, here are some sources to help with the next step: finding the actual titles and authors.

Cawelti, John. *Adventure, Mystery and Romance:* Formula Stories as Art and Popular Culture. Chicago: Chicago University Press, 1976. An influential and readable analysis of formula stories as popular culture. Provides an insight into the appeals of popular formulas.

Hackett, Alice Payne and James Henry Burke. *80 Years of Bestsellers, 1895-1975.* New York: R.R. Bowker, 1977. Provides lists of bestsellers. Very useful to indicate trends in popular taste.

Rosenberg, Betty. *Genreflecting: A Guide to Reading Interests in Genre Fiction.* 2nd ed. Littleton, CO: Libraries Unlimited, 1987. Invaluable for readers advisory work because it lists authors and books, grouped by genres, themes and types.

6.2.10 Integrating reference interview skills

King, Geraldine. "Open and Closed Questions: The Reference Interview," *RQ*, 12 (1972): 157-160.
Robertson, Carolyn. *Bibliography: The Reference Interview*. Ottawa: Library Documentation Centre, National Library of Canada, 1985. (pamphlet)
Ross, Catherine Sheldrick and Patricia Dewdney. "Reference Interviewing Skills: Twelve Common Questions," *Public Libraries* (Spring 1986): 7-9.

Video

The following Library Video Network tapes are distributed by ALA Video, a unit of the American Library Association, and are available in Beta, VHS, and 3/4" formats.

Does This Answer Your Question? Baltimore, MD, 1985. 17 min. On skills necessary for the reference interview.
The Difficult Reference Question. Baltimore, MD, 1986. 19 min. Describes and demonstrates basic communication skills for responding to difficult reference questions.
Who's First . . . You're Next. Baltimore, MD, 1980. 29 min. Skits represent problematic situations on the reference desk, which are then discussed by experienced librarians.

6.3 Coping with special situations

Many social service agencies, health organizations, and self-help groups publish pamphlets that increase understanding of specific disabilities and include tips for communicating. Ask your local organizations to provide you with multiple copies for your staff and your public. They may also provide speakers for staff training.

Dalton, Phyllis I. Chapter 4: "Two-Way Communication," *Library Service to the Deaf and Hearing Impaired*. Phoenix, AZ: Oryx Press, 1985. Skills for working with groups and individuals, including American Sign Language and other systems.
Hall, Edward. T. *The Silent Language*. Garden City, NY: Doubleday, 1959. The classic work on cross-cultural differences in communication.
Lucas, Linda. "Educating librarians to provide user education to disabled students," Chapter 9 in *Teaching Librarians to Teach: On the Job Training for Bibliographic Instruction Librarians*, edited by Alice S. Clark and Kay F. Jones. Metuchen, NJ: Scarecrow Press, 1986.
Schnapper, Melvin. "Nonverbal communication and the intercultural encounter" in *Small Group Training Theory and Practice: Selected Readings*, edited by J. William Pfeiffer and John E. Jones. La Jolla, CA: University Associates, 1977. (Reprinted from *The 1975 Annual Handbook for Group Facilitators.*) Provides useful examples of communication accidents due to cultural differences in behavior.

Thomas, Carol H. and James L. Thomas, eds. *Meeting the Needs of the Handicapped: A Resource for Teachers and Librarians*. Phoenix, AZ: Oryx Press, 1985. Helpful definitions, tips, and references for working not only with the physically disabled but also with students who are mentally retarded, have learning disabilities, or have emotional problems.

6.4 Awkward customers and problem patrons

Many libraries have prepared their own policy and procedure manuals for dealing with problem situations. Consult libraries in your area for examples.

Carparelli, Felicia. "Public Library or Psychiatric Ward?" *American Libraries* (April 1984): 212. A short provocative piece that blames library administrators for being too permissive.

Dowding, Martin. "Problem Patrons: What are they Doing in the Library?" *Quill and Quire* (November 1985): 4-6. Describes responses recommended by librarians and others for situations involving transients, alcoholics, psychiatric patients, and sexual deviants. Useful article for discussion.

Gothberg, Helen M. "Managing Difficult People: Patrons (and Others)," *Reference Librarian*, 19 (1987): 269-282.

Library Video Network. *A Library Survival Guide: Managing the Problem Situation*, 1987. 20 minutes. VHS, Beta, 3/4". This videotape presents six problem situations and suggests a variety of staff responses, with commentary from legal, health, and library professionals. Includes a five-page discussion guide for training programs. Available from ALA Video, the American Library Association.

Salter, Charles A. and Jeffrey L. Salter. *On the Frontlines: Coping with the Library's Problem Patrons*. Englewood, CO: Libraries Unlimited, 1988. Twenty-four case studies of problem patrons illustrate a variety of psychiatric disorders.

Shuman, Bruce A. *River Bend Revisited: The Problem Patron in the Library*. Phoenix, AZ: Oryx Press, 1984. Provides 40 case studies ranging from emergencies and theft to lost children and vandalism. Includes discussion guides.

Turner, Bonnie L. and Rondi Downs, comp. *Patron Relations: A Survival Manual*. Yakima Valley Regional Library, Washington, 1983. ED 254255 MF01

7 WORKING IN GROUPS

7.1 WHY WORK IN GROUPS?

The best idea from a group is almost always better than any one of the best ideas from individuals working alone. Group judgments are generally superior to those of one individual because the judgments are evaluated and refined by several people with varying skills and perspectives. Studies suggest that groups of individuals tend to accomplish more creative thinking than individuals who are isolated. The probability of productive discussion, however, is related to the quality of interaction within the group and to the purpose for establishing the group.

WHEN TO WORK IN A GROUP:
—to generate ideas or alternatives
—to use the resources of more than two people
—to explore a complex issue or solve a complex problem
—to share responsibility for a decision
—to develop motivation and leadership ability
—to gather information or opinions from people who have varying perspectives
—to teach people how to work together
—to allow people to share ideas or opinions about a film, book, or presentation that has been made
—to obtain feedback on decisions, instructions, or directions
—to encourage people to develop interpersonal contacts.

But group work is not always necessary, desirable, or even possible. When an emergency decision has to be made, valuable time can be lost in getting a group together. When the group cannot do the job better than a single individual could, don't work in groups.

WHEN TO USE SOME OTHER FORM OF COMMUNICATION:
—to give information that is not open to discussion or negotiation
—to give simple instructions or directions that require no feedback
—to gather background information from one expert.

Remember that the camel was a horse put together by a committee.

7.2 CHARACTERISTICS OF GROUPS

In this book, we use the word group to mean more than a collection of individuals. A group is a collection of individuals who have come together to achieve an explicit, shared goal (even if the goal is simply to exchange viewpoints) and who perceive themselves as members of the group. Group behavior is determined, or at least evaluated, by mutually accepted standards. Group members communicate primarily by talking to each other face to face. Groups may be further described in terms of their purpose, duration, size, personality, and communication structure.

Purpose. Although most groups regularly perform several functions at any one session, a group is usually established to achieve one primary purpose (which purpose may or may not be shared by particular individual members). Some reasons that people establish or join groups include:

—to get to know each other better
—to solve joint problems
—to explore issues of common interest
—to give or receive information
—to make decisions.

Think, for example, of the stated purposes of a staff meeting or a meeting of the board of trustees. The purpose of the group determines many of the other characteristics of the group. Individual members may also have hidden agendas that affect the nature of the group. For some individuals, the social purposes of the group may be more important than the task-oriented purposes.

Duration. Groups may be short-lived (such as an emergency meeting of people who normally do not meet together) or long-lived (such as regular staff meetings where there isn't much staff turnover, or a book discussion group of old friends who have been meeting for years). Voluntary groups survive when the members continue to share a common purpose and when the dynamics of the group are healthy.

Size. The optimal group size for productive group discussion is 12

DID YOU KNOW?

Groups of three solve easy problems more efficiently than larger groups, but groups of six are more successful in solving complex problems. Groups with more than six members tend to have more behavioral problems. The most common sizes of committees are five, seven and nine members; groups with an even number of members have more trouble reaching consensus (John K. Brilhart. *Effective Group Discussion.* 5th ed. Dubuque, IA: William C. Brown, 1986). Therefore the right size for a group depends upon the purpose of the meeting. 3M Canada, Visual Products Division, suggests the following guidelines:

For a problem-solving group, five people or less

For a group to identify a problem, ten or less

To attend a review or presentation, 30 or less

To attend a motivational or inspirational meeting, the more the better to 15 people. In groups of more than 15 people, the communication pattern changes in the direction of a more formal meeting structure, in which communication is channeled through the designated leader and the group can no longer be called a small group. Having fewer than 12 people limits the full range of group activities and abilities. Very small groups—such as buzz groups—of 3 to12 people can still operate productively as a group for certain purposes.

Group personality. Over time, groups take on a life of their own as they develop their own standards and cohesiveness. Groups are greater than the sum of their parts. The personality of a group may be completely different from the personalities of individual members. Notice, for example, how two groups of similar people working on the same issue can be very different.

Structure. The communication structure of a group refers to the way in which members interact with each other, the relationship between members, and the position of each member in relation to the leader. Communication structures are usually imposed externally, at least initially, and should be appropriate to the size and purpose of the group. For example, a budget committee is established with a specific number of members, a chairperson, and procedures for determining how members communicate with each other and with the parent organization. In very formal structures, the designated (or elected) head makes decisions about who can speak, to whom, when, and about what. A panel discussion is a group that operates for the benefit of a larger group—the audience, with whom the panelists may interact in a controlled and limited way, such as through questions and answers. A discussion group (for the purpose of personal growth or problem-solving) is designed for the benefit of participants, rather than for an audience, and works best with a small number of people who participate equally. Such groups may have a designated leader who facilitates discussion, but the group usually monitors itself. This latter type of group is usually what we think of when we use the term small group.

EXERCISE
Purpose of groups

1. List the groups to which you belong in your personal life. Classify them as formal groups and informal groups. What is it that makes each group formal or informal? For each group, consider (a) the stated purpose of the group, (b) the reason that

you initially joined the group, and (c) the reasons that you continue to belong to this group—what you are getting out of it.

2. Look at the following examples of groups and group meetings commonly found in libraries. Which of these groups hold meetings in your organization?

—Branch or departmental staff
—A union or staff association
—A board of trustees and their committees
—Management committees
—Task forces, ad hoc committees, special work groups
—Citizen participation groups for library planning
—Focus groups
—Discussion groups for staff
—Discussion groups for the public—book, film or issue oriented
—Library association committees, guilds, and round tables
—Social committees, orientation groups
—In-service training groups
—Seminars, classes, bibliographic instruction groups.

Choose three of these groups for discussion. What is the primary purpose of each of these groups? What are the secondary purposes? Could the primary purpose be accomplished in some other way? Why or why not?

7.2.1 Patterns of communication

Sometimes the leader controls communication within a group so that all discussion is channeled through the leader. Other members of the group talk to the leader but not directly with each other (Figure 1). This pattern is appropriate for a formal meeting but inappropriate for a small group discussion or joint problem-solving.

In Figure 2, more communication occurs between the group members, but the leader is still a strong focus. This pattern is not appropriate for a very formal meeting, where the chairperson needs to control who speaks when and about what. Nor is it the best pattern of communication for a small group. It works best for

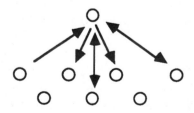

Figure 1: Formal or hierarchical communication

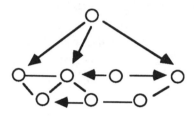

Figure 2: Semiformal group

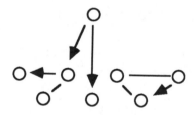

Figure 3: All-channel communication

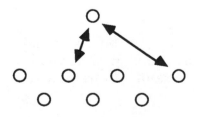

Figure 4: Splinter group

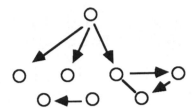

Figure 5: Monopolization

informal classes or large groups where some controlled interaction is desirable.

In a true small group, communication flows freely among group members with the leader appearing to take little or no part in directing the group's activities (Figure 3). Still, discussion is democratic and productive.

Each of these three basic patterns can be effective, depending on the size and the purpose of the group.

But some communication patterns never produce effective group discussion. Splinter discussions (Figure 4) occur when a few people in a group split off to talk with each other; they become their own small groups, excluding others and preventing the larger group from functioning.

Monopolization (Figure 5) is another common problem, in which one person does all the talking. See section 7.5.2 for some ways to cope with these situations.

7.3 GROUP DYNAMICS

In order for any group to achieve its goals, it must balance two functions: the *task* function (getting things done—making the decision, discussing the options, or whatever the group got together for) and the *maintenance* function (building a good communication climate in which people feel both free and able to participate). In addition, a third set of self-oriented functions can often be identified; these are discussed in a later section on problem behavior (7.5.1).

EXERCISE
Leadership in Groups
Divide into two groups, A and B. (If each group is larger than five participants, divide again so that you have two A groups and two B groups.) Designate a leader for the A group(s) but not for the B group(s). Designate a recorder (someone whose job it is to report results briefly) for each group (both A and B). The task of each group is to discuss what makes that group different from a simple collection of individuals (such as elevator riders) and to decide on three major differences. After ten minutes, reconvene. The recorders for each group report the list of differences, in turn. Discuss the

results with special attention to similarities and duplications, if any, between lists compiled by the A group(s) and the B group(s).

7.3.1 Task functions

These are the roles that people can take in order to facilitate the task functions of the group. A good group member often performs a number of roles at any one meeting, choosing the role according to what is needed at any particular time to further the discussion.

Initiating. Getting the group started, defining goals, problems, making group objectives explicit. "We're here today to talk about X. Let's start by going around the table and stating our individual interests in X."

Asking for information. Seeking facts. "Who was previously involved in this?" "What does STDG stand for?"

Giving information. Providing facts or information, defining. "STDG stands for Staff Training and Development Guild."

Asking for clarification. "I'm not sure what we're talking about." "I missed what you said—could you say it again please?"

Clarifying. Restating or paraphrasing. "What I mean by X is. . . ." "What you said means to me. . . ."

Seeking consensus. "Is there a basic condition that we all agree is necessary?"

Asking for opinions. Requesting others to state beliefs or make judgments. "What do you think we should do?" "How do you feel about the suggestion that we add a school librarian to the committee?"

Giving opinions. Stating beliefs or making evaluative statements. "I think this is too important to ignore. We ought to hire a fund-raiser."

Linking. Explaining relationships between ideas or information previously contributed. "Joe has been talking about the problems in the circulation department and earlier we heard from Rosa about the program in technical services. Could a similar program be applied in the circ department?"

Summarizing. Briefly restating group actions or concerns. "We've decided that we ought to do X, but we seem to disagree on exactly how to do this."

Testing. Trying an idea out in order to explore it more deeply. "Would that work in this situation?" "What happens if. . .?"

Expediting. Performing routine activities such as rearranging chairs, handing out paper, etc.

Recording. Writing down major points or decisions made by the group.

7.3.2 Maintenance functions

People rarely question the need for task functions in a group. But some are unaware of the importance of maintenance functions and may be inclined to label as a waste of time activities that are, in fact, crucial to the group's continued survival. Here are some functions that help in maintaining the group.

Supporting. Agreeing, praising. "That's a good idea, Barbara."

Harmonizing. Reconciling differences, mediating. "I can see why Jake is concerned, because it is a big risk. On the other hand, we should maybe look carefully at what Mario is proposing and see if that can be done in a way that won't hurt Jake's department."

Gatekeeping. Facilitating equal participation in the group, preventing monopolization, structuring discussion. "George hasn't said what he thinks yet."

Reflecting group feelings. "Maybe we've gone as far as we can with this point." "I think some of us are feeling a little lost."

Relieving tension. Telling a joke, story, or personal experience to defuse negative feelings.

DID YOU KNOW?
Almost all group behaviors can be categorized as task-oriented or maintenance-oriented. The classic study of group interaction is by Robert F. Bales. *Interaction Process Analysis.* Reading, MA: Addison-Wesley, 1950.

GETTING DISCUSSION STARTED

Suggest that each person introduce himself or herself and say something about his or her reasons for joining the group. Ensure that this doesn't turn into a status-definition procedure.

Ask each participant to contribute something from his or her own experience. For example, "Let's go round the table and each describe a recent problem we have had with the reserve system. Try to be brief and specific."

Help the group make an inventory of the problems or issues they would like to have discussed in the group. Write all suggestions on a flip chart or blackboard.

Begin with a provocative statement or radical proposition. Ask individuals to react. For example, "An extreme solution is simply to reduce library hours across the system. How do you react to that?"

Brainstorm for ideas. Generate as many ideas as possible, without evaluation or criticism.

Do these task and maintenance functions sound familiar? The microskills described in Chapters 1 to 3 are skills for group work as well as for one-to-one communication.

In any group, *attending skills* such as restatement (3.2) or eye contact (1.2) can function as maintenance skills by helping the group feel comfortable or as task skills by helping to focus on the task at hand. *Questioning skills* (3.5 and 3.7) contribute to the task functions of information gathering, checking out facts, comparing opinions, and probing. As in the interview, open questions (for example, "What are your expectations for this group?") work very well at the beginning of a group session. Neutral questions work well in finding out what has brought this group together, what their concerns are, what they need or want to find out, and what would help the group achieve its purpose.

Confronting (3.13) contributes to the maintenance of the group when it is used effectively to handle problem behavior. *Summarization* and *reflection of feeling* (3.7 and 3.9) are particularly important skills for group leaders because they convey to the group the leader's understanding of what has been accomplished so far and how the group feels. Research among politicians has shown that the most successful political leaders are those that can explicitly state the common feelings and opinions of the population.

ROLE-PLAYING EXERCISE

This exercise provides an opportunity for group members to examine the effects of task and maintenance functions in a discussion group. Each group member is given a card on which is described his or her role. The group member reads the card silently but does not let anyone else know what is on the card. Each person plays the assigned role in a group discussion, without explicitly revealing the role (the person who gets the supporter role supports other people's contributions but never says anything like, "Since I'm supposed to be the supporter . . ."). The topic of discussion should be a question on which there is likely to be diversity of opinion: for example, should the library be open on Sundays? When participants have read and understood their role, discussion begins and continues for ten to fifteen minutes. After the discussion, talk about these questions: what were the assigned roles? when did the roles emerge most clearly? what effect did each role have? how did each participant feel about his or her role?

[Note: The roles of opinion-giver and information-giver should be assigned to at least two people. The role of observer may be assigned to more than one member if group size warrants.]

Your role is to be the *group leader*. Get the discussion started by posing the question or topic. Keep it going by asking questions as needed. Encourage everyone to provide opinions and information. Don't give opinions or information yourself. End the discussion in approximately ten minutes.

Your role in this group is to be an *observer*. Contribute to the discussion occasionally, but focus on what others are doing and saying.

Your role in this group is to be a *supporter*. Agree with everything that has just been said. Show support by encouraging others. Do not give any new information or opinions.

Your role in this group is to be an *information-giver*. Volunteer facts (made up, if you like), and give information on what you have read or heard about this issue.

Your role in this group is to be a *tension-reliever*. Make humorous comments, encourage informality, help people to be at ease. Don't offer many opinions; just do your best to see that people are getting along and enjoying themselves.

Your role is to be an *opinion-giver*. Say what you think about the issue. Take the opposite view for the sake of argument, if you wish.

Your role is to be an *evaluator*. When a suggestion is made, encourage the group to test it out. For example, "Would this work if. . .?" "What would prevent this from working?"

Your role is to be a *harmonizer*. Try to reconcile different viewpoints. Suggest compromises. Smooth over the rough spots. Don't say much about your own opinions.

7.3.3 Group leadership

Every group has at least one leader. The leader may be the formal, designated leader (the chairperson, or the professor in a class) or an informal leader who holds no specified title but is able to influence

Exercise

SHARED LEADERSHIP

Practice shared leadership by working with a coleader to plan and lead a short discussion in a group of five or six people. Decide who will take the primary leadership role first and plan when you will switch roles. After the discussion is over, give feedback to your coleader. What helped you? What other help did you need? How flexible were you? What could you do to improve the way you work together?

QUICK TIPS FOR COLEADERS

Meet with your coleader well in advance of the group session to plan who will do what and when.

Share responsibilities for arranging the room, sending out notices, preparing materials, getting coffee.

Designate sections of the discussion to be led primarily by one person. The other person then acts in a supporting role only.

When you are in the supporting role, listen carefully so that you know where your coleader is taking the discussion.

When you are in a supporting leadership role, be alert to the general tone of the group—observe body language, note what's happening. Help your coleader to recognize members who want to have input.

group behavior and help the group work towards its goal. The leader's responsibilities are to:

—get the group started
—guide the group through the stages of information-sharing, exploration of ideas, and evaluation or decision-making
—keep the group on track
—encourage equal participation
—summarize group activity
—look after resources and physical arrangements.

A good leader is above all a good listener. An old saying attributed to the YM-YWCA describes how the effectiveness of a leader may be measured:

—not by the leadership he or she exercises, but by the leadership he or she evokes
—not in terms of power over others, but in terms of the power released in others
—not in terms of the goals he or she sets up, but in terms of the goals and plans of action people work out for themselves with the leader's help
—not by the products and projects completed, but by the growth of competence, sense of responsibility, and personal satisfaction among the participants.

LEARNING HOW TO LEAD

Studies of leadership show that leadership ability is not innate but involves skills that are learned. Many styles of leadership can be identified, but here we are concerned with facilitative leadership, or the ability to help a group identify, analyze, and reach its goals. Individuals who are formally designated as group leaders may or may not be effective leaders. The responsibility for effective group performance must be shared by everyone in the group. One way to provide leadership practice is to establish procedures for shared leadership. The designated leadership for an ongoing group may be rotated among all group members. An easy way to introduce this concept is to have coleaders: an experienced and an apprentice leader work together for one or two sessions, or for parts of a session. The apprentice leader then takes on the coleadership with a new apprentice leader until everyone has become more experienced as a leader.

7.3.4 Being a good group participant

When you are not exercising a leadership function in the group, you still need to be aware of what's happening and you need to be active in helping the group achieve its goals. First, pay attention to your own behavior. What are you doing to help the group? To hinder it? Second, help out by reinforcing positive group behavior ("That's an excellent suggestion, Bob") and not encouraging negative behavior ("That's interesting, but we do have a limited amount of time and maybe we ought to get back to the main issue"). Third, if there's a problem, bring it to the group's attention even if you can't think of a solution ("Look, I feel that we're going around in circles. What can we do to get back on track?"). You're not doing yourself or the group a service by bottling up your feelings of dissatisfaction with how things are going.

DID YOU KNOW?
Brainstorming produces better and more original ideas than ordinary problem-solving procedures, according to Sidney J. Parnes and Harold F. Harding, eds. *A Source Book for Creative Thinking*. New York: Charles Scribner's Sons, 1962.

DID YOU KNOW?
The Great Books Foundation pioneered the concept of shared leadership in small groups for the purpose of book-based continuing education. These leadership training courses were an early example of the microtraining precept, "Learn, do, and teach." Shared leadership in Great Books discussions meant that all participants learned basic discussion techniques and took turns acting as designated leaders.

7.4 GROUP WORK IN LIBRARIES: THREE TYPES

So far we have talked about group dynamics and leadership in general terms. The section that follows examines three representative types of group discusssions that commonly occur in libraries. We start with the book discussion group as an example of an informal group in which the leadership function is distributed. The problem-solving group, while still informal in its communication patterns, is usually more structured. And the formal meeting is the most structured group of all.

7.4.1 The book discussion

Contrary to what you might think, the desirable outcome of a book discussion is not to provide members with a comprehensive set of facts or a correct interpretation of the book. A book discussion is successful when it allows members to share their responses to the book, compare their differing interpretations, and ask each other questions. Something has gone wrong if the discussion turns into a lecture in which one person presents an expert opinion and everyone else listens.

Aidan Chambers in *Booktalk* speaks of the need to discover a repertoire of questions about the reading experience that helps rather than hinders the discussion of books. He developed what he calls the "Tell me" approach for use with children, but the questions are fruitful for discussing books with readers of all ages:

> Tell me . . . when you first saw the book, even before you read it, what kind of book did you think it was going to be? (probe: Can you tell me what made you think this?)
>
> What struck you particularly about the book?
>
> Was there anything that surprised you? puzzled you? bored you?
>
> Have you read other books (stories/plays/poems) like this? How does this one differ?
>
> Which character (or, in a nonfiction book, which section) interested you the most?
>
> Did you notice anything about the novel that made a pattern?
>
> If the author asked you what could be improved about this book, what would you say?
>
> We've heard each other's ideas on this book. Are you surprised by anything that anyone else has said?
>
> When you think about this book now, after all we've said, what is the most important thing about it for you?
>
> (*Booktalk*, pp. 168-73.)

The book discussion is one of the best ways to learn group leadership skills and to teach them to others, including library users. A volunteer leadership training program should include an introduction to group dynamics, basic listening and questioning skills, and a great deal of practice within the training group. The following tips for book discussion leaders can easily be adapted for discussions of film or video.

QUICK TIPS FOR BOOK DISCUSSION LEADERS
Be prepared: DO make an outline of questions and issues, but DON'T cling too closely to the outline.

DO let the discussion go on if it is relevant to the text.

Exercise

LEADING A DISCUSSION

Practice leading a book discussion using the Universal Declaration of Human Rights, or the introduction to some other code of human rights. Each participant takes turns being the leader for about three minutes. The task of the first leader is to get the discussion started by asking open questions to clarify meanings and get opinions about the statement "All men are created equal." The second leader continues this line of questioning, but probes more deeply, and so on.

DID YOU KNOW?

"Groupthink" is a term that refers to the excessive conformity in a problem-solving group that can occur either when high-status members control the communication process or when group membership lacks sufficient diversity. Groupthink results in decisions of low quality. (Irving L. Janis. *Victims of Groupthink*. Boston: Houghton Mifflin, 1973.)

DON'T try to cover the whole book. DO focus on about four issues but get the group to look at the book as a whole for a while.

Use questions only: DON'T make statements, answer questions, or give your own opinion.

DON'T ask leading questions (questions that appear to require some particular answer such as, "Everyone would agree that such-and-such, wouldn't you?")

DO keep your questions short. DON'T use double-barreled questions (questions that are really two questions such as "What was the most interesting part of the book, and what did you think was unusual about the literary style?").

DON'T stop with agreement. Go on to find out why.

Help the group to examine the author's ideas: DO probe the author's ideas to seek clarification, consider consequences, or look for consistency.

DO apply the author's ideas to imaginary situations or current events.

DO use provocative or "devil's advocate" questions to encourage opposing points of view.

Stay on track: DON'T let the discussion wander from the point. DO redirect the discussion from the monopolizer and nonreader.

DON'T encourage the group to bring in outside information about the author's time and place or cite other authorities or critics.

DON'T let the group attack the author's character; DO let them attack the author's ideas.

DON'T dispute facts. Either disregard them or assume they are true and examine the implications.

Maintain an open communication climate: DO get everyone into the discussion early.

DO encourage everyone to question each other.

DO keep an open mind. Entertain any notion as possible and get the group to examine it.

DO show patience and use humor. Be leisurely in attitude.

DON'T fear small silences.

These tips have been adapted from three sources: the Great Books Foundation's guide for discussion leaders; "A Guide to Group Discussion Techniques" compiled by C.D. Kent, London Public Library and Art Museum, London, Ontario, Canada; and the American Library Association's "Tips for leaders."

7.4.2 The problem-solving discussion

Basic attending and questioning skills are useful in all groups, including book discussion groups and problem-solving groups. In addition to these basic skills, problem-solving groups also need to use analytic and evaluative skills in a systematic, structured way. The following is a basic outline that a leader might use to prepare for leading a problem-solving group. These suggestions apply to committee meetings as well as to ad hoc groups that get together informally to address a problem.

1. Describe the problem: what is its nature and extent?
   —what background information is needed?
   —what is the specific question to be decided?
   —how serious is the problem?
   —what factors should be considered in deciding on a solution?
2. What solutions are proposed?
   —list solutions without evaluating
   —what are the advantages of each solution?
   —what are the disadvantages of each solution?
   —which solutions can be discarded because no one considers them workable
3. What is the group's initial reaction?
   —on what points does the group substantially agree?
   —what are the chief differences on matters of fact?
   —what are the chief differences on matters of opinion?
   —how fundamental are these differences?
4. Which solution, or combination of solutions, seems best?
   —can a compromise be reached that will find general approval?
   —if not, which solution, after debate, is favored by the majority?
5. How will the chosen solution be implemented and made effective?
   —what can this group do?
   —what can each member do?
   —how will the implementation be evaluated?

7.4.3 The formal meeting

Meetings may range from informal discussion groups to very formal meetings governed by specified rules of order. Some examples of formal meetings are the Annual General Meeting of the national library associations or the regular meetings of a Board of Governors or Trustees. Formal procedures are useful when:

—the decisions made by a group are important and must be formally recorded
—the topic is contentious
—the group is large
—a mass of routine business must be dealt with expeditiously.

If you become the president of the ALA, you will need to know how to conduct a formal meeting according to the rules of parliamentary procedure. These rules, which have been developed over the centuries as a way of maintaining order in democratic assemblies, are recorded in such standard works as *Bourinot's Rules of Order* (in Canada) and *Robert's Rules of Order*. But even if you are never called upon to preside, you still need to know the basics of how formal and semiformal meetings work in order to be an effective group member. This section is a basic introduction.

ESTABLISHING THE RULES

Your group need not adopt procedures exactly as set out in *Robert's*. Some adaptations may well be desirable to streamline procedures and suit the rules to the particular needs of the group. In general, the larger the group, the more formally the rules are followed. But keep in mind that rules are not ends in themselves: they should help in the transaction of business and not be used as technicalities to frustrate and obstruct the will of the majority. The basic principles lying behind the rules should always be honored:

—There should be justice and courtesy for all.
—The will of the majority should rule.
—The rights of the minority should be protected.
—Every proposition is entitled to a full hearing.
—Only one thing should be dealt with at a time.

PLANNING THE MEETING

The constitution and bylaws of your association or organization usually specify how often regular and general meetings must be held and who must be invited. When the date of the meeting is set, distribute a notice of meeting and brief agenda to members at least one week in advance (or more, if the constitution requires more advance notice). The notice should contain: the place, date, time, and the name of a contact person to notify regarding attendance. The agenda, or order of business to be brought before the meeting, usually consists of certain standard items:

—Approval of minutes of the last meeting
—Reports of officers and standing committees
—Reports of special committees
—Unfinished business
—New business

It may also include appendices containing material for group members to read before the meeting.

CONDUCTING THE BUSINESS OF THE MEETING

The *motion* is the main tool used to conduct the business of the meeting, although groups vary in the way they use motions. In some informal meetings, motions are not used: members make proposals and carry on discussion and debate until some consensus is reached. In formal meetings, members must formally move and second a motion before a proposal is open to discussion. In semiformal meetings, members may discuss a problem and consider a number of solutions before someone formally moves the adoption of one of these solutions in a motion.

What then is a motion? A motion is a proposal for the group to take a certain action. Most people, hearing the term motion, bring to mind proposals such as:

—I move that we adopt the committee's report.
—I move that we express our opposition to the proposed legislation on pornography by closing down library services for two hours on December 10.
—I move a vote of thanks to Betty for her excellent work on the Community Walks project.

These are *main motions*. Main motions, which constitute the majority of motions brought forward, are the only ones that introduce business for consideration and action. However there are three other categories of motions, any of which can be made while the main motion is pending: privileged, incidental, and subsidiary motions. Any motion in these three categories takes

DID YOU KNOW?
In general, the larger the group, the less involved each member is in the meeting. Therefore meetings with large groups should be shorter than meetings with small groups.

precedence over the main motion and must be dealt with before the group can return to the main motion.

Privileged motions have no connection with the main motion but are considered so important that they get immediate attention. Examples include motions to Adjourn, to Recess, to Raise a question of privilege (to point out that the room is stuffy and ask that the windows be opened), to Call for the orders of the day.

Incidental motions deal with questions of procedure that arise from the business at hand, usually another pending motion (to raise a Point of order, to Object to consideration, to Withdraw a motion, to Appeal the ruling of the chair).

Subsidiary motions are for the purpose of dealing with or disposing of the main motion. Examples include motions to Lay on the Table, to call for the Previous Question (close debate and vote immediately), to Limit debate, to Refer to a committee, and to Amend.

If you are going to chair a large formal meeting, make sure that you know the standard characteristics pertaining to different kinds of motions:

—What is the order of precedence for motions? (All other kinds of motion take precedence over the main motion.)
—Which motions require a second?
—Which motions cannot be amended?
—Which motions can be debated? Which ones can't be debated but must be voted on immediately?
—Which motions are carried by a simple majority? Which ones require a two-thirds majority? Which ones are settled by a ruling of the Chair?

Robert's Rules of Order, Newly Revised (1981) provides 45 pages of charts, tables, and lists intended to clarify these points.

As a member of a group, you can probably get through most meetings without ever encountering many of these privileged, incidental, and subsidiary motions. However, you do need to understand some basic procedures and use some ordinary common sense and courtesy. The outline for a meeting presented below presents only the common elements that are likely to arise in every meeting.

RESPONSIBILITIES OF THE CHAIR

The success or failure of the meeting largely depends on the Chair. The formal responsibilities of the Chair are easy to enumerate (though not so easy to carry off successfully):

—checking to see if there is a quorum (the minimum number of members required to hold a legal meeting, as specified in the bylaws)
—calling the meeting to order at the appointed time
—following the order of business as outlined on the agenda
—deciding all points of order
—recognizing members who are entitled to the floor
—guiding the discussion so that it does not digress
—stating and putting to a vote all legitimate motions
—ruling out of order motions that are deliberately frivolous or obstructive
—making sure that all points of view get a hearing
—adjourning the meeting.

In performing these responsibilities, the Chair should avoid expressing personal opinions on the merits of the proposals before the group. The presiding officer's job is to help the group discover the will of the majority by doing such things as sampling opinion, summarizing arguments, summarizing the feelings of the group, and suggesting procedural solutions. These activities can be carried out successfully only when the group perceives the Chair as impartial.

Be alert to physical problems with the environment and fix them. Is there something wrong with the arrangement of the chairs? Is the room too hot or too cold? Is sunlight pouring in through the window and blinding some members? Is noise from piped-in music or from a meeting next door drowning out the discussion? It shouldn't require a member's rising to a Point of Privilege to attract the Chair's attention to such problems.

While you listen to the speaker who has the floor, surreptitiously scan the whole room on a regular basis, watching for signs of difficulty such as puzzled expressions, raised hands, whispering, and inattention. Respond to these signs of difficulty. For example, if Bob Black looks puzzled at a speaker's proposal, wait until the speaker is finished and then call upon Bob to explain his difficulty with the proposal. If participants seem weary and inattentive, you can suggest a brief recess.

Facilitate discussion. The proper parliamentary practice for debate is that each speaker must first be recognized by the Chair.

Since this practice can be cumbersome and slow, it is common in semi-formal meetings for the Chair sometimes to allow two speakers to engage in rapid-fire, back-and-forth debate when this sort of exchange seems efficient. As Chair, you can allow this mode—what William Carnes has called the "self-disciplined Ping-Pong mode"—but be vigilant for signs that order is breaking down or that the debate has lost the interest of the group as a whole. Never allow speakers who have not been recognized by the Chair to speak at once or speak randomly on disconnected issues.

Listen for the sense of what is meant. If you can't understand what a speaker means by a proposal, probably no one else can either. As Chair, either you should ask the speaker to clarify or you should summarize (3.8) succinctly what you thought was meant and ask the speaker if you got it right.

KEEPING A RECORD

The purpose of minutes is threefold: to refresh the memory of those present about what was done at the meeting; to inform those who were absent; and to provide a historical record of resolutions, decisions, and acts. Timely minutes save time by providing continuity from meeting to meeting and by preventing the wasteful duplication of action. They also remind members what they agreed to do.

The minutes, which are written up by the Secretary and circulated to members (or sometimes read aloud at the next meeting), should contain the following information:

Details of Who, Where, When
—the kind of meeting (e.g., regular, special)
—the name of the group
—the date and time, and the place (unless the place is always the same)
—the names of those present, including whether or not the regular Chair and Secretary were present or who substituted for them (the names of those who sent regrets are sometimes included)

Approval of the Minutes
—whether the minutes of the last meeting were approved as read or circulated (or corrected and approved as corrected)

What Was Done at the Meeting
—a summary of what was done at the meeting in the order in which it happened.

SOME QUICK TIPS FOR WRITING MINUTES

Be tactful and avoid making personal references. Instead of saying, "Bill went on his usual rampage about user fees," the minutes might say, "One member expressed concerns about user fees."

Be selective, clear, and succinct. Minutes should provide a record of what was done without being encumbered with a mass of unnecessary detail. Highlight those things that furthered the objectives of the meeting.

Include a summary of strong minority points of view so as to acknowledge that these opinions were heard and taken into account.

For each main motion, it is necessary to record the exact wording of the motion, the name of the mover (and sometimes the seconder), and what happened to the motion. It is not desirable to record everything that was said. But it is often useful to record the reasons for a decision in sufficient detail that people consulting the minutes for guidance some time in the future can understand the rationale for decisions.

The Time of Adjournment

TEN COMMON FAULTS OF COMMITTEE LEADERS

Calling a meeting that is not necessary. Don't call a meeting just because it's the time for a regular meeting. If you can't write a one-sentence objective about what the meeting is supposed to accomplish, then don't call the meeting.

Not circulating in advance a meeting agenda that is specific enough that group members know what topics will be discussed and can therefore prepare in advance for the discussion.

Not sticking to the agenda during the meeting.

Coming to the meeting unprepared. ("Let's see. What are we discussing today?")

Losing control of the meeting so that the discussion goes off topic, splinter discussions develop, or monopolizers take over. Good leaders know when to practice closure (3.10).

Refusing to handle dysfunctional behavior. Do not permit unproductive or irrelevant discussion. Don't allow strong emotion to inhibit progress. Make sure everyone participates in an appropriate role and that decisions are made without bullying.

Not controlling the time: not starting the meeting on time; not ending on time; letting discussion continue unprofitably on some minor topic for so long that no time is left for the major topic. A good rule is to start on time, even if not everyone is present. Latecomers will soon learn. Finish on time, even if you have to refer an item to the next meeting. Allot a certain amount of time for each item on the agenda, then move on.

Monopolizing the meeting so that other group members get little chance to contribute.

Failing to encourage participation from all members.

Failing to show good humor and tact.

A MODEL MEETING OUTLINE

Chair: The meeting will now come to order. The first item of business is the minutes of the last meeting of October 17, which were distributed. Are there any errors or omissions? [An opportunity is provided for group members to point out corrections.] If there are no (further) corrections, the minutes are approved as read (or corrected).

[Some organizations prefer having a formal motion to approve the minutes, in which case the Chair says, "Can we have a motion to approve the minutes? Seconder? All in favor?"]

Chair: The second item is a matter arising from the minutes. At our last meeting we asked an Ad Hoc Committee consisting of Bob Black, Mary Brown, and Alice Green to look into the question of X and make recommendations. Bob, can I call on you to tell us what your committee discovered.

Bob Black: Thank you, Mme. Chair. Our committee . . . [summary of the committee's deliberations]. Therefore I am prepared to move that. . . .

Chair: Is there a seconder? [A main motion must have a seconder before it can be considered. The Chair acknowledges the seconder.]

It has been moved and seconded that [restatement of the motion]. Is there any discussion? Yes, Mr. White. [Only the person recognized by the Chair can speak. The Chair recognizes in turn everyone who wants to speak on the question, but disallows discussion that is not related to the present motion.]

Chris White: I move to amend the motion by deleting such and such (word, phrase, or sentence). [Motions can also be amended by inserting or adding words, or by striking words and substituting others. If the motion to amend is hostile or irrelevant to the main motion, it should be ruled out of order. Discussion, if any, follows as in the handling of the original motion.]

Jan Violet: I second the motion to amend.

Chair: We have a motion before us to amend the main motion so that it reads [statement of the amended motion]. Any discussion? [pause followed by a discussion, if any] If you're ready, I'll call the question. The motion before us is to amend the main motion by deleting such and such, so that it would read [restatement]. All in favor of the motion to amend? [Those in favor raise a hand.] Opposed? [Those opposed raise a hand.] Carried (or defeated).

The motion, as amended, now reads [restatement]. [If the motion to amend was defeated, the Chair would say, "The original motion is. . . ."] Is there any further discussion of the motion? [Pause] If not, I'll call the question. All in favor of the motion [restatement of the motion]? Opposed? The motion is carried (defeated).

Chair: The next piece of business is Item 3, the report from the Standing Committee on such and such. [Calls on the chair of the committee for a report.]

[And so on through the order of business.]

Chair: Is there any further business that you'd like to address? [Pause] If not, can we have a motion to adjourn?

7.5 WHEN YOUR GROUP HAS PROBLEMS

Problem behavior may occur because individuals have not yet learned how groups work or are unaware of the need for people to participate equally and constructively. People who are not used to working in groups often think, for example, that the person who has the most subject expertise or experience should do the most talking and, conversely, that people who have no expertise or experience have nothing to contribute. At other times, problem behavior occurs because participants do not yet have the skills for group work. They are not sure how to ask the right questions or

Exercise

how to express their feelings. A third reason for problem behavior is that some members of the group may have a hidden agenda that involves self-aggrandizement or perpetuating the problem that the group is trying to solve.

7.5.1 Self-oriented functions

In addition to the task and maintenance functions listed earlier (7.4), there is another category of group functions called self-oriented. These functions are destructive unless they are immediately addressed. Some common self-oriented functions are:

Blocking. Disagreeing without a rationale or alternative, preventing the group from moving on, repeatedly taking a negative approach.

Attacking. Criticizing individuals rather than their opinions and behavior, criticizing the group and its purpose without reason.

Attention-seeking. Bragging, recounting personal experiences in a self-important way, constantly seeking recognition.

Withdrawing. Refusing to talk or listen, doodling, behaving with excessive formality, conducting splinter discussions.

Monopolizing. Exerting authority or superiority, manipulating group behavior, interrupting, talking excessively.

Horsing around. Excessive joking, not taking people's contributions seriously.

One way for a leader to prevent problem behavior in a group is to describe the purpose of group work and to make the expectations explicit: "We are here today to discuss X. Some of us have had previous experience with this and some have not. Because we want to generate as many ideas as possible, it is important for everyone to participate in this discussion. We need to see the issue from everyone's perspective."

If a group is really committed to its task, the members themselves will eventually deal with problem behavior—sometimes very skillfully. Still, it is safer and more efficient for the leader to handle the problem promptly before it begins to affect the group's ability to function.

7.5.2 Handling problem behavior

QUICK TIPS FOR HANDLING THE TALKER

Individuals talk excessively in a group for various reasons—self-importance, enthusiasm, special knowledge or expertise on a topic, even nervousness. The talker may, in fact, be interesting, entertaining and have wonderful ideas and suggestions, but he's monopolizing discussion time to the exclusion of other people who may have equally wonderful ideas and who, in any case, are there to work through the group's task together, not to hear a lecture. Individuals talk excessively only because someone else lets them. The power to redistribute the discussion lies not only with the designated leader but also with the group. In any long-term group, the members will eventually deal with the talker but it's more efficient if the leader handles the problem promptly.

1. Use the skill of closure (3.10). Wait for the talker to finish a sentence or take a breath, then acknowledge her contribution or expertise, and shift the focus of discussion through a question directed to others: "That's useful information, Mary. We may get back to it when we write up the policy. Now, what do the rest of you think we should include?"
2. If the talker doesn't get the hint after you redirect the discussion, make your request more explicit. Interrupt if necessary. "Hold it, Mary. What you've said is useful, but one of the purposes of having this meeting is to get everybody's ideas, so I'm going to limit the next part of the discussion to those people who haven't said anything yet."
3. Mary may be dying to start talking again, with your permission. Don't make eye contact with her and don't acknowledge her gestures—if you do, that's an invitation for her to start all over again. Even if she's the only one waving her hand, look elsewhere or change the topic.
4. In large groups where there are a few people who do all the talking, try this: "One of the purposes of this meeting is to get everyone's ideas, but some people haven't had a chance to get a word in edgewise. For the next twenty minutes (or for today's session) I'm going to ask the people that usually say a lot not to say anything, and I'm going to ask the people who usually don't say anything to say a lot. You all know who you are, so let's start the discussion." This approach doesn't hurt anyone's feelings (never mention names) and reflects group feeling—

HANDLING THE KNOW-IT-ALL

The know-it-all wants everyone to know that he's an expert: he tried that plan before and it didn't work; he has read all the important literature; he alone knows what decision should be made. Handle the know-it-all as a special case of the talker and use the same strategies.

everyone knows that a balanced discussion is better. You may not think that this will work, but it almost always does!

QUICK TIPS FOR HANDLING TWO KINDS OF CLAMS

At the other end of the scale is the person who never speaks, but would like to. The shy person needs an atmosphere in which it is safe to speak without fear of saying the wrong thing or of being ignored.

1. Get the shy person into the discussion early—the longer a person goes without speaking, the harder it is for them to join in.
2. If necessary, call on that person by name and ask a question in a way that leaves the person in control, and does not demand too much. For example, "Jean, what do you think about that?" or "What experience do you have in that area?" If Jean answers, "I'm not sure" or "I haven't had any experience," follow up with a positive statement: "I think we're all a little uncertain about which way to go" or "This is a new experience for several of us—that's why we're here to talk about it." Pause to give Jean time to add more, and if she doesn't, move on.
3. Periodically, give Jean another chance to participate. When Jean does make a contribution, don't interrupt. Instead, be patient and use encouragers and restatement (3.3 and 3.8). Remember that shy people are often good listeners and will make more contributions in smaller groups.

But there is another kind of clam—someone who doesn't speak, not from shyness but for some other reason. He or she is usually not a good listener either, and may deliberately withdraw either by not showing up or by using body language that says "I don't want to be here."

1. Use the same questioning techniques as with the shy person, but when you get an "I don't know," probe further: "Do you mostly agree? Disagree? Give us an example."
2. In a long-term group where initial trust has been built up, use confrontation and reflection of feeling (3.9) to deal with the problem: "Joe, I get the feeling you wish you didn't have to come to these meetings. Am I right?" Then follow up: "What could we be doing that would make you feel more involved in this issue?"

HANDLING THE JOKER

This person is a grown-up version of the class clown, always ready with a smart remark, a joke, a funny face. His behavior can function positively by reducing tension and by helping people relax. But the behavior is negative when it happens so often that the group cannot concentrate on the task or members feel they are not being taken seriously. At first, ignore the behavior. Don't encourage the joker by acknowledging his behavior, not even by saying, "That's very funny, but. . . ." If you reinforce the behavior by commenting on it ("The class clown, I see") you may be typecasting the joker permanently and he may not be able to break out of it, even when he wants to get serious.

If necessary, use the DESC sequence (3.13): "You made a joke but, instead of helping us get this job done, it makes me feel as if our job isn't serious. I'd like us to get serious for a while and leave the jokes till after the meeting so that we can focus on the issue." You can also confront with nonverbal skills—a long, deliberately awkward pause, direct eye contact, all the disapproving gestures that your teachers used to use. This usually works in the short-term, but it may create an authoritarian image that inhibits shared leadership in a long-term group.

FOR FURTHER HELP

7.2 Characteristics of groups

Brilhart, John K. *Effective Group Discussion.* 5th ed. Dubuque, IA: William. C. Brown, 1986. This college textbook is highly recommended to trainers and students who want to read about group theory and practice. It contains many useful definitions, examples, exercises (which can easily be adapted for in-service training) and references. Chapter 2, "An orientation to small group processes," and Chapter 3, "Communication in the small group," provide a detailed and readable description of how groups work.

7.4.1 The book discussion

Chambers, Aidan. *Booktalk: Occasional Writing on Literature and Children.* London: The Bodley Head, 1985. An excellent book for anyone interested in children's literature, reading response, and talking about books.

7.4.2 The problem solving discussion

Brilhart, John K. *Effective Group Discussion.* 5th ed. Dubuque, IA: William. C.

Brown, 1986. Chapter 5, "Procedures for Effective Decision Making and Problem Solving," provides a discussion of the problem-solving process with a detailed example involving a group trying to solve the problem of theft and mutilation of library materials.

Delberg Andre L. et al. *Group Techniques for Program Planning: A Guide to Nominal Group and Delphi Processes*. Middleton, WI: Green Briar Press, 1986. Nominal Group Technique is a method by which problem-solving or decision-making is done individually but in the presence of others (hence nominal group). Chapter 3 provides detailed guidelines for conducting NGT meetings.

Johnson, David W. and Frank P. Johnson. *Joining Together: Group Theory and Group Skills*. 3rd ed. Englewood Cliffs, NJ: Prentice-Hall, 1987. Includes a chapter on problem-solving that provides useful strategies for problem-solving and lists eight barriers to problem-solving effectiveness in groups.

7.4.3 The formal meeting

Bianchi, Sue and Jan Butler. *Warm Ups for Meeting Leaders*. Ventura, CA: Quality Groups Publishing, 1984. Includes the alphabet game exercise to demonstrate that the best answers come from groups, not individuals.

Carnes, William T. *Effective Meetings for Busy People: Let's Decide It and Go Home*. New York: McGraw-Hill, 1983. An experienced chairman discusses, with helpful practical advice, his adaptation of parliamentary procedures for more effective decision-making in deliberative groups.

Parr, Jim. *Any Other Business: How to be a Good Committee Person*. Toronto, ON: Clarke, Irwin, 1977. Provides a common sense advice for committee procedures that are less formal than Robert's. There is a useful section on writing minutes that includes examples.

Robert, General Henry M. *The Scott, Foresman Robert's Rules of Order, Newly Revised*. Glenview, IL: Scott, Foresman, 1981. So far, more than 3,400,000 copies in print.

The 3M Meeting Management Team. *How to Run Better Business Meetings*. New York: McGraw-Hill, 1987. Contains chapters on preparing for the business meeting, room arrangement, participation skills, and visual aids as well as four chapters on specialized presentations like technical presentations, financial presentations, multilingual meetings, and staff meetings.

Xicom-Video Arts. *Meetings Bloody Meetings*, 1976. 16mm film or videocassette. Color. 30 minutes. John Cleese dramatizes five typical faults that make meetings unproductive.

8 PUBLIC SPEAKING

8.1 GENERAL CONSIDERATIONS

Who needs to be able to speak effectively in public? Anyone whose job involves any of the following:

—introducing or thanking a speaker
—doing a booktalk
—giving a library tour
—providing bibliographic instruction to groups
—speaking about the library to outside groups
—providing staff training.

Your choice is probably not between speaking in public or not speaking; it is between doing the job well or doing it badly. Think of the last time you heard an ineffective public speech. What made it poor? Probably something that, with some effort, could have been corrected.

Many speakers go wrong because they forget that a speech is intended primarily for the ear. They fail to consider the differences between an oral medium intended for groups and a visual medium intended for individual readers. Readers have more control than listeners do over how they receive a message and adapt it to their own needs. Readers can choose to skim a text, skip boring paragraphs, and read the end before the beginning. They can carefully reread passages that puzzled them the first time. They can speed up their reading for familiar content or slow it down for difficult unfamiliar content. They can examine the physical features of the text to determine, in advance of reading it, how long it is, how many sections it has, and what each of the sections is titled.

All audience members, in contrast, listen at the same speed to the same words in the same order. They can't go back to clarify something that they missed. And they never know in advance, unless you tell them, how long the speech is or where it is going. As a speaker, you must make allowances for these limitations of the spoken presentation. Keep your pace brisk enough that you don't bore your listeners but not so brisk that you leave them behind. Help your listeners get a handle on your talk by giving them, at the beginning, an agenda or brief outline of what you intend to speak about. As you go along, you can help your audience remember important points from your talk by putting key words on transparencies or flipcharts.

Remember, however, your advantage over writers: you have a direct relationship with your audience. Because you know who

Exercise

ORAL PRESENTATIONS

Consider the difference between oral presentation and written presentation. Suppose that you have written a 25-page report for your library system assessing the need for a new branch in a subdivision. You have been asked to present your report at a meeting of senior administrators.

(You realize, of course, that you can't simply read the report from page one onwards until some desperate audience member stops you.)

What steps will you have to take to turn a 25-page written report into an effective oral presentation? How does the difference between a written presentation and a spoken presentation affect your approach to the problem?

your audience is, you can tailor your message to this specific audience's needs. You can see how the group is reacting to your message and can correct problems as they occur. You can often provide an opportunity for your audience to ask you questions. And you can use gestures and qualities of voice to dramatize your message and give it impact. When you are giving a speech, take advantage of these strengths of an oral presentation.

8.2 ARRANGING FOR OTHER PEOPLE TO SPEAK

The only time when your audience thinks about the arranger's job is when something goes wrong. Then people ask: Who chose this dreadful speaker? Why didn't the speaker get here on time? Why didn't someone do something about the uncomfortable chairs/ unsuitable size of the room/ unbearably hot and stuffy atmosphere/ inadequate sound system?

QUICK TIPS: ARRANGING FOR SPEAKERS

Start your planning early. For some large, formal speaking occasions, starting six months in advance is not too soon. Assess your audience's needs and decide what kind of presentation will suit these needs.

Don't select a speaker on the basis of his or her written work. Interesting writers don't always make interesting speakers. Ask for an evaluation from someone who has recently heard the person speak. Make sure that this speaker's abilities match your specific needs.

Be forthright on the issue of fees and honoraria. You and the speaker should both clearly understand in advance whether or not a fee is being paid and how much it will be.

When negotiating with the speaker, don't just say, "Will you speak to our group?" Tell the speaker exactly what kind of presentation you expect (an amusing, 15-minute after dinner speech; a formal, 30-minute keynote address; a three-hour workshop on how to search online databases). *Be very clear about the amount of time*

DID YOU KNOW?

Studies of human perception can tell us much about the way audiences perceive and remember oral presentations:

Listeners infer large portions of the message from what they expect to be discussed.

Only one listener in four can summarize a message with reasonable accuracy.

The average audience member recalls less than half of the material presented.

(From research studies cited by Eric W. Skopec, "A Problem-solving Approach to Preparing Professional Presentations," *IEEE Transactions on Professional Communication*, PC-26 (March 1983): 30-35.

---

that is allotted for the speech. Describe the intended audience in terms of its size, its average age, its interests, and its level of knowledge about the topic. Explain any relevant details about the context of the presentation (the talk is last in a sequence of speeches on the same topic). Leave no room for misunderstanding.

Suggest a slant on the topic that you think would interest the audience.

Suit the room to the audience. Put forty people in a room with seats for fifty and the atmosphere seems cozy. Put them in a room with seats for one hundred, and it looks as if half the audience stayed home.

Arrange to have refreshments if possible. Refreshments do wonders to improve the audience's frame of mind.

In good time before the presentation, ask the speaker if he or she will need any special equipment or facilities. Well-prepared speakers, taking nothing for granted, always specify their needs for transparency machines, slide projectors, lecterns, tape recorders, blackboards, special seating arrangements, etc. But don't wait for your speaker to tell you. Ask. Avoid having the speaker show up and say, "Oh dear, I just assumed that all rooms would have a screen for showing slides."

A day or two before the actual presentation, find some excuse to call up your speaker. Your real purpose is to remind her of the time of the speech and confirm that she is actually coming. But, when you call, say something like this: "Can I help you with anything before your talk tomorrow?" If the speaker lives in town, you can ask if she needs a ride. With a speaker from out of town, you might say you are calling to confirm plans for meeting her plane. This precaution is well worth the effort for the one time in twenty when the speaker says, "Good heavens. Tomorrow? Isn't it *next* Tuesday that I'm supposed to come?"

The day of the presentation, look after your speaker. Meet her and take her to the room at least half an hour before the audience is due to arrive. Suggest that she will probably want to check out in advance the room and the equipment. Remind her once again about the length of time allotted to her speech.

After the speech is over, don't abandon her. Make arrangements to get her home (or to the hotel or airport).

Thank the speaker in person after the talk. Thank her again in a letter, mentioning favorable comments from the audience and any initiatives that may have been sparked by the talk.

8.3 INTRODUCING A SPEAKER

The speech of introduction has an important function. It focuses the audience's attention, settles people down, and prepares them to listen with interest to the speaker. All this can and should be done briefly. In four to six sentences, you can:

1. State the title of the talk:
   Today's topic for our Noon Hour Speakers' Series is: "Franchising: Is it for you?"
2. Say briefly but specifically why this topic will interest this particular audience:
   Not: I'm sure all of us here are interested in this topic.
   But: In our fall survey of the interests of the group, franchising came out in first place, which is why we invited. . . .
3. Explain the speaker's qualifications to talk about the topic and end with the speaker's name:
   Our speaker opened her first Yum-yums store three years ago to sell chocolate specialties. Since then she has franchised and now has over 40 stores selling her treats. She has agreed to tell us some of the things she learned the hard way about franchising. I'm pleased to introduce to you—[one second pause]—Mary Maddox.

Make sure that the microphone works and all the necessary arrangements have been made before the audience arrives. The first words of your speech of introduction should not be excuses for why something isn't working.

Create a positive atmosphere for the talk to come. Don't embarrass the speaker or put him at a disadvantage. Don't

Exercise

CLICHES

Make a list of cliches to avoid when introducing a speaker. Here are some obvious ones:

Without further ado. . .

Here is a speaker who needs no introduction.

You didn't come here to listen to me.

How many more can you think of?

overdo your praise: overpraise can embarrass the speaker and lead to disappointed expectations on the part of the audience.

Don't talk about yourself or take over the role of the invited speaker by expressing your own views on the speaker's topic.

Never apologize or dwell on the negative aspects of the event. It only depresses the audience to hear things like: "It's too bad we have such a poor turnout tonight" or "We hope you won't find these chairs too terribly uncomfortable" or "Thank you for coming out on this stormy night to hear our speaker when you'd probably rather be home watching the football game."

Be selective. The audience doesn't want to hear a detailed list of the speaker's every university degree, administrative role, honor, affiliation, and publication. Mention those accomplishments, especially recent ones, of particular relevance to the audience, the occasion, or the topic of the speech. The better known the speaker, the less you need to say.

Write down the title of the talk and the speaker's name on a card and keep the card handy but unobtrusive. This way you avoid the embarrassment of: "I'm pleased to introduce—um, um, er."

Don't let your voice go up at the end of your sentences, as if you are doubtful or hesitant about your statements, "Our speaker opened her first Yum-yums store?" (See 1.5)

End decisively with the call: the speaker's name. Don't say, "I'd like to introduce Mary Maddox [the beginning of applause] but before I do, let me remind all those who haven't signed up for the next session to do so before they leave. There is coffee available following the talk, and we hope as many of you as possible. . . ."

Be brief.

Give the speaker your full attention, once the speech has started. Do not distract the audience by whispering, gesturing, fiddling with your notes, or writing out your thank you speech.

8.4 THANKING A SPEAKER

The speech of thanks can be even briefer than the speech of introduction. It should include these elements:

—a sincere thank you
—a specific reference to something significant and interesting in the speech. Be concrete and not general.
—a statement about why this particular item was valuable to the audience
—another sincere thank you.

Following this, you lead the audience in applause.

8.5 CHAIRING A PANEL

The chairperson plays an important role in the success of the panel. But remember that your role as chair is to choreograph the speaking of others, not to give a speech yourself. Limit yourself to the following facilitating activities: double-check the arrangements; briefly introduce the topic and the speakers at the beginning; call upon each speaker in turn; control the time they speak; handle questions from the audience; and provide a definite ending point to the event by briefly thanking contributors and leading the audience in applause. Your biggest problem will be controlling the time. Every speaker thinks his or her speech deserves at least ten minutes longer than the allotted time.

SOME QUICK TIPS

Make sure that, well in advance, both you and the panelists understand and agree upon the agenda and format. Be specific about what each panelist is expected to talk about and for how long. Put this in writing.

Timing is crucial. To help panelists stick to their time allotment, you might say to them ahead of time, "It's often hard for a speaker to keep track of how much time is left. So when I give you this sign [demonstrate it], you will know that you have three minutes left."

If this doesn't work (and often it won't), you can always stand up. Begin moving toward the microphone if there is one. This body language conveys a powerful hint that you mean what you say about timing.

Before the audience arrives; check to make sure that chairs, tables, lecterns, and screens are positioned properly; that the microphones work; and that water is available for the speakers.

Write down on a card the names of the speakers and key information about them. If you go blank on a name during your introduction, you can glance at your card. Practice pronouncing difficult names in advance so that you don't stumble over them during the introduction.

Your introduction of each panelist should be even briefer than an introduction of a single speaker. In most cases, all that needs to be said about each panelist is the name and why this person is qualified to speak on the topic under discussion.

During the panel discussion itself, be prepared to help panelists as needed with lights, slide projectors, overhead transparencies, etc.

The audience will want an opportunity, at the end, to ask the panelists questions. Your job is to control the question period by soliciting questions, calling on the questioners in turn, and then repeating the questions so that everyone can hear them. Limit the number of questions so that the program ends promptly at the advertised time. You could say, "We have time now for one more question." Then move on firmly to thanking the panelists briefly and leading the audience in applause. Don't let the question period drag on so long that audience members are trickling away, one by one.

8.6 MAKING A SPEECH

8.6.1 Knowing your purpose

Ask yourself why you are making this speech. Some possibilities are: to make Mary feel good at her retirement dinner, to entertain the audience and make them laugh, to explain a process, to present information, to change or confirm attitudes, to persuade the audience to some course of action, or to sell an idea or proposal. If you can't explain to yourself in one sentence what you would like to see happen as a result of your speech, your efforts will lack focus. It helps to write down, in specific behavioral terms, your objectives. Here are examples of specific objectives:

For informative talks: Staff members will learn enough about the new computers to start using them immediately for interlibrary loan.

For persuasive talks: Library board members will approve a change in policy with respect to handling Young Adult materials.

For inspirational talks: The reference staff will will be filled with new energy and enthusiasm for answering people's questions.

For ceremonial talks: Listeners will feel that the new branch library was opened with style and dignity.

8.6.2 Analyzing the audience

Ask yourself these questions about the audience. Why is this audience coming to hear me? Have these people chosen to come or is attendance compulsory? What are they hoping to get from my presentation? What do they already know about my topic? Are they receptive to my message or are they hostile? How large is the audience? What is their age/ gender/ political affiliation/ ethnic origin/ educational level, and how will these factors influence the way they will receive my talk? You can use the Checklist for Audience Analysis to record your answers to these questions.

CHECKLIST FOR AUDIENCE ANALYSIS
1. What is your purpose in giving this talk? What do you want to happen as a result? What do you want/expect your audience to do/know?
2. Who will make up the audience?
3. How many people do you expect?
4. What are your audience member's reasons for being at your talk? What do they want/ expect to happen?
5. What is your audience's most pertinent problem? How can you help audience members to solve it?

6. How much do they already know about your topic?
   —They are specialists.
   —They have a good, general background.
   —They know a little bit.
   —They are new to the topic.
   —I don't know their level of knowledge but will find out.
7. How receptive are they to your message? They are:
   —Very receptive
   —Somewhat receptive
   —Indifferent
   —Somewhat hostile
   —Very hostile
8. What do you know about their age, gender, ethnic origin, educational background, cultural interests, political and religious affiliation, or other factors that will affect their reception of your message?
9. What kinds of material are most likely to succeed with this audience? (Inversely, what probably won't succeed?)
   —Stories and anecdotes
   —Facts
   —Statistics
   —Testimony
   —Analogies
   —Demonstrations
   —Other (specify)

8.6.3 Finding a topic

Often your topic will be decided for you by the context in which you give the speech or presentation. It is probably because you are considered an expert in some topic that you have been asked to speak in the first place. For example, a high school teacher asks you to tell his history class about the documents in your regional history collection; a local reading group invites you to give a book talk; the Association of Special Libraries asks you to discuss the implications of copyright legislation; your job requires you to provide library tours and bibliographic instruction. In these cases, the main challenge is to find the right slant on the topic to suit the interests and level of understanding of the particular audience.

Sometimes, however, you will have considerable freedom of choice in selecting your topic. Suppose a men's service group has asked you to speak after dinner at the annual meeting for the men and their wives. The topic is to be "anything you like." You could

Exercise

CHOOSING A TOPIC

Suppose that you have been asked to give a talk related to libraries to some group. (Specify the group and keep it clearly in mind for this exercise.) To find a topic suitable for this group, go through the following steps:

1. Brainstorm. Write down on a piece of paper all the topics you can think of that satisfy these two criteria: the topic is related to libraries; the topic is something that you know about *from your own personal experience.* Don't evaluate the topics at this stage. Write down as many as you can. For example:

   answering reference questions

   telling stories to children

   choosing an author in residence

   automating the catalog

   putting on library programs

   selecting new popular fiction

   finding resources in the library to help with job hunting (or some other topic)

   local authors

2. Consider each topic in terms of its appeal to your selected audience. Rule out topics that would interest only a portion (or none) of your audience. Keep the best three.

3. For each of the best three topics, think what you could say about the topic: How much material do you already have at hand? What more work will you have to do? What can you do to slant the topic to the interests of your audience?

talk about your birdwatching hobby, but after all you have been invited because you are a library professional. This is your chance to increase community awareness about the library and what it does. On the other hand, an after-dinner speech should be lively and entertaining: after the double chocolate layer cake, few would want to hear a factual speech on international standards for serials. See the exercise on choosing a topic.

Consider how you might adapt your chosen topic to accommodate the audience's known interests. For example, suppose your topic is reference service. If the service group you are talking to is dedicated to helping young people become entrepreneurs, you could focus on the variety of unusual resources in the library helpful to anyone starting a small business: government statistics; census data; statutes and regulations. Illustrate this talk with interesting and little known examples. For a more general audience, you could talk about how the library answers questions and use as illustrations three diverse cases where the questions were challenging and unusual and the answers were interesting, surprising, or funny.

8.6.4 Developing the topic

There are two elements in a speech: 1) a governing idea, message, or thesis and 2) supporting materials that develop or reinforce the governing idea. Let us suppose that you have a topic: burnout among librarians. That's the *subject,* but you don't have a *message* or governing idea until you know what you want to say about burnout: for example, "Burnout is the number one problem facing public librarians today" or "You can recognize burnout by these telltale signs."

The first step, then, is deciding upon your message or governing idea. With your message clearly in mind, you can proceed efficiently to the next step of gathering the supporting materials. Supporting materials that are not directly related to your governing message should be ruthlessly rejected as irrelevant. Your sources for material are:

—yourself—your professional expertise, your memory of examples and anecdotes (this is the most important source)
—your own research
—talking with other people
—reading other people's material and research (in most cases, you should use this one only as a supplement)

To develop your governing idea, use one or more of the following kinds of supporting materials:

STORIES, ANECDOTES, CASE STUDIES

One of the most interesting and effective ways of developing an idea is to tell a story. For retirement tributes, anniversary lunches, ceremonial occasions, and after dinner speeches, the best material is often a series of well-chosen and appropriate anecdotes that have some bearing on the occasion.

FACTS AND STATISTICS

Use statistics sparingly. Remember that long lists of numbers are hard for the ear to take in. Space out your facts. If a number is important, repeat it. Translate the fact into terms that make sense to the listeners—the needed library budget increase would cost taxpayers the price of one cup of coffee a week.

TESTIMONY

Quote respected authorities on the topic. Of course, the quotations must be accurate and must not be distorted by being taken out of context.

ANALOGIES

Compare a lesser known subject with a more familiar subject in order to make a point. In explaining the classification system to students, you could say that methods of ordering books on the shelf are like methods of organizing food in supermarkets. Although each store is different, all supermarkets put meats together in one place, cereals together in another, condiments in another, and so on, and they do so for good reasons. Likewise, libraries have good reasons, for grouping related materials.

DEMONSTRATIONS AND MODELING

When you want an audience to understand an object or a process, you can show it to them or model it for them. For example, you could demonstrate how to search indexes on CD-ROM by actually doing the search. (If your audience is too big to crowd around a computer monitor, you will have to display the output on a large screen.)

8.6.5 Choosing a good structure

The supporting materials discussed above are the basic building blocks of the speech. But they are still just raw materials until you organize them into an effective pattern.

Exercise

IMPROMPTU

This exercise on developing a topic can be done on your own, but it's more fun in a small group.

Put a number of topics chosen at random on small pieces of paper inside a hat or bowl (e.g., apples, dust, paper, skiing, holidays, retirement savings funds, molasses, solar heating, life rafts, high fashion).

Each person in turn draws a topic from the hat. He is given three minutes to organize a two-minute talk on the topic, after which he gives the talk.

Suppose the topic apples is drawn. The first step is to decide on the governing idea, such as: "The apple has been a source of mischief to humanity ever since Eve" or "The apple that we find in stores today is a designer product" or "Here's an inexpensive but exotic dessert you can make with apples."

The next step is to develop this governing idea through one or more kinds of supporting materials: anecdotes of disasters caused by apples; an explanation of how new apple species have developed through genetic selection; or instructions on making the apple dessert.

Experienced speakers have found that certain standard formulas work well as frameworks within which to organize materials. Here are some suggestions:

1. TELL 'EM

A popular design for presenting information is the old "Tell 'em" formula, where the message is hammered home through repetition:

—Tell 'em what you're going to tell 'em
—Tell 'em.
—Tell 'em what you told 'em.

This is a good design to use when you want the audience to learn something. It takes into account the situation of listeners. Unlike readers, they cannot skim over the text in advance to orient themselves and they can't go back to review points they missed. Therefore the preview, in a speech, is useful as an advance organizer that tells listeners what to expect. It helps them comprehend, assimilate, and remember the details. The summary reinforces and confirms the main message. Use this direct strategy with audiences who 1) are receptive to your message or 2) are busy and want a straightforward approach.

The structure of a talk using this formula looks like this:

Introduction: Catch the audience's attention with a brief illustrative story, a startling fact, or a vivid quotation from an authority (One out of every four North Americans lacks basic literacy skills: they can't read instructions on a bottle of medicine or figure out a menu in a restaurant.) The introduction prepares the audience for the substance of the talk at the same time that it indicates the importance of the main message.

State the message and provide a preview of key points (So how do these findings about literacy affect us in public libraries? I'm going to tell you today about three implications: [one], [two], and [three])

Body: *First point*—Examples, testimony, statistics, facts, or other supporting data

Second point—Examples, testimony etc.

Third point—Examples, testimony, etc.

Three main points are usually enough for all but the longest of speeches, and the number three has a satisfying ring to it. For

DID YOU KNOW?

Here is a useful framework for clarifying your ideas about a persuasive talk:

I want the audience to . . .

which they will do because it will benefit them by . . . .

So I must. . . .

(Suggested by Don Vincent)

DID YOU KNOW?

When presenting unfamiliar material to an audience, you should explain the unknown in terms of the everyday and the familiar. For example, tell the story of a particular concrete case before generalizing. Or use an analogy to compare an unfamiliar concept with a familiar one.

It is also a good idea, when explaining difficult concepts, to restate the idea in several different ways and to provide examples.

suggestions about putting the points into an appropriate order, see the patterns of organization of written texts—section 4.5.

Conclusion:
—Summary of key points
—Repetition of main message

2. HWFS

A variation that works well for persuasive speeches is one first recommended by Richard C. Borden in his *Public Speaking as Listeners Like It* (New York: Harper & Row, 1935, p. 3). Use it when you want to get the audience to act:

—Ho Hum.
—Why bring that up?
—For instance.
—So what?

In other words, first you grab the listener's attention (perhaps by a story, a startling statistic, analogy, or testimony); then you show why your message is relevant to the listener's interest; then you reinforce your point with specific cases (the illustrative examples); finally you ask for action (You can help in the fight for literacy by participating in our 'Bookmates' program).

3. MOTIVATED SEQUENCE

With an indifferent or hostile audience, the Tell 'em-right-away approach runs the risk of provoking resistance to your message. People tend to become defensive and stop listening (see barriers to listening—2.2). Therefore, you should delay your real message. First you highlight a problem that the audience faces. Then you reveal your message, which you present as the solution to the audience's problem. Alan Monroe and Douglas Ehninger have developed what they call the motivated sequence, which ties the speaker's message to the audience's needs:

—Attention. You catch your audience's attention.
—Need. You focus that attention on a problem or concern.
—Satisfaction. You present your solution to the problem.
—Visualization. You explain the benefit of your solution to your listeners (the What's-in-it-for-you theme).
—Action. You ask for approval of your solution.

8.6.6 Using audiovisual aids

Well presented audiovisual aids can hold your audience's attention and help people remember the important ideas in your talk. But your aids should supplement your talk, not upstage you. You don't want to reduce your role to that of technical support for the equipment.

GETTING AUDIOVISUAL AIDS READY

There are two kinds of aids that you can use: ones that you prepare ahead of time and ones that you create during the presentation. Convenient and inexpensive aids that you prepare in advance include:

—35mm colored slides
—large cardboard charts or posters
—transparencies, sometimes in color, to present diagrams, charts, tables of figures, or key words
—audiotape to present oral material such as role-played interviews for staff training
—handouts to provide the audience with material to take home and consult.

These aids give you control over your presentation, but they cannot accommodate participation from the audience. To involve participants in a spontaneous way, you might write down their suggestions on one of the following:

—a blackboard
—a flipchart
—blank overhead transparencies.

The single most common fault with visual aids is that they are too small for the audience who is intended to see them. Almost everybody makes charts that can't be read past the third row. Too many speakers create transparencies by reproducing from books or reports pages which have been set in a type size intended for the individual book reader. And some speakers even wave tiny objects in front of their audiences and say, "Unfortunately, you can't really see this. But if you could, you would notice. . . ." This point cannot be stressed too much: *your visual aids must be big enough for the audience to see; your audio aids must be loud enough for the audience to hear.* Check out ahead of time, preferably in the room

DID YOU KNOW?
If you plan to make 35mm slides containing text, you can use a pica typewriter so long as you limit yourself to what can fit, double-spaced, in an area of 4" x 6". From David Nadsiejka, "Can They Read When You Speak?" *Bulletin of the American Society for Information Science,* 13 (April/May 1987): 22-23.

DID YOU KNOW?
When you are giving a talk in English to people whose first language is not English, it helps the audience if you write down key points on transparencies. People often can understand the written text better than the spoken word in a second language. (Suggested by Jean Tague)

you will be using for the talk, the visibility or audibility of your aids.

MAKING TRANSPARENCIES

Choose a size of type or lettering that is large enough for the audience to read without strain. Here's a guideline for transparencies used in a medium-sized conference room: minimum typesize for titles is 20 point (about 5/16 inch); the rest of the text should be at least 16 point (about 3/16 inch). Lower case type is easier to read than all capitals. For hand lettering, use a dark marker pen (black, not yellow) and draw bold lines. For printed lettering, a sans serif typeface like Helvetica works well. Avoid *italic* or script (like cursive handwriting), which are hard to read when projected on a screen.

Use key words and expand on these key words as you talk. (Never, under any circumstances, try to put the whole talk on the transparencies themselves.) Some authorities recommend the rule of six—no more than six words to a line and no more than six lines to a page.

Don't make them all the same. Avoid showing a series of transparencies that are all alike—all tables or all text or all graphs.

Keep charts uncluttered. Your audience cannot see or absorb a lot of detail. Label all charts clearly (see 4.6).

Give transparencies an interpretive title that headlines what the transparency is about.

Spell words correctly. Do your own proofreading, but also get someone else to check for errors that you've missed.

Rehearse your presentation using your audiovisual aids, paying attention to such details as where you will stand, how you will operate the equipment, and how loud you will speak. Practice until you feel so comfortable with the machinery that you can look at the audience and not at the buttons and controls. Put your slides or transparencies in the correct order and number them. Know which way the transparency goes on the machine, so that you don't find yourself saying, "Sorry, this must be upside down." Since the fans on slide projectors and overhead projectors can be noisy, compensate when using these aids by speaking more loudly than usual.

A sampler of point sizes

HELVETICA TYPEFACE

6 point Helvetica

10 point Helvetica

12 point Helvetica

16 point Helvetica

20 pt Helvetica

24 pt Helveti-

36 pt He

48 pt

Compare Helvetica 14

Times 14

Things can go wrong: bulbs can blow; extension cords can be too short; there may be no chalk. So bring your own emergency kit, stocked, as appropriate, with such items as a spare bulb, pens, chalk, blank transparencies, an extension cord, or masking tape.

Adding color to your transparency.

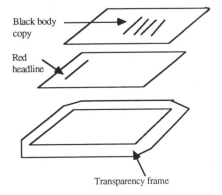

Black body copy

Red headline

Transparency frame

On the day of the talk, get to the room early and set up your equipment. Plug in the slide projector or overhead projector to make sure that the light works, that the image is in focus, and that the screen is visible from everywhere in the room. Test out your cassette player to make sure that it still works and is audible from the back. Then cue the tape so that the desired portion will play when you hit the Play button. (This way you will avoid the embarrassment of having to search backwards and forwards in the tape, saying apologetically, "No, that's not it. I guess it must be a bit further on.") The point to remember is that you *do all the set-up work before the audience arrives;* during the talk itself, all you need do is turn the machine on.

USING AUDIOVISUALS EFFECTIVELY

Make sure that the members of your audience know *why* you are showing them these particular slides, transparencies, etc. Don't make them guess what point the aid is intended to demonstrate. Tell them. And tell your audience *what* they are seeing.

Control *when* your audience sees your visual aid. Keep your visual aid hidden until the time comes in the talk when you want to use it. Your audience should be listening to you and not puzzling over the significance of a map, model, or chart that you have not yet started to talk about. When using a transparency, you can control what the audience reads: use a piece of cardboard to cover up all but the first part of the transparency and gradually move the cardboard down to uncover points as you come to them in the talk. After you have finished with a particular transparency, turn off the overhead projector until you need it for the next transparency. Erase writing from the blackboard.

Don't distract the audience from your talk by introducing competing materials. If you have produced a kit of handouts, don't hand it out till the end. If you want audience members to be able to consult handouts during the talk, hand out the kit at the beginning but ask people to put it away. Say that you will let them know when they will need to refer to something from the kit. Don't pass out materials like books, pictures, etc. while you are talking. When each person is examining some different item, no one is listening to you and you will lose your audience. Instead, set aside some time solely for the purpose of examining the materials.

8.6.7 Delivery

Excellent delivery can sometimes rescue a weak speech, but a badly delivered speech almost always fails. Important elements of good delivery include: good vocal quality; use of appropriate gestures (and absence of distracting gestures); pauses; and eye contact with the audience.

A good rule of thumb is: Never read a speech if you can avoid it. Actors can read without sounding as though they are reading, but most people can't. Know your material well enough that you can speak from your notes as if you were having a conversation with your audience. Tape record one or two rehearsals of the speech so that you can listen for qualities of voice that need improvement (see section 1.5). Your voice should be loud enough to be heard, clearly articulated enough to be understood, and expressive enough to keep the audience interested.

Think of yourself as on stage. Use the resources of a good actor: variety of pitch and emphasis; changes of pace; pauses for effect; gestures and movement. Look at your audience and not down at your page or at some spot on the ceiling. Vary your visual focus. Don't look mostly at people on one side of the room or the other. If your audience is large, divide it into quandrants and make sure that you look at each quadrant on a regular basis. Every member of an audience of hundreds will think that you have been looking directly at him.

8.6.8 Overcoming stage fright

Stage fright is a normal part of making presentations in public. All speakers experience it. But good speakers are able to use their nervousness to charge their talk with energy; they don't let it cripple their performance. A good strategy for dealing with anxiety is to ask yourself: what is the *worst* thing that could happen? Your secret phobia may be:

—tripping on your way up to the podium; falling over; falling off the stage
—dropping your notes and having them get out of order
—shaking uncontrollably

—not being able to get out even the first sentence
—losing your voice
—stuttering or mispronouncing words
—going blank and forgetting your whole speech
—making some horrible mistake that the audience will all laugh at and remember with merriment for the rest of their lives
—boring your audience so much that they all fall asleep or else leave
—discovering in the middle of your speech that your slip is showing; that your fly is undone; (or even that you have on no clothes at all).

Whatever your fear is, the strategy is the same: 1) plan what you will do to prevent this mistake from happening; and 2) plan what you will do to recover if it does happen. Successful speakers are not people who make no errors; they are people who make fewer errors and have a recovery plan to deal with the ones they do make. For example, if you fear you may trip, wear comfortable, safe shoes that are easy to walk in. If you fear your notes may get out of order, write them on cards and use three rings to attach the cards together. If you do make a mistake, pull yourself together, maintain the appearance of calm, and don't draw attention to the gaffe by apologizing. If you can forget about the mistake and carry on, the audience will be able to do so as well.

A useful formula for overcoming stage fright is 70% preparation ahead of time, 15% good breathing technique, and 15% strategies for coping with problems. Here are some specific things you can do to lessen anxiety about speaking.

PREPARE THOROUGHLY

After you have developed your speech, rehearse it. Tape record your rehearsal so that you can play it back and correct problems. You might also want to rehearse your talk in front of friends who can offer suggestions for improvements. If possible, rehearse it aloud in the room in which you will actually deliver the talk. Time your speech; if it is too long, make cuts. Remember that it takes longer to deliver a speech to an audience than to a tape recorder. If you plan to use audiovisual aids, always rehearse with them. Feeling prepared will give you confidence.

USE NOTES

Don't try to memorize the speech word for word. With a memorized talk, the danger is that either you will go completely blank or you will rattle through your speech at top speed. Instead of

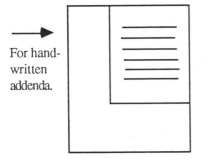

For hand-written addenda.

NOTES FOR YOUR TALK
On 8.5 by 11 paper, you can use the rectangle formed by the top, right 2/3 of the page for your typed notes.

Leaving the bottom blank means that you never have to look down.

(Suggested by Don Vincent)

memorizing, speak from notes on which you outline the key ideas of your talk. If you find regular 8 by 11 inch paper hard to hold and liable to rattle, transfer your notes to cards (4 by 6 or 5 by 7 inch). Do *not* do any of the following:

—Don't clutch your notes. Instead place them on a lectern or desk.
—Don't fiddle or fidget with your notes.
—Don't try to conceal that you have notes.

BE POSITIVE ABOUT YOUR ROLE AS SPEAKER

Act confident even if you don't feel confident. Walk briskly to the platform. Stand straight. Look as if you are enjoying yourself. Look directly at your audience, smile, and take a deep breath. Pause for a moment before you begin speaking. Be enthusiastic about your topic.

RELAX

If you are offstage and out of sight, do some neck rolls. Let your head droop forward to your chest, allowing your muscles to relax and your cheeks sag. Inhale. Turn your head to the right and hold while you count five. Exhale and let your head drop back to your chest. Inhale. Turn your head to the left and hold while you count five. Exhale and let your head drop back to your chest. Repeat. This exercise helps to get rid of the tension in your neck and shoulders.

You can do this exercise right in the conference room and no one will notice. Take a deep breath, keeping your upper chest still and expanding the diaphragm and abdomen. Let out the breath slowly in a sigh. (But don't hyperventilate.)

COPE WITH SIGNS OF NERVOUSNESS

For a *dry mouth,* keep a glass of water handy and take a small sip, not a gulp. If there is no water available, you can stimulate saliva by biting (not too hard) the side of your tongue. Avoid hard candies, which will interfere with your articulation and may choke you.

Shaking is caused by an excess of energy. You can't stop shaking by going rigid, clutching the lectern, and trying not to move. But you can use this energy in a positive way by directing it into motivated movement and gestures. These movements should not be fidgets and random pacing but movements that reinforce the meaning of what you are saying or that bring you into closer connection with your audience. It is reassuring, however, to realize that trembling that seems violent to the speaker is not noticeable to the audience. If you think the shakes may be a problem, put your

ROOM SETUP FOR OVER-HEAD TRANSPARENCIES

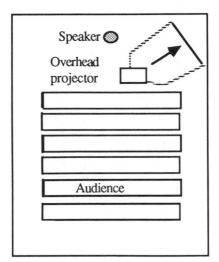

Speaker does not block the screen but can see the images. Audience can concentrate on speaker or on images at different times.

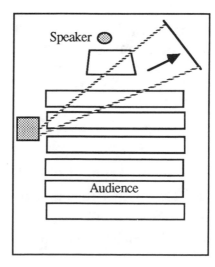

35mm projector on a high stand.
(Suggested by Don Vincent)

notes on cards of heavy stock that won't rattle and don't wear jangly bracelets.

If you suddenly *go blank* and can't remember the next sentence, pause. Take a deep breath. Exhale. Look down at your notes to find your place. Do not fill up the silence by babbling. A pause that seems excruciating to you will not seem long to your audience.

If you *garble* your words, don't draw attention it by saying, "Oh dear, I've made a mess of this." Make the correction smoothly and confidently and go on. Television announcers sail right over errors: "The spokesman for inside workers—outside workers, rather—said that he expected. . . ." If you make total nonsense out of a whole thought, say, "I'll repeat that last point to make sure it's clear."

The good news for anxious speakers is that people in the audience can't tell how nervous you feel. Your heart may be pounding, your palms sweating, your mouth dry, and your stomach fluttering—but the audience can't tell.

8.6.9 Public speaking: a checklist

BEFORE YOU GIVE THE TALK

Do you clearly understand what kind of speech you are being asked to give?

Have you analyzed your audience? Have you geared your speech to your expected audience?

Have you rehearsed your presentation, including your visual aids, ahead of time?

Is your clothing appropriate for your intended audience? Is it consistent with a professional image?

Can you operate the equipment (including the microphone) that you plan to use?

Have you checked to make sure your notes and audiovisual materials are in the right order?

Did you come to the room early enough to correct for problems with seating or audiovisual equipment? (Set up the overhead projector; focus the slide projector; test the microphone; rearrange the chairs if necessary; get a glass of water.)

Have you checked your appearance and clothes, at the last minute, for embarrassing slipups?

DURING THE PRESENTATION

Do you respect your audience—their intelligence, point of view, and way of life? Never condescend.

Will your talk entertain as well as inform your audience? It helps some speakers to think of the presentation as a performance.

Are you looking at your audience?

Are you paying strict attention to timing? Starting on time? Ending on time?

Are you providing variety and a change of pace?

Are you observing your audience's reactions and adjusting your presentation accordingly? Cut short a section that seems to be boring the audience.

Have you kept your visual aid hidden (transparency, slide, model, blackboard) until the moment in your talk when you plan to use it?

WHAT NOT TO DO

Never apologize. Don't say at the outset that you fear that the talk may be a waste of time; that you are nervous; that somebody else would probably do a much better job; or that you really know very little about the topic. If this last claim is really the case, you should have declined the invitation to speak.

Don't speak inaudibly. At the beginning, ask the audience if you can be heard from the back.

Don't turn your back to your audience to speak to your visual aid.

Don't stand in front of your visual aid. Ask whether the audience can see the visual aid. Make changes if anyone cannot.

Don't use transparencies that are unreadable from the back of the room.

Don't pass out competing materials like books, pictures, etc. while you are talking.

Avoid irritating mannerisms (rattling change in your pockets, twisting a strand of hair, rubbing your chin, or saying *um* or *you know* too often).

Avoid the "I know it's here somewhere" syndrome. Put a marker in the book at the passage that you intend to read. Cue your tape so that it is ready to play. Put your transparencies in order and number them.

Don't draw attention to the fact that you have had to cut something out. Don't say, "It's too bad that we didn't have time to talk about X because X is probably the most important aspect of the topic."

Don't run overtime.

8.7 WORKSHOPS AND CONFERENCE SESSIONS

You may be asked to give a longer presentation, either at an in-house training session or at a conference or workshop. In addition to paying close attention to the topics discussed in section 8.6, you should be aware of some considerations peculiar to longer sessions. The most important thing to remember is that the longer the presentation is, the more energy you need to put into keeping your audience interested, comfortable, awake, and involved. A low-key delivery that succeeds for a brief talk may put an audience to sleep during a three-hour talk. Chairs that are acceptable for thirty minute talks may be intolerable for a six-hour workshop. And unless you are Bill Cosby, long presentations without audience involvement are almost always deadly (see 8.7.6). The longer presentation is harder and takes more confidence and expertise. Get experience with the shorter ones first.

8.7.1 Accepting the invitation

Are you capable of giving the kind of presentation that is expected? If not, don't be afraid to say "No" when you are first invited. Later on, it will be too late to back out.

Once you have decided to accept the invitation, confirm your acceptance in a letter to the organizers. Your letter should include:

—a confirmation of the terms agreed upon
—a list of the equipment and supplies you will need

EXAMPLE OF COPY TO SEND TO WORKSHOP ORGANIZERS

This workshop will help participants to:

—deal with reference queries about unfamiliar topics
—identify common communication accidents occurring in the interaction between user and librarian
—become more aware of their own communication behavior
—learn and practice new interview techniques
—apply new approaches to the online presearch interview
—assess the user's level of satisfaction with the information provided.

Workshop format

This workshop is a series of structured learning experiences, including role-playing, group exercises, mini-lectures, simulation, and discussion.

Registrants may participate as much or as little as they wish. Everyone is encouraged to share real examples of difficult interviews.

—specifications for the set-up of the room
—a statement of any other special arrangements as applicable (for example, that you will send them the camera-ready originals for ten handouts that they should print on colored paper and assemble into a kit for participants.)

8.7.2 Publicity

Often longer presentations are advertised ahead of time in posters, flyers, etc. It's safest if you supply the organizers with your own copy that they can adapt for their advertising. Include the following:

—your name in the form in which you wish it to appear
—the exact title of your talk
—biographical details of relevance, including your qualifications for giving this talk (you have been responsible for the design and implementation of the system you plan to talk about)
—what your audience can expect as a result of hearing your talk (they will learn X or will be able to do Y or will experience Z)
—the format (workshop involving mini-lectures, role-plays, and group exercises; slide-presentation followed by group discussion; straight lecture, etc.)

8.7.3 The agenda

Prepare two agendas—one that you give your audience and one that you use yourself. Providing your audience with an agenda has two advantages. The process of preparing the agenda in advance (either as a transparency or as a handout) helps you by forcing you to think realistically about the timing and structure of your presentation. Having an agenda helps the audience members listen better because they know what to expect. In drawing up the agenda that you give your audience, don't be either too general or too detailed. Leave some flex time.

The agenda that you prepare for your own use should be more detailed (see next section).

8.7.4 Designing the presentation

In drawing up the agenda that you will follow yourself, be detailed. Plan exactly what you are going to do, minute by minute of the presentation, whether it's one and a half hours, three hours, or six hours. Don't imagine that you can wing it. (You might be able to, but that's just lucky.) Work out in five minute blocks exactly what you plan to do. In your design, pay special attention to pacing and to providing flexibility.

PACING

All of us have relatively short attention spans, possibly as short as fifteen minutes when we are listening to a lecture. This means that variety is important to recover the audience's flagging interest. So after you've done one kind of thing such as lecture for fifteen minutes, do something else. Involve the audience by asking questions. Let the audience ask you questions. Do a role-play. Tell a joke. Get your colleague to do something. If one voice has lulled the audience, the switch to another voice may wake it up.

If you are talking to a group who has just come back from a large lunch, you will have to use extra energy to combat post-lunch drowsiness. One way of keeping the audience awake is to encourage its active participation. Instead of lecturing, involve the audience in an exercise, a discussion, or a role-play.

PROVIDING FLEXIBILITY

Make a very detailed plan in advance, but be prepared to be flexible if necessary. Work out in advance alternate strategies of what to do in case something goes wrong or in case you need to respond to the group's concern.

It often happens at a conference that things get behind schedule. You may have been billed to start your 1 1/2 hour presentation at 10:30 a.m., but it is actually 11:15 before you can get going. There are three things that you should *not* do in this situation. Do not run over into the scheduled lunch hour; your audience will be hungry and blame you. Do not try to dash through your talk at double speed; it won't work and you will ruin your delivery. Do not present the first half of your talk and then say at noon, "Too bad we ran out of time before we got to the most important part." Instead, make a silent cut so that you do cover the most important things in the time you have. Be prepared for this contingency by planning ahead what, if necessary, you will cut. Conversely bring extra material to use if you get ahead of schedule.

Adapt your presentation to the needs of your audience. Don't go on doggedly with uninteresting material just because it is in your plan. If you see that your audience is losing interest or has grasped something faster than you thought it would, cut short your presentation on this point and go on to something else. Cutting it short does not mean running through the same material at a faster clip; it means eliminating transparencies, dropping out illustrative examples, and providing summaries instead of a detailed development.

8.7.5 Rehearsing

Rehearse until you are thoroughly familiar with your material (see suggestions for preparation in 8.6). It is a paradox that the more thoroughly you have rehearsed, the freer you will feel to depart from your plan if neccessary, and the more flexible you can be. Then you can wing it.

8.7.6 Getting the audience involved

We know from experience that there are definite limits to how many facts we can absorb from a lecturer who stands at the front and talks at us. People learn best when they are actively involved. So try interspersing your lecture presentation with opportunities for your audience to participate. The following ways of involving the audience are popular techniques used by trainers.

At workshops, participants welcome the opportunity to meet other people who share their concerns. So, if the participants don't already know each other, you can give them a chance to introduce themselves briefly at the beginning. With a small group, you can ask each person to say who he is and where he's from. With a group of more than fifteen, you won't have time to hear from everybody, but you can ask for volunteers. Suppose that you have come to speak to a group of librarians from different libraries on problems of doing legal reference work. Ask participants to tell the group what particular problems they are facing. Get a few different experiences by asking questions that invite sharing: Has anybody here had a different problem? Anything else? What else?

Ask your audience questions to get their input as you go along. Questions encourage active participation because all audience members, not just the ones who actually answer, get involved in thinking about their response.

DID YOU KNOW?

The body language of audience members gives clues about their response to a presentation. When interested, people look directly at the speaker. They may lean forward slightly or lean to one side and make small, responsive noises or slight head nods at particular points in the talk. They may smile from time to time.

When audience members disagree with a speaker, they may sit with heads straight and erect, arms folded. They may signal boredom by slumping in their seats, stretching out their legs, looking away, staring into space, yawning, and shuffling.

Be aware of the effects of the kinds of questions you use (see 3.5). Three kinds of questions usually *don't* work in generating discussion: 1) closed questions that can be answered with a yes or no answer; 2) questions with only one right answer, such as "What was the name of the first Librarian of Congress?"; and 3) questions that are too broad, such as, "Are there any questions?" "What do you think about x [the topic of the presentation]?" Instead ask open questions that:

—get participants to share relevant experiences
—elicit opinions or feelings
—invite critical scrutiny of an issue.

You could say, "How do you handle this problem in your library?" "What do you think would be the hardest part of this plan to implement?" "How do you feel about this way of handling grievances?" "What reservations do you have about using this skill?"

When you ask a question, wait for an answer. It often takes participants a while to formulate their ideas. Don't confuse them by asking another question or by rephrasing the first one. And don't answer the question yourself. Treat with respect all answers that you get.

An application of the questioning method is the structured discussion. For example, instead of telling your audience of children's librarians what to look for in a good book for children, you can ask people what they look for themselves. Write down points, as they are suggested, on an overhead transparency. Adult learners learn best when they are encouraged to draw upon their own past experiences.

One consideration is that many people with excellent ideas are reluctant to express them to a group of 40, although they may be happy to share them with a group of five. So another option is to break up the audience into small buzz groups of from three to seven people. This way you get more individuals actually involved. Buzz groups are given a task to work on, a specified time to work on it, and the responsibility of later reporting their findings to the group as a whole. Therefore, before they break up, tell the buzz groups clearly what they are supposed to be discussing and how long the discussion can last. Ask them to appoint a spokesperson to report the group's response to the task (its recommendations; its list of important questions; its best one or two ideas on the topic, etc.). A tip for the set-up of the room: buzz groups are easiest to manage if participants are sitting at round tables.

Case studies are useful in getting participants to deal with concrete specifics. Participants receive a printed description of some particular problem situation. Their task is to bring problem-solving skills to bear on the case in order to come up with a solution, decision, recommendation, or plan of action. Fruitful cases are usually ones in which more than one good solution is possible. Case studies are popular tasks to give to buzz groups.

In a training workshop, you can give the audience members an exercise in which they can use the information or skills you have just presented. The exercise provides an immediate application in which the learner can test out what has been learned. You can get participants to do the exercises individually, in pairs, or in groups of three to five.

Involve the audience in simple role-plays. For example, in a workshop on answering reference questions, you could ask for volunteers who will play the part of the users. Make it easy by giving cards to the "users" from which they can read off their reference question. Ask audience members to take the part of the "librarian." The librarian responds to the "user" by using the skill that you have just taught. If the "librarian" succeeds only partially at demonstrating the skill, focus on the strength, not on the weakness, of the performance (see 3.14). When learners are learning a new skill, they rarely get all of it right on the first trial. But they get some of it right. Reinforce what they do well. People learn by successive approximations to the desired behavior.

Two things are important with role-playing: never put anyone on the spot; and never set up a situation in which the volunteer can be made to feel foolish or incompetent.

Get your audience to ask you questions during the course of the presentation. You can either encourage your listeners to ask for clarification as you go along. Or you can specify when you will be allowing time for questions and ask them to hold their questions until then. Your handling of the first few questions determines whether or not the audience will ask anything more (see 8.7.7). If you imply that questions are silly, further questions will dry up. Input from the audience is valuable, but you should control how much and when. If someone asks you to discuss a point that you had planned to cover later, you may want to say something like, "That's an extremely important aspect. I'm going to discuss it in this afternoon's session, after lunch, so I'll ask you to bring up your question again then." But give a brief answer at the time so that you don't appear too smug.

8.7.7 Answering questions

Here are some suggestions for handling the question period at the end of a presentation:

Do your homework. Prepare answers in advance for questions that you can anticipate being asked.

Provide a positive climate by treating each questioner with respect and each question as valuable. You can say, "That's an interesting point to raise, because. . . ." or "I'm glad you asked that because it's a question a lot of people may wonder about."

Repeat the question to make sure everyone has heard it before you begin your answer.

If you don't know the answer, say so and promise to find out. Don't waffle.

These techniques can help you with troublesome questioners.

Incomprehensible questioners: If, instead of a question, you get a long, rambling, incomprehensible statement of opinion, don't ask for a clarification. The second attempt probably won't be any clearer. Instead, agree with the participant on some point that you were able to understand from the rambling: "I agree with you, sir. It is certainly true that libraries are very different places from what they were fifty years ago." Then turn away and look at another questioner.

Monopolizers: Handle a monopolizer by taking one step toward him and looking at him as you answer his question. Or say, "That's a good point. You're right." When you've finished your answer, don't provide another opening by saying, "Does that answer your question?" Instead, break eye contact, look away to another part of the room, and field a question from someone else.

Hostile questioners: The important thing is to keep cool and not be baited into going on the attack yourself. It sometimes works to turn the question back on the questioner: "I see that you are doubtful about my solution. How would you handle the problem?" If this doesn't work, use the "monopolizer tip." Don't get drawn into an argument.

Workshop Evaluation Form

TITLE OF THE WORKSHOP

Name of the sponsors of the workshop

Place of workshop

Date of workshop

Please help us to evaluate this workshop by completing this form and handing it in at the end of the session.

1. Briefly describe your position and the kind of contact that you have with the public (or the amount of online searching that you do on your job or whatever background information is relevent to the topic).

   [The answer to this question lets you know how accurate you were in your analysis of the audience and its level of knowledge.]

2. What aspects of the workshop were *most* helpful to you? How did they help you?

3. What aspects of the workshop were *least* helpful to you? What kind of help would you have liked instead?

4. Generally speaking, was the workshop a worthwhile experience for you? (Please circle one)

   1   2   3   4   5

   (1 = Not at all worthwhile; 5 = very worthwhile)

5. Would you recommend this workshop to a friend or colleague?

   Yes   No

Please use the back of the page for further comments.

Thank you for helping us evaluate this workshop

8.7.8 Evaluating the presentation

The test of your presentation is how well you satisfied the needs of your audience. Get feedback by asking audience members to fill out an evaluation form.

The decision about when to collect the forms involves a trade-off. If the evaluation form is completed and collected at the end of the presentation, you will get a response from everyone. But you won't be able to ask questions about the usefulness of the presentation to participants once they return to the job.

On your evaluation form, use a combination of open and closed questions: the closed question "Would you recommend this workshop?" or some variant thereof provides clear-cut evidence as to how many participants were satisfied. The open questions allow participants to make suggestions in their own words about what helped them and what didn't.

Keep the form short—usually a single page is enough. See the Workshop Evaluation Form for an example.

8.8 BOOKTALKING

The purpose of booktalking is to turn people on to books they will enjoy reading. Two essential elements are: 1) selecting books appropriate to the intended audience; and 2) talking about the books in such an interesting way that people want to read the book. A booktalk is not the same as a book review or a piece of literary criticism. It does not evaluate or offer a balanced assessment; it sells the book. You start with a book that you like and that you think the audience will like. Then you entertain with a come-on for the book. You tell what was funny, interesting, exciting, scary, or moving about the book. You want your talk to result in people borrowing and reading the books you've discussed. Good booktalks boost circulation and generate excitement about reading.

Booktalks vary. They can be given impromptu on-the-floor to one person who has asked for a good book, or they can be presented more formally to a whole classroom. They can be aimed at children, young adults, or adults. They can be presented in the library, in schools, and community settings, or they can be broadcast over the local radio or TV. A short booktalk on a single book may be less than a minute long, and a long one may last three to five minutes.

SOME QUICK TIPS ON BOOKTALKING

Don't generate a demand that you can't fill. Talk about enough titles that you can spread the demand over a number of books. But have multiple copies available of books you expect to be most popular.

Don't spill all the beans, or your listeners will feel they don't need to read the book. Never tell the ending.

Read sparingly, if at all, from the text—four or five sentences at most. Listeners usually find it boring to hear long passages read, no matter how well you read.

Sketch out the essential action of the book in bold strokes. Don't get bogged down in complicated details and long descriptions.

Your booktalk should convey the essential flavor of the book. If a novel is a study in character, don't imply by your discussion that it's full of exciting action. Don't over-sell a book or your audience won't believe you next time. If, however, the book has a slow beginning, warn your listeners that it is worth persevering to chapter two.

Anticipate and avoid problems. For example, Mary Chelton points out that it can be dangerous to start off a booktalk with something like, "What do you suppose it feels like to be the fattest girl in the whole school and have everybody call you Blubber?" The entire audience may simultaneously turn and look at the fattest person in the room.

Keep records of which books you've talked about with which audiences. When you talk to the same group again next year, you won't want to repeat yourself.

In preparing to do a booktalk presentation, you analyze the audience, just as you would before giving any presentation. Questions to ask include: What is the nature of the group—grade nine English class? Senior citizens? Naturalists' club? What is the ratio of males to females? What is this group interested in? What is the reading level of group members? What are their reading tastes? What books have you presented to this group before? How long a presentation are they expecting to hear?

In making your presentation, keep in mind all those things that are crucial to the success of any talk: delivery, the use of eye contact, controlling stage fright, etc. (see 8.6).

Usually a formal booktalk presentation consists of a series of booktalks, varying in length from long to short and strung together with transitional sentences. As you begin to talk about each book, you pick it up and show it to the audience, stating clearly the author and title. Your first sentence grabs the audience's attention by introducing the main character or by leading up to the action. By the second sentence, you are well into the main action, theme, or dilemma of the book, which you elaborate with a few concrete details. The last sentence is a cliffhanger that restates the author and title, while leaving unanswered questions in the listeners' minds. Then you move on to the next book.

Aim for variety in the books you select and in the way that you present them. Alternate a long book talk with a short book talk. If you start off with an action book, the next book you discuss may be a bit quieter and more reflective. Suggest some challenging books that stretch the best readers in the audience but make sure that you also talk about some books within the reach of the less practiced readers. At the end of the presentation, you invite the audience to look at the books and ask questions.

EXAMPLE

O. R. Melling. *The Druid's Tune*. Markham, ON: Penguin, 1983: Seventeen-year old Rosemary and her younger brother Jimmy are sent to spend the summer with their uncle and aunt in Ireland. They expect to be bored. But what happens is that they are trapped in a Druid's spell and taken back in time to an ancient Celtic battle-camp. There, they meet vivid characters like Maeve, the blood-thirsty warrior-Queen. And they meet Maeve's greatest foe, Cuculann . . . [more details but not a plot summary]. The two Canadian teenagers become key players in a legendary story of war, love, and treachery. O.R. Melling's *The Druid's Tune* is a fantasy book, but you will find that it feels very real.

Exercise

GIVING A TOUR

Take one or two friends on a ten-minute tour of a place that you know well and where the tour isn't going to be disruptive. (Explain that you're practicing giving a tour.) Practice personalizing the tour to meet their interests. After the tour, ask for feedback. What did they remember most clearly? What seemed most interesting? What did they learn that might be useful in the future? What was most boring or tiring? What could you have done to make this a more interesting or useful tour?

8.9 GIVING TOURS

A tour provides participants with first-hand experience of a particular physical area, giving a sense of context or atmosphere that description alone can't provide. A guided tour for an individual or a group is useful for:

—supplementing an orientation process
—introducing staff members in their own environment
—encouraging people who wouldn't normally use your library or who aren't motivated to visit on their own.

But consider your purpose carefully. If you simply want to describe the functions of a department, give a history of the building, or demonstrate particular reference sources, don't organize a tour. Instead, use a lecture or display format—or just give people a map.

Consider your audience carefully, too. The kind of tour you organize for the Board of Governors or for new staff members is going to differ from the kind of tour you organize for freshmen in your bibliographic instruction course or for people from a local service club. Assess the level of motivation, interests, and needs of the group. How is the tour going to help this group? What do you most want the group to understand about your library through this tour? Keep your objectives simple. You may have achieved your purpose if your students see for themselves that there are five floors in the library and meet some pleasant, accessible librarians. It may be enough for your new board members to get an impression of the complexity and variety of library services, or for nonusers to find out that you have more than books or for new staff members to be able to associate a few faces with locations.

QUICK TIPS FOR TOURS

Keep the group size manageable. Arrange several tours for small groups rather than trying to conduct a large group tour, which may be disruptive to normal operations and may not be informative for participants. The maximum number is usually 12 to 15 people.

Speak clearly and slowly. Don't shout. At the beginning, ask if everyone can hear you. If not, take a deep breath, pitch your voice to the person furthest from you, and ask again. Use short sentences.

Don't talk while you walk. Stop periodically, face the group, pause, then make your point or ask your question. Don't get involved with private conversations with individuals in the group as you walk along. Very experienced leaders can talk while they walk backwards (but first they check for kick-stools in the aisles).

Don't use the tour as a lecture platform. Make only essential points and leave the rest for another time. Inexperienced tour leaders provide too much or irrelevant information. Don't overload people.

Involve participants. Use questions as well as statements. For example, when demonstrating an index, ask someone to suggest a topic of interest. Or ask people to guess the age of a building. If you can, find out the interests of your group in advance. Address people by name if possible.

Introduce staff members as you go along. At the very least introduce the group. For example, "Hi Mary, these are visiting guidance counsellors. [To the group] Mary is one of the people who prepares book orders." Staff members like to be acknowledged and respected for their work. Moreover, when you introduce employees, you give tour members the confidence to approach these people for help later. To vary the pace of the tour, you might ask the staff member to answer a simple question: "About how many books do you process each month?" Avoid leading questions ("You enjoy working here, don't you?") or questions to which the staff member may not immediately know the answer.

Keep the tour short. People don't learn when they are tired or overloaded with information. A reasonable attention span in a tour is probably twenty minutes or less.

Combine formats. Arrange a meeting or short lecture before the tour to present factual information and give an overview. Or bring people together after the tour so that they can ask questions about what they've seen. You might provide a short break between two parts of the tour. This helps to solve the problem of information overload. Consider combining classroom discussion with self-guided tours that use a guidebook or audiocassette. If necessary, you can motivate participants to take a self-guided tour by providing an easy exercise or assignment (like a treasure hunt) that will take them through all the areas of interest.

8.10 PROVIDING BIBLIOGRAPHIC INSTRUCTION

Increasingly, librarians are being called on to provide bibliographic instruction or user education to teach people how to use library resources. Bibliographic instruction (BI) may take place in the classroom, in a lab, on a tour of the library, or on a one-to-one basis. Effective BI requires the instructor to master, in addition to subject expertise, three types of teaching skills:

—organizing skills, including the ability to assess needs, set objectives, and design the curriculum or program
—writing skills and skills of graphic presentation
—interpersonal skills for communicating effectively with individuals and groups

Much of the library literature on bibliographic instruction concerns the first two categories of skills. Excellent articles and books are available on the following: instructional approaches such as problem-solving and critical thinking; curriculum content; and creative ways of teaching basic reference tools, online searching, and other specific topics. See, for example, the topics included in the bibliography prepared by Hannelore B. Rader, "Library Orientation and Instruction -1986," *Reference Services Review,* 15, 2, (Summer 1987): 65-76. Most formalized bibliographic instruction also involves the writing skills described in Chapter 4 and in other sources for preparation of course or program outlines, exercises, pathfinders, handouts, and visual aids.

However, very little seems to have been written about the personal communication skills required of the instructor, perhaps because these skills are necessary for any kind of effective teaching. Since bibliographic instruction provides an excellent example of a specialized application for many of the nonverbal, listening, and speaking skills described in Chapters 1 through 3 of this book, this section focuses on ways in which selected skills may be used in bibliographic instruction.

8.10.1 Attending and influencing skills for BI

Experts in BI now recommend a variety of "teaching modes"—not only lectures, but also labs, discussions, demonstrations, tours, individual assistance at the point of service, and computer-assisted instruction with minimal intervention from the instructor. The particular interpersonal skills needed depend on the instructional format. One-to-one instruction requires all the nonverbal and speaking skills described in Chapters 1 through 3, but these skills are also essential when working with groups. Listening (Chapter 2), acknowledging (3.2), and encouraging (3.3) are basic attending skills that help to establish a productive communication climate in which potential library users feel that their problems, experiences, and ideas are respected. Inclusion (3.12), the skill of explaining what you are doing, is useful in BI demonstrations where you need to describe or explain a procedure as you carry it out. This is especially the case when instructing large groups, since not everyone can see exactly what you are doing.

Instructions and directions (3.11) need to be clear and specific so that there is no doubt as to what is required. In a group situation, it's important to wait until the group is ready to hear the instructions (you may need to pause until you have everyone's attention) and to ask for confirmation of your instructions: "Now, before you begin, tell me what I've asked you to do."

8.10.2 Questioning skills for BI

Asking questions is a skill useful not only for one-to-one instruction but also for working with groups. Questioning is a more versatile technique than many teachers suspect and need not be limited to the usual "test" question ("What are three points of access to a catalog?") that anticipates one correct response from the keenest student. Questions can be used to perform other functions. First, open questions (3.5) and the more structured neutral questions (3.7) can encourage participation, motivate students, and establish a good communication climate. "Tell us a little about your first experience in using a library" is a good icebreaker that also provides an opportunity for the instructor to assess the diversity of experience, expertise, and motivation in a group. Encourage a variety of responses. Listen carefully and keep your comments brief and nonjudgmental.

DID YOU KNOW?
The average student's attention span in a lecture is 20 to 30 minutes.

Questions may also be used to instruct. Draw on expertise within the group ("Who has used *Psychological Abstracts?* Tell us briefly what you used it for and how it helped you"); brainstorm ("If you were looking for information on X, where would you begin? Tell me all the possible places you can think of"); identify unexpected problems using an open question ("What problems did you have when you did this search?"); and find out what's missing in the student's understanding by asking neutral questions ("How did this index *not* help you? What got you stuck? What else did you want to find out?").

Questions can also help you to evaluate both student progress and your own. Giving and receiving feedback (3.14) is an essential part of any instructional program and should occur periodically throughout a program, not just at the end. By requesting and receiving feedback, you learn what aspects of your teaching are helpful (or not helpful) to the students and what you could do to improve the program or your teaching techniques. For example, "Last session we talked about business databases. How did that discussion help (or not help) you? Give an example of something it helped you do or understand" or "What could be done to make this course more helpful to you?"

When you give feedback (written or spoken) to the students, you are letting them know how they are doing. Use the steps suggested in section 3.14 on giving feedback: start with something positive ("You found the two most important periodical indexes"); describe rather than judge ("Your literature search included only popular articles and no other types of sources" rather than "Your literature search wasn't very good"); be concrete ("You did not mention *Dissertation Abstracts*" rather than "Your literature search was incomplete"); be realistic ("For the next assignment, try to find two more different types of reference tools" not "You must list all types of reference tools"); limit suggestions to two or three; and suggest rather than prescribe ("You might want to look at X").

QUESTIONS THAT INSTRUCT

Suppose I've never used an index before in my life. Explain this to me so that I understand.

If you had to find a biography of this artist, what would you do first? Next? Next?

What does this citation *not* tell you?

QUESTIONS FOR ONE-TO-ONE INSTRUCTION
To assess the need:
What are you working on? [not, Is this for a term paper?]

What have you done so far? Where have you looked? [not, Have you looked in the catalog?]

What happened? What got you stopped? [not, Are you having trouble with the headings?]

To assess the gap:
What do you want to find out? [not, Do you want a review article?]

What do you already know about this index? [not, Do you know how this index is arranged?]

What don't you understand about it? [not, Why are you having trouble?]

To assess the help required:
What do you want this [tool] to do for you? [not, Do you want abstracts?]

What would help you most?

What other help do you need to do this? [not, Do you need to know how to operate the machine?]

8.10.3. Group skills for BI

Understanding how groups work (Chapter 7) helps in teaching small or large groups of potential library users. Discussion, exercises, and demonstrations also provide necessary variation in the pace of the session. Handling problem behavior (7.5) sometimes becomes necessary in a group, especially where students are not equally motivated to attend the session. When the BI program involves a lecture, public speaking skills are important (8.6 and 8.7). First, examine the purpose of the lecture and the audience by using the checklist in 8.6.2. Consider the structure of the lecture (the "tell 'em" approach described in 8.6.5 works perfectly for BI); use audiovisual aids skillfully (8.6.6); and work on your delivery skills, including overcoming stage fright if necessary (8.6.8). Use the public speaking checklist (8.6.9) if this is your first attempt to

Exercise

STRUCTURED CRITICISM

Structured Criticism is a technique developed by C. J. Marino to obtain feedback from students in any type of course and can be used with classes of 10 to 20 students who are enrolled in a BI course over several weeks. Use "Structured criticism: a technique for student feedback" as a hand-out for your students and explain the purposes of feedback. For the first session, ask for structured criticism about the technique itself; that is, ask each student to write two things they like about the idea of this particular feedback technique and one concern. At the next session, discuss the feedback and decide with the class whether or not to continue using the system in your BI course.

Exercise

ROLE-PLAYING THE MEDIA INTERVIEW

Practice the media interview by role-playing with an audio or videotape recorder. Practice one skill (for example, responding to questions, pausing or eye contact) at a time. Ask for feedback from friends or colleagues.

teach BI in a large group. Don't forget your nonverbal communication (Chapter 1): eye contact, posture, and vocal qualities can help to make "using the library" a more interesting topic than your audience may have anticipated. These skills are also important in giving tours of the library (8.9), which are often part of user education programs.

STRUCTURED CRITICISM: A FEEDBACK TECHNIQUE

A structured criticism is a short statement listing two or three positive aspects of a class session followed by a single concern, if you have one. The *positive* aspects are things you personally liked, learned, or understood in a new way as a result of your participation in the class. The *concern* could be a goal, a wish, or a problem.

The last five minutes or so of each class session will be set aside for you to write a structured criticism on that session. At the beginning of the next class, I will summarize those structured criticisms and tell you what I intend to do in response. These criticisms obviously involve some effort on your part and I take them very seriously. To write a structured criticism:

1. Be specific. State as precisely as possible what it is you like or were concerned about in a particular class.
2. Be personal. I am interested in your own personal opinion, not in "we all learned...." or "everyone liked...." Use the pronoun "I."
3. Be careful. Especially in the beginning, if you have a concern (the loaded part of a structured criticism) state it in one of the following ways: a. My goal is.... b. My wish is.... c. My concern is how to....
4. Be balanced. Each concern must be preceded by two positive statements.

If you have more than one concern, state two positives and then the first concern; repeat the process until you have taken care of all the concerns.

Please hand in your structured criticisms (no names, please) at the end of the class.

© 1982 by C.J. Marino, York University, Toronto. Used by permission.

Exercise

TELEVISION INTERVIEWS

Watch two or three televised interviews on your local station. For each, pay attention to one aspect of the interviewee's behavior—body language, voice quality, appearance, or structure of responses. What behavior contributes to a good interview? What behavior distracts or is dysfunctional?

SOME QUICK TIPS FOR RADIO INTERVIEWS

If the reporter doesn't tell you when the recording is to start, ask.

If you use notes, put them on cards, not on paper that rustles.

Speak loudly, from the diaphragm, not from the throat. Vary your vocal quality for emphasis (see 1.5).

8.11 THE MEDIA INTERVIEW

The media interview is a hybrid. It differs from the other kinds of public speaking discussed in this section while at the same time it shares characteristics with both the interview (Chapter 6) and PR, publicity, and promotion (9.14). In the media interview, your communication with the public is mediated through an interview, which is then edited into either a newspaper article or a recorded radio or television clip. This mediating and editing process, over which you have little control, is what makes the media interview challenging. Many of the tips offered in this section are related to the problem of reducing distortion and ensuring that you are conveying the message that you want to convey.

Usually, media interviews with library representatives occur in response to your media release or because the reporter wants to obtain an informed opinion on a library-related issue. The interview may take the form of a short telephone conversation (recorded for radio) or a television interview taped at the library or at the studio. The interviewer will sometimes go over questions with you in advance, and may or may not ask exactly the same questions in the recorded interview. For all media interviews, be prepared. Ask how long the interview will be (so that you can give shorter or longer answers) and what the main focus will be (so that you can address the major points). Have facts at your fingertips—don't guess. Never speak off the record; assume that everything you say will be reported, even small talk. Treat the interviewer as a friend, not an adversary, and the interview as a conversation with a purpose.

GETTING YOUR POINTS ACROSS

Define for yourself in advance the position statements that you would like to make about the issue or topic, whether or not you get asked about them. During the interview, fit them in, using a transition such as, "I'm glad you mentioned that because [position statement]" or "You may not be aware of this but [position statement]" or "Your viewers would probably be interested to learn that [position statement]."

Communicate enthusiasm, concern and authority ("I'm delighted to be able to tell you. . .," "This is an important issue for the library

SOME QUICK TIPS FOR NEWSPAPER INTERVIEWS

Make sure that what you say is what you want to see in print. Rephrase or repeat your answers if necessary.

Don't expect to review the article before it appears. This is rarely permitted.

Provide background facts (including spelling of names, full titles or positions, and statistics) in writing to avoid errors. Encourage the reporter to call you for further information or clarification if necessary.

SOME QUICK TIPS FOR TELEVISION INTERVIEWS

For on-site television interviews, be prepared with suggestions about where the interview should be recorded. Consider background noise, whether or not privacy is important, equipment facilities, and the visual background. But follow the crew's advice; they are the experts.

Wear appropriate clothing—lightweight (because the lights are hot) in solid, midrange colors. Avoid white because it tends to cause glare on camera, and avoid shiny or noisy jewelry.

Maintain eye contact with the interviewer. Look at the camera only when you are introduced or to make a special point.

Gesture naturally. Don't fold your arms across your chest, wring your hands, or fidget.

Stay calm and don't lose your temper, no matter what the interviewer says.

and for the taxpayer," or "We've been studying this very carefully. . . .")

Listen carefully to the question; if you don't understand, ask that it be repeated. If the question is difficult, pause first and think what you want to say before you begin to speak.

Use the inverted pyramid structure for your responses (see 4.5). Give a general reply, then make it more specific, and finally give examples. If, as often happens, the whole interview is cut to 20 seconds, the editor can use your first few sentences which encapsulates the key points.

Use short words, simple sentences, and analogies that the audience can understand (see 4.2 and 4.4—many of the hints for writing clear, understandable prose apply here too). Avoid jargon and buzzwords.

Don't repeat an interviewer's words if they contain false premises; instead, correct or rephrase the question. Explain why the premises are wrong.

Set the record straight by saying "A lot of people think that . . . but that's not true and here's why. . . ."

Don't try to answer hypothetical questions. Instead, state your general position and offer your own example.

FOR FURTHER HELP

8.2 Arranging for other people to speak

"Ten Tips for Preparing Guest Speakers: Good Advice from the Connecticut Friends," *The U*n*a*-b*a*s*h*e*d Librarian*, 59 (1987): 9.

8.6 Making a speech yourself

Bareham, S. "Improving your public speaking," *Emergency Librarian*, 16, 1 (September/October 1988): 21-25.

Ehninger, Douglas et al. *Principles and Types of Speech Communication*. 10th ed. Glenview, IL: Scott, Foresman, 1986. A basic text.

Hart, Lois B. and Gordon Scheicher. *A Conference and Workshop Planner's Manual*. New York: AMACOM, 1979. A systematic presentation of the steps of putting on a conference or workshop, enhanced with many sample checklists, letters, schedule sheets that the reader can adapt.

Hunt, Gary T. *Effective Communication*. Englewood Cliffs, NJ: Prentice-Hall, 1985. See Chapter 12, "Planning and Preparing Your Speech."

Leech, Thomas. *How to Prepare, Stage, and Deliver Winning Presentations*. New York: AMACOM, 1982. A thorough coverage, written for people in business but valuable for anyone making presentations. Contains a useful bibliography of suggested further readings.

Munter, Mary. *Guide to Managerial Communication*. 2nd ed. Englewood Cliffs, NJ: Prentice-Hall, 1987.

Page, William T. "Helping the Nervous Presenter: Research and Prescriptions," *Journal of Business Communication*, 22, 2 (Spring 1985): 9-19

Stone, Janet and Jane Bachner. *Speaking Up—A Book for Every Woman Who Wants to Speak Effectively*. New York: McGraw-Hill, 1977. Geared especially to women speakers.

IEEE Transactions on Professional Communication. New York: Institute of Electrical and Electronics Engineers. Published quarterly. Frequently publishes articles dealing with making speeches and presentations. The whole March 1980 issue of *IEEE Transactions* is devoted to articles on public speaking. For a useful bibliography, see Fearing, Bertie E. and Thomas M. Sawyer. "Speech for Technical Communicators: A Bibliography," *IEEE Transactions on Professional Communication*, PC-23, 1 (March 1980): 53-61. Cites 178 selected resources for technical communicators who want to improve their speaking skills: associations, speech courses, bibliographies, textbooks, and articles.

8.6.6 Using audiovisual aids

Turnbull, Arthur T. and Russell N. Baird. *The Graphics of Communication: Typography, Layout, Design, Production*. 4th ed. New York: Holt, Rinehart and Winston, 1980.

Woelfle, Robert, ed. *A Guide to Better Technical Presentations*. New York: IEEE Press, 1975. A compilation of practical articles on topics related to making technical presentations, including preparing visual aids.

8.7 Workshops and conference sessions

Anderson, Ronald H. *Selecting and Developing Media for Instruction*. 2nd ed. New York: Van Nostrand Reinhold, 1983.

Baird, Lloyd S., Craig Eric Schneier, and Dugan Laird, eds. *The Training and Development Source Book*. Amherst, MA: Human Resource Development Press, 1983.

Craig, Robert L., ed. *The Training and Development Handbook*. 2nd ed. New York: McGraw-Hill, 1976. Sponsored by the American Society for Training and Development.

Laird, Dugan. *Approaches to Training and Development*. 2nd ed. Reading, MA: Addison-Wesley, 1985. The distillation of the author's more than thirty years' experience as a trainer and training consultant.

McLaughlin, W. Keith and Evelyn Piush. "Planning Checklist for Seminars or Workshops," *Canadian Library Journal* (June 1980): 175-177.

O'Donnell, Peggy. *Public Library Development Program: Manual for Trainers.* Chicago and London: American Library Association, 1988. Excellent suggestions for preparing staff training workshops.

Pfeiffer, J. William and John E. Jones. *Annual Handbook for Group Facilitators.* LaJolla, CA: University Associates Press, 1972.

8.8 Booktalking

Bodart, Joni. *Booktalk! 2: Booktalking for All Ages and Audiences.* 2nd ed. New York: The H.W. Wilson Company, 1985. An excellent how-to-do it guide on booktalking for librarians and teachers. Contains over 200 pages of examples of booktalks, classified for various audiences: young children, older children, young adults, and adults.

Chelton, Mary K. "Booktalking: You Can Do It." *School Library Journal*, 22 (April 1976): 39-43. Includes a one-page "Guide for Booktalkers" that contains 19 useful tips.

Edwards, Margaret A. *The Fair Garden and the Swarm of Beasts: The Library and the Young Adult.* New York: Hawthorn, 1969. A classic.

Nilsen, Alleen Pace and Kenneth L. Donelson. *Literature for Today's Young Adults.* 2nd ed. Glenview, IL: Scott, Foresman, 1985. A helpful survey of books of interest to YA's.

Rochman, Hazel. *Tales of Love and Terror: Booktalking the Classics, Old and New.* Chicago and London: American Library Association, 1987. A school librarian shares her booktalking techniques. Also available from the American Library Association is a 25 minute video *Tales of Love and Terror* in which Rochman discusses and demonstrates booktalking. VHS, Beta, and 3/4" formats.

8.10 Providing bibliographic instruction

Preparation for providing BI requires knowledge of the theory and practice of teaching, such as can be found in the classic work by Malcolm S. Knowles, *The Modern Practice of Adult Education: From Andragogy to Pedagogy*, rev. ed. New York: Cambridge Book Co., 1980. Another practical book is *What's the Use of Lectures?* 2nd rev. ed. by Donald A. Bligh. Exeter, UK: Briarhouse, n.d. Or consult your local college or university, which may have an office that provides materials and workshops on teaching skills.

Breivik, Patricia. *Planning the Library Instruction Program.* Chicago: American Library Association, 1982.

Clark, Alice S. and Kay F. Jones, eds. *Teaching Librarians to Teach: On the Job Training for Bibliographic Instruction Librarians.* Metuchen, NJ: Scarecrow Press, 1986.

Dewdney, Patricia and Catherine S. Ross. "Effective Question-asking in Library Instruction," Library Literacy (guest column), *RQ*, 25, 4 (Summer 1986): 451-454.

Hoffman, Irene and Opritsa Popa. "Library Orientation and Instruction for International Students: the University of California-Davis experience," *RQ*, 25, 3 (Spring 1986): 356-360. Describes a program for teaching library awareness to international students and cultural awareness to librarians.

Lubans, John Jr., ed. *Progress in Educating the Library User*. New York: R.R. Bowker, 1978.

8.11 Doing the media interview

Many of the quick tips in section 8.11 have been adapted from *Effective Media Relations*, a booklet prepared for faculty members by the Department of University Relations and Information, University of Western Ontario, London, Ontario, Canada. Your local university or media representatives may be able to provide you with a similar handbook.

Read, Nat B. Jr. "How to Prepare for the TV Interview," *IEEE Transactions on Professional Communication*, PC-23 (March 1980): 45-47.

WRITING

9.1 WHEN TO WRITE AND WHEN NOT TO

The first decision you must make is whether or not to write down your message. You might do better to communicate it in person— either over the telephone or face-to-face. Here are some guidelines.

WHEN TO WRITE

To create a permanent record of the communication. A written memo can be filed and used later to resolve a dispute over what was actually said. A written thank you for an excellent job can be included in a dossier and used at performance appraisal time to document a success.

To convey complex or detailed information. Written instructions decrease the chances of misunderstanding or error. You should write down dates, times, deadlines, individual responsibilities, or numbers that you don't want the reader to forget or confuse.

To aid the memory. Handouts given out at staff training sessions and minutes of meetings are both examples of aids to the memory.

To convey routine information that doesn't require a response.

To allow the reader time to consider your question or request before formulating an answer.

To communicate efficiently to a number of people who are separated geographically. It can take much longer to telephone than to send out copies of a letter or memo.

WHEN TO TELEPHONE

To *avoid* creating a record of the communication. A message committed to paper is easily photocopied and distributed. If you don't want the message to be reread later by unauthorized third parties, then it may be prudent not to write it down.

To make sure that the person does take note of the message. Often, people file or discard messages without reading them.

To convey information that is sensitive or painful. Face-to-face, you can see how the other person is reacting and can correct misunderstandings immediately.

To encourage dialogue and discussion. The person you are talking to can ask questions and can contribute ideas of her own.

To get an immediate answer.

To make a direct, personal contact.

Sometimes it's best to combine both written and spoken communication. Staff training is a good example of a situation that benefits from the use of both: the spoken presentation makes a direct contact with participants and fosters interaction; the handouts are permanent records that aid the memory.

9.2 INTERNAL VS. EXTERNAL COMMUNICATION

Before you start writing, consider: are you writing for readers who are internal to the library (administrators, library technicians, librarians?) or are your readers external to the library (members of the public, applicants for jobs, newspaper reporters, government officials). Writing for an internal audience differs from writing for an external audience in the following ways:

You can make some assumptions about what an internal audience already knows. Since you share with your readers a common language of jargon, acronyms, and technical terms, you may be able to use terms like bib. checking, OCLC, CIP, Sears, L.C., in the expectation that your readers will understand them. The specialized language of jargon develops because it allows insiders to communicate concisely about matters specific to a field. When writing for an external audience, you should either avoid such terms or else explain them.

You can use a more conversational and informal style because you are writing to your colleagues (see Appropriate style, 4.2). Use contractions and first and second person pronouns (I, we, you). The two lists below suggest the variety of communications commonly written by people in libraries. Later in the chapter, we will look at some of these forms in more detail.

INTERNAL COMMUNICATION

Memos and Letters
—Good news (congratulations, compliments)
—Bad news (complaints, refusals)
—Routine requests

Reports
—Committee reports
—Reports of meetings
—Progress reports
—Incident reports
—Trip reports
—Feasibility studies
—Planning reports
—Reports to recommend

Manuals
—Procedures
—Policy

Instructions
—Operating instructions

Records of meetings
—Minutes
—Notices and agendas

Performance appraisals
—Written evaluation

Training materials
—Handouts
—Transparencies

Staff newsletter

Bulletin board announcements

EXTERNAL COMMUNICATION

Signs

Letters
—Good news (congratulations, compliments)
—Bad news (complaints, refusals)
—Routine requests, orders for materials

Reports
—Annual reports
—Reports of research

Instructions

Briefs to commissions or government bodies

Publicity announcements
—Book spots
—Media releases
—Public service announcements

Bookmarks

Booklists
—Annotated bibliographies
—Pathfinders

Book reviews

Flyers
—Service announcements
—Orientation to the library
—Program announcements

Policies
—Edited for the public (i.e., book selection)

Project proposals
—Requests for funds

Newsletters
—Circulated to the public

9.3 MEMOS

With some exceptions, memoranda or memos are written to people within an organization, whereas letters are written to people outside. Hence the format of the memo, which dispenses with some formalities of the letter in order to achieve speed, directness, and consistency. Many organizations provide memo forms, printed with headings like these:

To:
From:
Date:
Subject:

Memos are generally not signed, although many writers like to initial their typed name on the *From* line.

Memos are a flexible form for communicating vertically or horizontally within an organization. A memo may serve the same purpose as an ordinary letter—providing information, asking for information, making a request, giving instructions, etc. But a problem-solving memo is close in function and form to a report (see 9.5.1).

The most common problem with memos is that they beat around the bush and waste the reader's time. Write your memo with the needs of your reader in mind. Unless there is some evident reason not to (see 9.4.2 for the indirect approach to use with bad news), start by explaining:

1. why you are writing
2. what, if anything, you want the reader to do about it.

The following opening gambits are useful because they answer the reader's tacit question, "What's this got to do with me?":

This memo is to let you know the details of the new X.

Please read the attached plan for X and let me know if you approve of it.

You will be pleased to learn that. . . .

If you are in category A (e.g., have people in your department who will be requesting maternity leave), then you will be interested in the following details. [This saves time by telling a reader not in category A not to bother reading the memo.]

You asked me to let you know when Z was completed. . . .

I read with great interest your report on X and am writing to respond to your recommendations.

If you are making a request for action, don't bury your request in the middle of paragraph three, where it may be missed. Instead try something like this:

To: xxxxxxx
From: xxxxxxx
Date: xxxxxx
Subject: xxxxxx

So that [purpose explained—we can measure the effectiveness of our new safety procedures], please do the following:

1. request 1
2. request 2

[After you have made your request, you provide any necessary background information, for example, explaining why the requested action is important.]

SOME TIPS FOR WRITING MEMOS

Be personal and conversational. Try reading your memo out loud. If you would never say anything like this in a face-to-face encounter, there is probably something wrong with the memo's style: too stuffy; too formal; too bureaucratic. Don't say, "Please be advised that your report was received today by our department." Say, "Thank you for your report, which arrived today in our department."

Use the word "you" to emphasize the way the situation looks from the perspective of the reader, not the writer. A writer-oriented statement is: "I am pleased to report. . . ." A reader-oriented statement is: "You will be happy to learn. . . ."

Be concise. If possible, get your memo all on one page. But remember that your motive for conciseness is to save the reader time. If your memo is so short that it leaves out essential information, your reader will have to waste time in writing you another memo asking for clarification.

Make your message complete. Anticipate and include in your memo all the details that the reader will need to know.

Be specific. On your Subject line, don't just say: Draft proposal or Recommendations. Better to say: Draft proposal of the Computer Users Committee or Recommendations on choosing a jobber.

Use headings to divide up the text of longer memos, such as Need for a Quick Decision, Action requested, Rationale, Background. Headings make information easier to find and assimilate.

Use checklists if you are making a number of requests. The reader can check off the requests as he or she complies with them.

9.4 LETTERS

Letters come in two categories: 1) Good news or neutral messages and 2) Bad news messages. Letters in the former category are straightforward and easy to write because your reader will be receptive to your message. You may, for example, be writing to supply requested information, to place an order, to make a routine claim, to grant someone a request, to congratulate someone, or to offer a job. Bad news letters require more care. You may have to turn down a request or make a negative evaluation. The challenge is to say "No" in a way that makes your position clear but respects the feelings of the reader.

The sort of message you are writing determines the approach to take in organizing the letter. The governing question to ask is: how can you best accommodate the needs of your reader? To which approach will your reader respond best?

9.4.1 Good-news and neutral letters

Take the direct approach. Get to the point immediately, without minor preliminaries. If you are writing good news, your reader will be anxious to hear it right away and not be left in suspense. If you are placing a routine order or making a routine claim, your reader will appreciate that your directness is saving time.

DID YOU KNOW?

The average business letter gets about 45 seconds of attention from its reader—not a long time to get the point across. Michael H. Murray, "Making a $4.17 Letter Worth It," *Banking,* 69, 5 (May 1977): 124-28.

This formula is most commonly recommended for good news or neutral letters:

1. Start with the main point
2. Provide explanations or supporting detail
3. End with a statement of goodwill.

This means that if you are able to make a favorable reply to a question or request, your opening sentence should be the answer. Instead of writing, "Thank you for your letter of January 10" try: "The answer to your question about X, raised in your January 10 letter, is. . . ." Instead of writing, "Thank you for your letter asking about reserving rooms in the Central Library," try: "We have booked Room 3 for your Reading Group on Thursday, October 15 from 8:00 to 10:00 p.m." (More later on how to write the letter turning down the request to book a room.)

EXAMPLE [LETTER TO GRANT A REQUEST]
Main idea

Here is the book list that you requested containing suggestions for good books to share with your preschool children.

Supporting detail

This reading list is a good starting point, but if you want more information you might want to come to the library and look at some of our books written for parents like yourself. In particular, I would recommend Margaret Meek's *Learning To Read* and *The Good Book Guide to Children's Literature.*

Positive ending

I would be happy to show you these books and answer your questions about our collection of books for children.

This same direct approach works when you are making routine claims. You may think that, because claims are prompted by some failure of performance or service, you should follow the indirect approach of the Bad News letter. But the direct approach has two advantages: it appeals to the idea that companies want satisfied customers and need to know when things go wrong; and it gives strength to the claim.

Start by specifying what action you want from the reader. Then provide, as supporting detail, an explanation of why the requested action is warranted. Use unemotional, measured language when describing the problem. Avoid gratuitous insults or threats. By your tone, you indicate that you have confidence in the fairness and goodwill of the other party.

EXAMPLE [CLAIMS LETTER]
Ineffective version

Until now, we have always found your reference tools very reliable and have a number of them in our library. Therefore you can imagine my surprise when a user tried to look up Chrysanthemum in *The Complete Gardener's Encyclopedia,* and couldn't find it anywhere. It took us quite a while to discover that all the entries were missing for B and C. Somebody has been guilty of pretty shoddy workmanship somewhere. Please remedy this situation.

Note that this poor version makes several mistakes. It starts off with general statements and includes irrelevant details about how the problem was discovered. Remarks about poor workmanship are unnecessarily abrasive. The main point of the letter is buried in the last sentence. Moreover, the writer fails to specify exactly what remedy is wanted.

Better

Please send another copy of *The Complete Gardener's Encyclopedia,* to replace the imperfect copy that I am returning. I have enclosed the invoice that came with the book.

The returned copy apparently lacks an entire gathering. You will see that 32 pages are missing so that entries starting with B and C are missing.

If you could send the replacement copy soon, I would be grateful.

9.4.2 Bad news letters

The indirect approach usually works best when the news that you have to give is unpleasant. Since your main point is unwelcome to the reader, you don't announce it flatly in the first sentence. You delay it until you have explained the reasons for the bad news. By the time the reader gets to the actual refusal, he or she will be psychologically prepared for it.

As you write the bad news letter, you should put yourself in the place of the reader. Ask: How would I respond to this language, this opening paragraph, this letter? Does the message seem too abrupt? unnecessarily negative? You want the reader to finish

DID YOU KNOW?
If the news is partly good and partly bad, it is usually best to write the letter as a good news letter, playing up what you can do, not what you can't. However, you will have to use your common sense in deciding which approach to take.

reading the letter, with self-respect intact, thinking that your explanations, though disappointing, have been fair and reasonable.

The pattern commonly recommended for the bad news letter is:

1. Start with a pleasant, neutral statement that is related to the topic. Begin, if you can, with an area of common agreement.
2. Explain in general terms the reasons for the refusal. If the reason is library policy, point out why this policy ultimately benefits everyone, including the reader.
3. State the bad news, as gently and as briefly as possible. Leave no room for misunderstanding, but don't belabor the point.
4. End with a statement of goodwill. When you can, offer an acceptable alternative or a helpful suggestion. Avoid referring again to the refusal.

This organization goes from general (the policy or the conditions for granting requests) to the specific (the refusal of the particular request). You explain, for example, that your library rooms are made available to nonprofit groups. Then when you refuse the use of the room to a small business, the refusal does not seem personal but the logical outcome of the general policy. Then as a goodwill close, you provide the names of facilities that do make their rooms available to small business groups.

EXAMPLE [TURNING DOWN A REQUEST TO REMOVE A BOOK FROM THE SHELF]
Ineffective version

You will be disappointed to learn that we have decided to turn down your request to remove from the shelf Maurice Sendak's *Outside Over There*. Your son's response to the book, though unfortunate, is not typical. If you have any other concerns, don't hesitate to let us know.

Better

We appreciate the care you took in discussing your four-year-old son's response to Maurice Sendak's *Outside Over There*. We share your concern that a child may be frightened by a particular book, especially since it is very hard to predict responses.

As you know, the Children's Department is responsible for providing the public with picture books of high quality. As a book by an award-winning illustrator, *Outside Over There* is in great demand both by children themselves and by students of children's literature. That is why we must continue to make this book available.

The best we can do is to encourage parents to make the judgment about suitable books for their own child. Since all children are different, parents are usually the most qualified persons to withhold a book they think might be frightening.

Thank you for this opportunity to explain.

SOME TIPS FOR WRITING BAD NEWS LETTERS

Don't use a form letter if you can avoid it. People who have put a lot of time and energy into sending a proposal, coming for a job interview, etc. find a "Dear Sir/Madam" letter particularly heartless and uncaring.

Avoid negative or accusatory language. Don't start off your letter with phrases like: *We regret, we must refuse, we have turned down, we have rejected, I'm afraid you may be disappointed, unfortunately, impossible, cannot, will not, unable*, etc. If your reasons for the bad news have to do with the reader's behavior, don't use words like *negligent, irresponsible, careless*, or say you *failed, disregarded, neglected, refused*, or *forgot* or *if you had read our policy statement, you would realize*. Avoid referring to a statement made by the reader in terms suggesting distrust such as *although you claim, according to you, as you allege*.

Use the passive voice. This is one of the few cases in which the weakness of the passive is an advantage. Instead of "*You left the records in a hot place, which caused them to warp*," try: "*The warping was caused because the records were left in a hot place*." Instead of "*The committee voted overwhelmingly against your proposal*," try: "*Your proposal was not adopted*."

Explain your reasons. Don't just say that library policy prohibits granting the request. Explain why you have this policy and why the policy benefits all library users.

Don't overdo your apologies, if you have to turn down a request. It won't sound sincere, given that your refusal has been based on a good reason. On the other hand, if you or the library are at fault, then you should convey your genuine regret and acknowledge the problem.

Don't talk down to your reader. People resent condescending comments like "*we know from long experience that*."

Play up the positive. If you cannot satisfy the reader's request, you could explain the conditions under which you would be able to satisfy it. Instead of saying, "*We can't do X*," you might say, "*As soon as* [specify condition], *we will be pleased to do X.*" Or you might be able to suggest an acceptable alternative: "*The best we can do is Y.*"

Avoid ending with a cliche. A perfunctory conclusion like "*Don't hesitate to contact me if I can be of any further help*" is especially galling if you have been of absolutely no help so far. The more you can personalize your ending for the particular reader, the better.

9.5 REPORTS

Written reports vary in length, appearance, purpose, and formality. They may be a page long or 100 pages long; they may be in the form of a memo, a letter, or a bound, professionally printed document; they may be written to answer a request, supply information, or help in decision making; they may be an internal communication or an external one. What they have in common is that they are all organized presentations of material, written to convey the impression of objectivity. Reports present accurate factual information as the basis for informed evaluation. Kinds of reports typically written in libraries include progress reports, feasibility reports, investigative reports, committee reports, monthly and annual reports, planning reports, and research reports.

Reports may be either formal or informal. Informal reports, often written as a letter or memo, include only the essentials—an introduction containing background information, a body that tells the reader about the investigation of the problem, and a conclusion containing whatever recommendations there may be. Formal reports often include, in addition to these essentials, the following: a cover, title page, abstract, table of contents, executive summary, bibliography, and appendix.

9.5.1 General characteristics

These defining characteristics of reports influence how they should be written:

1. Reports are usually written for busy readers who want to grasp the essentials quickly and not hunt for the main points. They should be able to get the gist of the report without having to

read the whole thing. Therefore you should begin with a summary statement that puts the essence of the report in a nutshell.

2. Report writing is often an assigned job. The person or group who asked you to write the report usually knows what kind of report is wanted and should tell you. If not, you should ask.

3. A report is often written initially for a small number of identifiable readers who have authorized the report for a specific reason. (The report may later, of course, be read by secondary readers.) Identify your readers and analyze their needs (see 4.1 on analyzing the audience).

4. A report may go up a hierarchy—to directors, boards, legislative bodies, and the like. Therefore, in analyzing your audience, you need to keep in mind the needs of readers at all levels in the hierarchy.

5. Because a report usually presents a lot of complex information, reports must be well organized. Organization is a matter of putting like things together into groups and then ordering the groups into a helpful sequence. There is no single best way to organize (see 4.5 on organizing). Everything depends on the topic and how you have investigated it. For a short informal report, it may be enough to arrange three or four points in an itemized list. For a long formal report, a classification system may be desirable to show the reader the parts of a report and their organization. Here are two popular options:

Method 1	Method 2
1.0	A
1.1	1
1.2	2
1.3	3
2.0	B
2.1	1
2.1.1	a
2.1.2	b
2.2 (etc.)	2 (etc.)

Layout, or the way the report looks on the page, is important, especially in a long report. Page after page of uninterrupted text discourages readers (see 4.8 on formatting). Help your readers deal with masses of evidence and complex arguments by using these techniques: headings and subheadings in bold type; numbered lists; and graphic aids such as tables, graphs, charts, and flowcharts (see 4.6 on charts).

9.5.2 Informal reports

Most of the reports written in libraries are informal reports, written for an internal readership. Because you are writing for colleagues, your tone is informal (see 4.2 on appropriate style). Your report may be in the form of a letter or a memo, but it should be divided into sections, and sometimes subsections, with headings.

PARTS OF AN INFORMAL REPORT

1. Introduction stating the purpose. Sometimes a single sentence is enough, explaining why the report was written and what are the major findings. For example, "As requested, I have investigated the feasibilty of Sunday opening and recommend that we open the Martindale branch on Sundays from 1:30 to 5:00 p.m. on a trial basis for six months." In an investigative report, this section might discuss the problem, outline its previous history, refer to earlier reports on the same problem, and define the scope of the analysis to follow (sometimes in the form of a list of questions to be answered).

2. Body. This section presents the facts and explains where these facts came from. In an investigative report, you say what you were trying to do in your investigation, what you actually did do, and what you found out. In a progress report, you answer questions about the status of the project: is it on schedule? is it within budget? are there any unexpected problems or requirements for new resources? In a periodic report, you talk about work performed during the period, special accomplishments, problems encountered and remedies taken, and project plans. In a feasibility study, you point out alternatives and present evidence, as fairly and objectively as you can, both for and against each alternative. (Don't forget that one of the possible options is to do nothing: to buy none of the products considered or to make no changes to the policy, etc.)

3. Conclusion and recommendations or discussion. The conclusion is your interpretation of the evidence presented in the body of the report. Recommendations advise what to do about a conclusion, what course of action to follow, which alternative to prefer. For example, if you are writing a report to evaluate different microfiche readers, evidence might include facts such as these: Brand C is less expensive; Brand C is just as reliable

and easy to use as the rival brands; surveyed users report a slight preference for Brand C. The conclusion would then follow: Brand C is the best buy. And the recommendation would be: Buy Brand C.

Of the many different kinds of informal reports, the following are most often encountered in libraries.

9.5.2.1 Trip report

Employees who go on work-related trips are often encouraged to write trip reports, usually in the form of a memo to a supervisor. The trip report provides a record of the trip and its achievements so that the information gained by one person can be shared by others. Your report should include a statement of purpose (why you made the trip), where you went, who you talked to, and what you achieved or found out. In providing details, be selective. Don't start at the beginning and tell everything that happened, hour by hour. Highlight the significant events or discoveries. The bottom line for a trip report is that it should answer the question: Why was this trip worthwhile?

Adapt the following outline to the demands of your own trip report:

Summary, containing the following:

—why you went
—places that you visited
—the names of other people who went with you
—summary statement of the main payoff of the trip (important benefits, significant discoveries, recommendations).

Details of the trip, in which you highlight significant events or discoveries.

Conclusion, in which you provide, in more detail, your conclusions and recommendations. You may also discuss the need for similar trips in future or acknowledge people who have helped.

9.5.2.2 Accident report, incident report, or trouble report

When an accident or breakdown occurs, the person in charge may be required to write up a report of the incident. Sometimes the report is written solely to provide information, as in this case of a building superintendent writing to a library director: "I thought you should know that there were two dead cats in the book chute again this morning." At other times, an accident report will include recommendations for action, such as "A handrail should be installed on all staircases."

It is particularly important to be factual, accurate, and prompt in writing up accident reports because they may be used as evidence in the case of lawsuits, insurance claims, and the like. Include the following kinds of information:

—the exact time, date, and place of the incident
—what happened, described in objective factual terms
—who was present
—the precise nature of the injuries or damage
—treatment or remedies undertaken
—what has been done (or should be done) to correct the cause of the incident
—any other pertinent information.

In your analysis of what you think caused the problem, omit speculations and interpretatons unsupported by evidence. Avoid a heated, condemnatory tone.

Here is an outline for a typical trouble or accident report:

Summary, stating in a concise sentence or two the essence of what happened ("The mayor collapsed from a heart attack while at the circulation desk. An ambulance came promptly and took him to Memorial Hospital, where he is now out of danger.")

Details of the incident, in which you specify time, date, place of the incident; who was present; what happened.

Conclusion, in which you evaluate the implications of what happened. Here's where you would make any recommendations, if appropriate, on how to prevent a recurrence of the problem (or on how to draw up a disaster plan).

9.5.2.3 Investigative report

An investigative report is written to supply a demand for information and is used as the basis for making a decision. For example, you might be asked to to find out what users think about the new phone-in reference service; to discover what other services are available in the city for young adults; to assess whether buying a new piece of equipment is warranted; to evaluate the success of a staff training program; or to investigate options for automating a library system. A memo format is common for this kind of report.

Here is an outline for an investigative report:

Introduction, in which you get right to the point. Explain what you were supposed to find out and what you *did* find out: "As you requested, I have assessed our need for desktop publishing. My judgment is that we should buy our own equipment and I am recommending X." In other words, start with what the reader wants to know.

Supporting details, under headings like:

—Background of the problem (What happened that made a decision necessary? What is the extent of the problem? What are the present and anticipated needs?)
—Criteria for the solution
—Analysis of options (pros and cons for each option)
—Sources used (what you did to investigate the problem; who you talked to; what the literature says).

Conclusions and recommendations, detailing who should do what—and when, where, why they should do it.

9.5.2.4 Progress reports

Progress reports inform the reader (usually a supervisor or funding body) about the status of a project. The reader wants to know, as quickly as possible, the answer to the question: "How is the work going?"

A typical format for a progress report on a project is:

Summary, including a succinct statement on the following:

—Time period covered

—Status of the project (Is the project on schedule? Ahead of schedule? Behind schedule?)
—Budget (Have there been cost overruns? Cost savings?)
—Forecast (Will the project be done on time?)

Details of the project, in which you explain and justify what you have said in the summary by discussing:

—Work completed
—Work in-progress as you write the report
—Work still to be done
—Problems encountered or anticipated at each of these stages.

Revised plan, in which you forecast what will happen during the next reporting period.

Periodic reports discuss the achievements and problems occuring during regular time periods—monthly, quarterly, annually. Monthly reports are written to inform supervisors of work accomplished. You will be expected to provide certain routine information, sometimes using a preprinted form. However, you can make the report more useful if, in addition to providing the required routine information, you highlight the nonroutine event. Mention the success of a new innovation or special program.

Annual reports are a type of periodic report, but they differ from routine monthly reports in three important ways: they are formal reports, written for an external audience, for the purpose of public relations. The purpose of the annual report is to highlight, for trustees and the library's public, how well the library is using resources to satisfy objectives.

9.5.3 Formal reports

As you would expect, formal reports share many characteristics of informal reports, differing in being longer and more elaborate.

PARTS OF A FORMAL REPORT
Cover

Title page. Includes the full title of the report, the name of the person or organization receiving the report, the author's name and position (Head of Technical Services), the place, and the date of the

FRONT MATTER
The front matter is made up of all the prefatory material that must be provided before the real reporting can begin. In various forms, the front matter provides the reader with condensed indications of what the report is about. Normally the pages of front matter are numbered with roman numerals (iv, v, vi, etc.). While formal reports may do without some of these elements, all should have a title page and a table of contents.

report. Titles should be specific enough to indicate clearly the purpose and scope of the report.

Abstract. By condensing the essentials of the report to about 150 words, the abstract allows readers to decide whether or not they need to see the report in full.

Table of contents. Lists in order all parts of the report together with page numbers, except for the title page and the table of contents. It includes all the headings and subheadings of the body of the report to help readers go directly to particular sections.

MIDDLE
The heart of the formal report includes the same elements that go into the informal report, but often in longer and more complex form.

Summary. Explains in a page or two the following: 1) Why was the report written? 2) What were the procedures used to gather the evidence? and 3) What are the major findings or recommendations? You write the summary last, although it appears first in the report. In business reports, this part of the report, called the executive summary, may be all that busy managers will read.

Introduction or background. Provides readers with information they need in order to orient themselves to the report. The introduction should state the purpose of the report (to investigate the feasibility of a micrographic facility), explain the history of the topic or problem, indicate the scope (aspect of the topic covered, time period covered, etc.), and briefly summarize the main finding(s) or recommendation(s).

Body. This is the longest part of the report and is usually subdivided into sections with headings like: Methods of investigation, Findings, Present needs, Predicted needs, Factors affecting X, Alternatives, etc.

Conclusions and recommendations. This is the payoff of the report—the place where you pull together the results of your study. Don't scatter your recommendations (putting one on page 9, another on page 14, another on page 17) but pull them all together in a numbered list so that the reader can't miss them.

BACK MATTER
This contains material that is not essential, but may be helpful.

Bibliography. An alphabetical list of sources consulted.

Appendix or appendices. If readers do not need to read something in order to understand the report but may want to consult it, put this material into the appendix. Good candidates for the appendix include long charts, supplementary tables, copies of a questionnaire, copies of policy statements, lists of authorities whose advice was solicited, and the like.

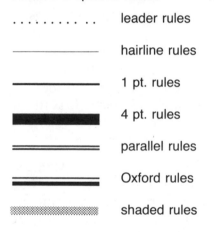

Glossary. Contains definitions of specialized terms that you have used in your report.

9.6 SIGNS

Signs are a good way to communicate with the public. Consider using signs for the following purposes:

—to orient the public to the layout of a building (you can use a floor plan with an arrow and the message, "You are here") and to provide directions (with arrows) to destinations such as the circulation desk, information desk, periodical reading rooms, special collections, regional history, washrooms, and exits
—to identify these destinations so that people recognize them when they come to them
—to explain regulations (restrictions on eating or smoking) or provide instructions (how to use catalogs, microfiche readers, or other equipment).

Used in a library context, the term signage refers to a system of informational graphics created to help the public understand the library's physical layout and use its services. Too many libraries take the higgledy-piggledy approach, producing signs as needed on an *ad hoc* basis. Planning is necessary to produce an integrated totality that provides the needed information in a graphically consistent form. Designing a coherent system of signs involves two activities: 1) deciding what questions users have about the library that can be best answered by signs, and 2) choosing suitable design elements including lettering, graphics, color, and the shape and placement of the sign.

To decide what signs are necessary, here are some suggestions:

Analyze your audience into its constituent user groups. Who are you making your signs for—general adult users, children, students, ethnic group members, the visually impaired? What special minority needs must be taken into account (braille signs for the visually impaired)?

Ask yourself, for each of these constituent groups: What is a typical destination for members of this group? What will they

Exercise

POSITIVE MESSAGES

Make a list of all the messages on signs you can think of that convey a negative tone:

No loud talking.

Do not remove.

Students are not allowed to use this machine.

Rewrite the messages so that the meaning is still clear but the tone is more positive.

DID YOU KNOW?

Studies have ranked color combinations used on signs in descending order of readability as follows:

black on yellow
black on white
yellow on black
white on blue
yellow on blue
green on white
blue on yellow
white on green

(Pollett and Haskell, *Sign Systems for Libraries*, pp. 238-239).

need to know as they move along their route? What signs will be needed to give directions? for identification? to provide instructions?

Try entering your library and walking through it as if you were a first-time visitor. What will you need to be told to help you find your way around? (Notice that at the entry point you need only a broad overview of the whole. As you get closer to your destination, you need more specific details.)

Monitor the questions library users ask about locations of things and use of services. What do these questions tell you about problems people are having finding their way around the library and using its services?

DESIGN ELEMENTS

Once you decide what signs are needed, you need to consider the following design elements:

Words and/or graphics. What are you going to put on the sign? Graphic symbols are efficient and can be understood by people who don't speak English (internationally recognized symbols used to indicate male and female washrooms, facilities for wheelchair users, lost and found, telephones, parking, no smoking, etc.). If you are using words, be brief, clear, and specific. Cut out all unnecessary words. Avoid unfamiliar words or library-system jargon. Be consistent in your choice of terminology: don't use the term "reference desk" on one sign and "information desk" on another.

Lettering. A sans serif type like Helvetica has a clarity that works well for display lettering. (Serifs and tapered strokes make it easier to read long texts printed in small point sizes, but are not so legible at a distance.) In general, lowercase letters are easier to read than all capital lettering because the ascenders and descenders on lowercase letters provide additional clues for the reader.

Color. The greater the contrast in brightness between the print and the background, the easier to see at a distance. Therefore you should use a combination of colors that enhances legibility such as black on white, black on yellow, green on white. Black on white is much easier to read than type printed in reverse lettering (white on black). Remember that green and red look similar to people who are color-deficient or color-blind (5% to 9% of viewers). Most color-deficient people can distinguish blue from other colors.

Size of the sign. Figure out how far away from the sign most

SOME QUICK TIPS FOR SIGNS

Keep it simple. Signs are minimalist forms.

Make the tone as inviting and as positive as possible (see 4.2 on tone). Consider the differences in tone: "No smoking," "No smoking please," and "Thank you for not smoking." Instead of "No food allowed except in lounge," you could try "Food is allowed only in lounge."

readers will stand and make sure that the sign is big enough to be read from that distance. For example, one inch lettering can be read without strain at eight feet, but four inch lettering is needed for signs intended to be read at 30 feet. Make your sign big enough that you can leave margins of white space around your text.

Placement. Your sign should make information available where users are likely to look for it—at the entrances and along the major traffic routes. (But don't put your signs in places where people reading the signs will block traffic.) Place the sign where it will be seen—not too high, not too low, not obstructed by a post. Be consistent so that people learn where to look: don't make some signs free-standing, hang others from the ceiling, and attach others to walls.

When you have installed your sign system, document it in a sign manual. Record how the signs were designed and made so that all new signs can be made identical in style to the old ones. The sign manual should include the following information: rules governing the choice of wording; design specifications (panel size, layout, lettering, arrows, symbols, colors), placement (height from the floor or ceiling, distance from door frames), and specifications (materials, mounting details).

Exercise

REVISING INSTRUCTIONS

Find a set of instructions used in your library or place of work. Revise the instructions, following the suggestions outlined in this section.

9.7 INSTRUCTIONS

You may find yourself writing instructions for the public (how to use the fiche machines, how to search indexes, how to find consumer information) or for fellow staff members (how to enter a new cardholder into the computer, how to operate some new piece of equipment. See also 9.8 on procedure manuals).

Often you will give instructions face-to-face, a method that allows you to demonstrate a procedure. However there are times when written instructions are useful, either used alone or accompanying spoken instructions:

—when procedures are complex and hard to remember. In such cases, you may want to provide both a demonstration and written instructions that can be consulted later to refresh the memory

—when people need help at times when nobody is available to help them

—when a lot of different people need help at different times with the same procedure

—when it is useful to document a procedure for the sake of continuity when new staff are hired.

Written instructions too often evoke in their readers responses of either frustration or laughter. Sometimes it seems as if writers of instructions are translating from a foreign language (as, for example, this sign in a hotel room: "In case of fire, do your utmost to alarm the hall porter.") Here are some suggestions for avoiding common problems and making your written instructions more helpful.

GETTING READY

Analyze the audience (see 4.1). How much do these readers already know about the procedure? What gaps do they have in their understanding? What will your readers need to be told? If your readers are beginners at using, say, computers to search indexes on CD-ROM, you will have to explain everything from the very beginning, including where to find the On button.

Analyze the procedure. Break it down into its constituent parts. Consider the time sequence: what must be done first, before something else can be done?

Distinguish steps that are necessary from steps that are merely recommended. Ask yourself particularly: Is there something that is crucial for the reader to know? (for example, don't do X because doing X will cause an explosion.)

WRITING INSTRUCTIONS

Provide a You emphasis. Use a second-person construction to highlight what the *reader* has to do. Say "Turn the printer off" rather than "The printer should be turned off."

Use parallel structure. In most cases, it works best to start off each step with a verb that indicates the action that the reader should take. For example:

1. Turn the printer off
2. Remove the cover
3. Set the release lever

DID YOU KNOW?

The following typographic factors *lessen* the clarity of graphic materials:

—reversed lettering (for example, white letters printed on a black or dark background)

—show-through (the print from the back of the page showing through)

—words set at an angle to the horizontal

—lines that haphazardly connect labels to reference points

—using a large variety of type sizes and styles.

From James Hartley, "Eighty Ways of Improving Instructional Text," *IEEE Transactions on Professional Communication*, PC-24, 1 (March 1981): 26.

Reversed lettering

4. Grasp
5. Lift
6. Place

Arrange the steps in chronological order and number them.

Anticipate problems and questions that the reader might have. For example, warn the reader that, after being turned on, the machine takes ten seconds to warm up before it starts. Explain that a certain amount of buzzing is normal and does not indicate that the machine has broken down.

Explain the reasons. Say why the optional steps are recommended. Explain why the required steps must always be followed. People are more apt to follow instructions when they understand the reasons.

Use plain, everyday language (4.4). Say "shake" rather than "agitate"; "start" rather than "initiate" or "commence."

Cut out all unnecessary words. Consider the difference between these two headings:

IMPORTANT!

IMPORTANT INSTRUCTIONS TO READ
BEFORE OPERATING THE EQUIPMENT!

Use common sense. Don't warn people not to do things that no one would ever be likely to do.

FORMATTING

Highlight crucial information. Put crucial information at the beginning: Never do X. (If you delay your warning, the reader may do the proscribed thing before reading the warning.)

Give further emphasis by using a typographic device like a pointing finger, red ink, or bold type to draw attention to crucial information:

Do not do X.

Or use a word like "Caution" or "Warning."

CAUTION!
Do not do X.

Use headings to cluster together related steps. People cannot easily take in any more than seven unrelated units at once—seven digits in a telephone number, seven unrelated words in a list, seven steps in a procedure. So if you want readers to assimilate 20 steps in a procedure, you can help by organizing these steps under three or four headings that correspond to major subdivisions of the process. In this example, the reader has four units to keep in mind, not 14:

Before you begin	Operating the machine
-1	-8
-2	-9
-3	-10
	-11
Setting the adjustments	-12
-4	
-5	Putting everything away
-6	-13
-7	-14

Use diagrams to illustrate concepts difficult to explain in words. Label parts of your diagram clearly. If you use lines to point to parts of the diagram, don't let the lines cross over each other. Place the diagrams on the page so that they are close to the text that they are intended to illustrate.

Leave white space. Instructions that are crowded are hard to read and intimidating.

CHECKING THE INSTRUCTIONS

Scrutinize for possible problems. When you have finished writing the instructions, read them over carefully, looking for ambiguities or omissions. Have you used any words/sentences/constructions that could possibly be misunderstood? Don't take anything for granted. If there's a way of misreading the instructions, then some reader will do it. Have you left out any important steps in the instructions?

Field test your instructions. Ask a colleague unfamiliar with the task at hand to try to do the task by following your instructions. Watch for areas of uncertainty, difficulty, or error. Afterwards, ask your colleague for feedback: What did she find hard to understand? Which part of the instructions did she find unnecessary? What would she like explained more fully?

Revise and field test again, if necessary.

9.8 POLICY AND PROCEDURE MANUALS

An effective organization usually has two kinds of written (or electronic) manuals: policy and procedure. Although some organizations combine policies and procedures into one manual, the distinction between the two is important. A *policy* is a statement intended to guide long-range decision making and usually reflects the basic responsibilities and principles of an organization. Because a policy usually has legal implications and requires the approval of a governing body (library board or management committee), production of a policy manual differs from production of a procedure manual. The most frequent users of the policy manual are managers or supervisors, board members, and sometimes the public. On the other hand, procedure manuals are most often used by front-line workers. A *procedure* is a set of steps, or series of actions or operations, that must be carried out to achieve a specific result. Writing procedures is a special case of the more general activity of writing instructions just discussed and the same considerations apply (see 9.7). Organizations may also have a third kind of administrative manual: the *organization* manual, which includes descriptions of organizational structure, lines of authority, and job descriptions. All three types of manuals are very useful for orientation and training of new staff.

Some general considerations for producing administrative manuals:

Consider the needs of the reader. Who will use this manual? For what purpose? Under what circumstances? Will the reader understand the manual? What might happen if the reader misinterprets or fails to understand the policy or procedure?

Organize the manual clearly, logically and simply. Choose from a variety of standard numbering systems (see Chapter 5 in Travis's *The Handbook Handbook* for examples) according to the needs of your organization. For a complex manual, you might need a system of arabic numerals with one or two decimal places or dashes (for example, 2-23.1); in a smaller organization, you might opt for a simple alphabetic arrangement (A, B, and C). The system should be no more complex than necessary. Every section and subsection should also have a brief descriptive title or heading.

Exercise

WRITING STYLE FOR MANUALS

Choose a procedure from one of the ARL (Association of Research Libraries) Spec Kits or from some other accessible procedure manual. Examine this procedure for instances of good manual style and poor manual style. Rewrite the instances of poor style to make them better.

Exercise

POLICY: SPECIFIC OR NOT?

Find several examples of written policies about materials selection. Compare those sections that deal with the same issue (for example, censorship) for readability, clarity, and specificity. For what reasons might a policy not be very specific? How does this differ from the need for a procedure to be specific?

Index. People using a manual want to know about something in particular and want to find it quickly. A manual that lacks an index is frustrating and hard to use. Provide an index as well as a table of contents. Index keywords and topics by page or section number. Remember that automated indexing may look easy to do, but the resulting index almost always requires editing for clarity and consistency. Consider a global index if you have more than a few manuals.

Cross-reference. Provide enough cross-references that readers will easily be able to find related sections or manuals, but avoid cross-references that are too detailed or too general. You can help the reader by using headings as well as the section number (for example, see also filing procedures, 2.5, rather than See also 2.5.)

Keep the layout simple. Use lots of white space. Avoid cluttering the manual with logos, signatures, lines, and excessive cross-references. (See Formatting, 4.8)

Keep the manual up-to-date. An outdated manual may be misleading. Include issue dates for each revision. Use a loose-leaf format to accommodate revisions. Periodically request department heads to submit revisions.

Ask for feedback. In business and industry, user reviews are an important part of manual production. Ask staff to evaluate the accuracy, completeness, and readability of your manuals and to suggest changes if necessary.

One way to write procedures. If the procedure has never been written down, begin by observing an experienced staff member performing the procedure. Ask him to describe what he is doing step by step as he does it and as you take notes. Be alert to routine activities that need to be described in more detail. For example:

"First, I do the mail."

"How exactly do you do that? Tell me a step at a time."

"Well, I go to the main office at ten o'clock, and ask for the mail for Technical Services. Then I . . . etc."

Reformulate this procedure as a directive: "Each working day at ten a.m., go to the Administration Office and ask for the mail for Technical Services . . . etc." After you have a complete draft of the procedure, test it by asking someone (preferably an inexperienced person) to follow the procedure exactly as you have written it. Problems, omissions, and redundancy become clear immediately.

Exercise

WRITING A PROCEDURE

[Note: Do not choose a dangerous procedure for this exercise!]

Write a procedure for changing paper in the photocopy machine (or charging out a library book, or operating the microfilm machine). Ask a partner to carry out the procedure exactly as you have written it. Ask for feedback.

Revise the steps and repeat the test until the procedure is clearly and completely described.

QUICK TIPS FOR WRITING PROCEDURE MANUALS

Place warnings and cautions first. Placing safety instructions at the end can be dangerous. Put this type of instruction first: "If the red light goes on, stop immediately and unplug the machine."

Speak directly to the reader. Use the imperative mood ("Stack the books on the truck") not the indicative mood ("The worker first stacks the books on the truck.") Use the active, not the passive voice; avoid "X should be done by Y" constructions.

Be clear and specific. For example, "File the report within four days" is better than "as soon as possible," but does it mean four working days or four calendar days?

Use simple words and terms. A procedure manual should require no more than tenth-grade reading skills. (See 4.2 on readability.)

Use parallel constructions for your headings. If the first heading is "Selecting periodicals," a subsequent heading should be "Reviewing selection decisions," not "Review of selection decisions" or "Methods of reviewing."

Be consistent. Procedure manuals should not differ greatly in style from department to department. Centralize the editing and production.

9.9 STAFF NEWSLETTERS

When an organization gets so big that its members don't regularly see each other face-to-face, then it may be time to develop other channels of communication. A staff newsletter is one way: it can be useful for maintaining morale and for making people feel part of a community. A staff newsletter is a good way to inform people about the following: news items about staff members ("Congratulations to Carol on the safe birth of triplet daughters Margo, Marsha, and Marlene"; job openings within the system; progress reports ("Architect promises that the new Whiteoaks branch will open on schedule June 1"); news items of professional interest; and announcements ("Anyone interested in forming a bowling league should come for an organizational meeting. . ."). A newsletter provides an informal channel for a community of people to share information with each other.

However there are some things to think about before launching into the production of a newsletter:

Can you give the necessary commitment of time, energy, and resources? Producing a newletter requires an ongoing effort at newsgathering, copywriting, editing, and layout, not to mention the more routine job of typing or keyboarding.

Who has editorial control? Will the newsletter be perceived as a tool of the administration for downward-flowing messages or as a channel of communication for all kinds of news and messages—downward, upward, sideways, etc.?

If you do decide to produce a staff newsletter, consult the books listed in *For further help* to help with problems of writing and layout as well as with the following kinds of basic decisions:

—How often will it be published?
—What size will the pages be?
—How many pages per issue?
—How many columns of type per page?
—How will it be produced? by typewriter for the informal look? by desktop published, laser printing for the professional look?
—How will it be printed—by mimeographing? photocopying? offset printing?

9.10 ONLINE PRESEARCH FORMS

The job of writing useful forms requires the combination of a number of writing and questioning skills—especially writing briefly (4.4), formatting the page (4.8), and asking appropriate questions (3.5 and 3.7). In this section, we will not try to deal with those aspects of form creation that are related to record management. Instead, we use one kind of form—the presearch form—as a specific example of how to adapt the questioning skills discussed in Chapters 3 and 6 to the new context of written forms.

In section 6.2.6 tips are provided for conducting the online presearch interview. Before this interview, the user is often asked to fill out a form describing his requirements for the online search. Use of the form may save time in the interview but it may also cause other problems, especially when the questions are worded in terms of the information system rather than in terms of how the information can be expected to help the user. System-oriented questions can confuse the user and sometimes force him to choose between options that he doesn't understand.

Think of your form as a written reference interview. To replace the usual "What is your topic (subject)?" or "Do you want X or Y?" or "Provide keywords, synonyms, descriptors," use some of the questions recommended in Section 6.2.6.

QUESTIONS FOR THE ONLINE PRESEARCH FORM

Please describe in your own words what you would like to find out as a result of this search.

What other terms or phrases may be associated with this topic?

What have you done so far?

What has helped you so far? (Please indicate useful names of people, organizations, or publications.)

How do you plan to use this information?

Then, use this completed form to provide a structure for the personal interview, in which you clarify and further explore the written responses.

9.11 BOOKLISTS

The booklist provides a way of overcoming the problem that books can be put on library shelves in only one order—Dewey, LC, alphabetical by author, or whatever. But readers often want books and other materials brought together in other orders. For example, they want a list of authors of mystery stories (or gothic romances or horror stories or westerns); or they want everything related to Arthurian legends—myths, recent fiction based on the legends, accounts of staging of *Camelot,* historical maps of Wales, literary criticism of Thomas Malory; or perhaps they want fiction and nonfiction materials brought together that can help in particular situations (for example, coming to terms with cancer or getting back into the work force).

Lists are much more useful when they are specific and narrowly focused. Don't draw up a list called Good Books You Might Like. Think of topics for which you think there is a demand in your library where the materials are scattered and hard to find. For example:

—recent books on women's issues
—fiction books about native Indians
—Dracula
—new short story collections
—local writers
—fiction and nonfiction materials to help a reader cope with divorce/ illness/death of a loved one.
—materials on coping skills for the new mother.

SOME TIPS FOR BOOKLISTS

Be selective in the books you recommend. The reader, faced with hundreds of books to choose from, often feels overwhelmed. Your booklist provides the service of selecting a manageable number of the best/newest/most interesting works.

Don't put too many items on your list. Instead of a booklist of 100 titles, try a shorter list of 15 annotated books to narrow the field for the reader and help her choose. You can alert the reader to the existence of other items by saying, "These books are only a selection of those available on X. Ask us about finding others."

9.12 ANNOTATIONS

Good annotations provide information that can help readers decide whether or not a book is worth their time. An annotation answers questions like: Is this book on a topic that I would be interested in? Does it address the problems I'm concerned about? Is it written at a level appropriate to me?

A short annotation can be done in one sentence. Fiction books in particular lend themselves to a short annotation of the sort intended to whet the reader's interest in the book:

[Gothic Romance] When Sarah arrives as a governess in Holyrood House, she is enchanted by her new situation—until she begins to suspect that someone is trying to kill her.

The Progress of Love. Alice Munro's most recent collection of award-winning short stories explores with unusual sensitivity the "pain of human contact."

Longer annotations (two to three sentences) are sometimes written for annotated bibliographies. An annotation of a work of nonfiction answers questions like:

—What is this book about and how well does the book deal with its topic?
—What approach does the book take—is it theoretical? practical?
—What are the qualifications of its author(s) to write this book?
—What special features does it have that might interest the reader—illustrations, practical exercises, an annotated bibliography, appendices containing useful tables, etc.
—Who is the intended audience for this book—a beginner? a specialist? a professional group?

The challenge is to condense a lot of information into just two or three readable sentences.

EXAMPLE

Written by [a Professor of English/ a skydiver], this [textbook/ manual/ collection of critical essays] provides an [introductory treatment/ a specialist's analysis] of [topic].

Readers may be willing to overlook [the rather dull opening chapter/ the jargon-ridden writing style/ the confusing graphics and tables/ the lack of an index]

because the [strong point of the book] is so valuable.

To pack the most into the fewest words, annotation writers often write sentence fragments: "Fast becoming the standard work in the field" or they start right in with the verb: "Provides a detailed discussion of," "Deals with theoretical aspects of," "Gives practical information on."

SOME TIPS FOR WRITING ANNOTATIONS

Be brief—one or two sentences. An annotation is not a review.

Consider your audience. For whom are you writing the annotation? What kinds of information do your readers want from your annotation?

Consider your purpose. Are you trying to attract the reader's interest to a book on a reading list? Or are you providing a balanced and informative assessment of books in a field for an annotated bibliography?

Use active verbs rather than passive verbs. Better to say "This practical how-to manual explains how to deal with five common troublesome situations" than "Five common troublesome situations are dealt with."

Let the reader decide. Instead of saying "a poor book," provide the specific grounds for your evaluation (the black-and-white illustrations are muddy) and let your reader decide whether this factor matters.

Try to get some variety in the annotations by varying the sentence structure and the approach. Because a list of annotations is usually read all together as a group, you don't want them all to sound the same.

9.13 REVIEWS

Reviews can range from something just slightly longer than an annotation to a review article of a thousand words or so. Which kind you write depends upon your audience and where your review will be published. Usually professional journals for librarians favor short, current reviews that quickly provide enough information to enable a purchasing decision. Scholarly journals that are discipline-oriented are more leisurely in their approach to reviewing, trading off brevity and currency for critical insight and thoroughness of treatment. Since one of their purposes is to provide current awareness to academic readers, these reviews tend to summarize key arguments of the book. Whatever the length, however, the primary purpose of the review is to provide balanced information that the reader can use to make a decision: Is this book worth seeking out and reading? Or is it worth buying?

Before you write your review, read other reviews published in the journal in which you expect to publish yours. This will give you an idea of the style expected of you. In any case, stick to the number of words your editor allots you (200 words, 700 words, 1200 words) and get your review in by the deadline.

As you are thinking about what to say in your review, it may be useful to think about where you stand on the issue of reviewing. Reviewers can be divided into two ideal types, depending on what they think they are doing when they read books and write reviews. One type thinks of the text as having an objective, autonomous existence apart from any reader. Such reviewers, therefore, consider it their job to make objectively true statements about the text:

the book is about the Petroleum Industry; it has ten chapters; it has a 30-page index. Evaluative judgments, if provided, are phrased as objective attributes of the text: the book is enlightening/ dull/ disturbing.

The second type of reviewer considers that all reading is a transaction between reader and text in which the reader is actively engaged in creating meaning. These reviewers tend to see themselves as offering, not objective statements about the book, but statements about their own response to the book: I found the book enlightening/ dull/ disturbing (with the implication that, if you are like me, you will find it this way too). These reviewers often provide a few brief details about themselves so that readers of the review can judge whether or not their tastes are like the reviewer's ("I usually prefer the British country-house mystery to the hard-boiled San Francisco type, but I found this hard-boiled mystery thoroughly enjoyable and stylish.") This approach requires tact, so that the review doesn't sound like a biography of the reviewer's own reading taste. However, its advantage is that it is based on a theory of reading that takes into account what actually does happen in the review process. Your review evaluates the book. But then your reader evaluates your review to decide if you should be trusted.

What should go into a review? At a minimum, a review should answer the questions that are answered in a good annotation (see 9.13): Who is the book for? What is this book about? How well does it do what it sets out to do? What approach does it take? What special features does it have? What are the credentials of the author? Provide factual statements, but go beyond facts to an evaluation. After all, your readers want to know more than that the book is about the petroleum industry. They want to know: How good/accurate/thorough is this treatment of the petroleum industry?

In addition, reviews often do one or more of the following:

Comment generally on the field to which the book belongs. (A reviewer could say that the commonest critical approach for literary studies in the particular field has been thematic, so that the new book's semiotic approach is a welcome new direction.) The focus of discussion could be:

—generic (What characteristics of the thriller does this particular thriller share?)
—national (What advances have been made in the past decade in, say, Canadian retrospective bibliography? And how does this

particular retrospective bibliography fit into the context of other similar work?)

—theoretical (What theoretical controversies divide this field? Where does this book fit in?)

—methodological (What methodologies are available to investigate questions in this field? How does the research methodology used here measure up?)

Relate the reviewed work to other comparable works in the field. The reviewer could say that this new directory supercedes some former standard work in the field. Or that the book, though not comprehensive, is the only available book that treats the subject. Or that the book is a good popularization of topic X but provides nothing new to readers already familiar with works Y and Z.

Compare the reviewed book to other works by the same author. A reviewer might show how this latest book by an author fits into the total canon of the author's work. For example, the book returns to a preoccupation addressed in the author's first book; it shows the maturation of the author's thinking; or it will disappoint readers who want a repeat of the previous bestseller but will delight readers who appreciate risktaking.

Discuss the underlying assumptions of the book, the theoretical stance taken, or the ideology espoused by the book. The reviewer could point out that that the book has illuminated its topic from the perspective of Marxism/ behaviorism/ Jungian psychology/ feminism/ supply-side economics/ phenomenology/ structuralism and so on.

Analyze specific features of the book. The reviewer could analyze the style of a literary work, the development of character and plot in a novel, the relation of pictures to text in a picture book, the use of primary sources in an historical or biographical work, the use of tables and graphs in a report, the choice of methodology in a research study.

Test aspects of a reference work such as its accuracy, its currency, its ease of use, the balance of its coverage, etc. You could read a picture book to a group of children to test its appeal.

SOME TIPS FOR WRITING A REVIEW
Read the book thoroughly. Skimming isn't fair to the author or to your readers.

Exercises

REVIEWING

1. Select two professional reviewing journals for librarians and two discipline-based journals for academics. Browse through reviews in these journals. Compare the styles of reviews in the two types of journals. What differences do you notice? What similarities?

2. Select several reviews that you find particularly good. What specific things did you like about the review? What made the review helpful? On the basis of this analysis, what tips for reviewers can you add to the list provided at right?

Don't review a book in a case where there is a conflict of interest (you dislike the author or the author is your best friend; you have spent your lifetime combating the position taken by the book).

In your review, try to convey the flavor of the book.

Keep things in proportion. Don't give a disproportionate amount of attention to some minor feature.

Review the book that was written, not the one you wish had been written. Don't complain that the author didn't do something that he or she never intended to do.

Use criteria appropriate for the type of book being reviewed. It's not fair to make a negative evaluation on the grounds that a book on Husserl uses unfamiliar Germanic terminology or that a work of YA realism dwells too much on the downside of adolescent experience. (You can, however, point out such things as features that the reader may wish to know about.)

For a nonfiction work, summarize the main arguments of the book. But never give away the plot of fiction in which suspense is important to the reading experience.

9.14 PR, PUBLICITY, AND PROMOTION

PR or *public relations* is the ongoing communication between your organization and the public—how people perceive your services, staff, and organization. Public relations is not something you choose to have—you just have it, good or bad. Your formally designated "public relations staff" use specific skills to enhance the positive image of the library. But everybody in the organization is a PR person whether or not that person realizes it. A positive or negative impression of your library may be created instantly by a particularly helpful janitor (or an especially surly librarian). Public relations extends beyond the formal communication channels of the library. A satisfied user can be your best advertisement; a disgruntled employee can be your worst. Although the library's image is generally positive, most people (including funders) do not have a complete picture of what libraries can do for them or they may not think of the library as relevant to their own personal lives—this is where publicity and promotion come in.

Publicity is what results when public attention is directed to some aspect of the library, and that publicity can be positive or negative. We can influence the kind of publicity we get. For example, we may notify the newspaper of a new service to create public awareness of the service. If the editor throws away our notice, we get no publicity. If he writes a story about the service, we get publicity. If we achieve our objectives through this publicity, the publicity is positive; if not (imagine that public demand exceeds the library's ability to deliver the new service, or that the new service isn't available after all), negative publicity results. Communication accidents are just as apt to happen with mass communication as with one-to-one communication; the trick is to recover from them and, if possible, to turn them to advantage.

Promotion is a deliberate, controlled effort to draw attention to the organization in order to increase positive public response. Much of what is called public relations or publicity is really promotion; the difference lies in the amount of control exercised over the resulting effect. Promotion includes such communication methods as public service announcements, media releases, newsletters, signage, advertising, special events designed to increase the library's profile, and informal but planned efforts whose primary purpose is to enhance the library's image and/or enhance public awareness of specific services or events.

Finally, remember that publicity and promotional tools must be part of a larger, planned program of public relations that includes everything from market surveys to training staff in public communication skills. Many excellent articles and books have been written on public relations programs for different types of libraries. The next few sections provide only a general introduction to common promotional techniques and offer some new practical tips.

9.14.1 Public service announcements

A PSA or media spot is a brief, written announcement intended to be printed by a newspaper or read aloud by a radio or television announcer. Public service announcements are free—most national broadcasting regulations require television and radio stations to donate time for community service announcements. On the other hand, because you pay nothing, you can't specify when (or if) the announcement will be run. Well-written radio announcements that take the fancy of the announcer may get prime time and an ad-libbed endorsement. Poorly written, dull announcements may never get aired. Use public service announcements to inform the public of new services, library locations, changes in hours, or similar information—but not news or feature items. Public service announcements aren't just for public libraries, either. Academic libraries can use campus newspapers or radio stations; special libraries can use staff publications or other channels.

SOME QUICK TIPS FOR WRITING PSA'S

Analyze your audience. Who are the people you want to reach? Do they read the paper? What radio stations do they listen to? When do they watch TV? Look at readership or audience surveys.

Head up the announcement with a release date and contact information (name and telephone number). Double-space the announcement.

Begin with a short sentence or question to attract attention ("Do you live in the Whiteoaks area?")

Give the essential facts (what, where, and when). For example, "The XPL bookmobile now stops at the Whiteoaks Park gates every Tuesday afternoon from 2 pm to 4 pm."

Finally, add or repeat important details, ending with your library's name: "That's the bookmobile stop at Whiteoaks Park gates every Tuesday from 2 to 4 pm—a service of the XPL."

For radio/TV announcements, read your announcement aloud to ensure that it is no longer than 15-30 seconds in length.

Don't try to use a single announcement to promote two programs or to promote services at more than one location.

If you want your announcement repeated over any length of time (for example, a month), send the announcement in more than once.

Send your announcements well in advance. Check with the newspaper or station for schedules.

Evaluate. Ask your staff and public if they have heard or seen the announcement, and how it came across.

9.14.2 Media releases

A media release is meant to attract the attention of news editors and reporters who may then contact you to do a story. Unlike a public service announcement, a media release is not usually read or printed exactly as it has been received, although this sometimes happens. If you have fast-breaking news, telephone the assignment editor of the newspaper, radio station, and television station. Then hand-deliver the media release. Use media releases for:

—a good news item—your budget has been approved; a new director has been hired; you are automating the catalog.
—a human interest story—someone returned *The Art Of Memory* and it was sixteen years overdue.
—news that can be supplemented with an interview or photograph of an interesting visitor—a famous author, politician, or a public figure opens your new branch.
—issues and problems of public interest—new trade legislation has implications for book budgets.

Excellent guidelines for writing media releases are provided in books on library promotion. The basic rules are: be clear, concise, and brief. Use the five W's (Who, What, Why, Where, When). If you feel it's necessary or desirable to provide more details (biographical information on a visiting bigwig or specifications of your new online system) include this as a one- or two-page enclosure and make sure the media release can stand alone.

Always give the name of a contact person. For policy and issue-oriented news, one of these contact people should be at the highest administrative level—the information they give out must be authoritative. A general rule of thumb is to give the name of the person who knows the most about the item and who is the one you want quoted or interviewed. Make sure this person is available and informed before you send the release. (See Section 8.11 for tips on the media interview.)

NEWSPAPER ADVERTISING

Seek advice from the advertising sales department on layout and placement.

Avoid an overcrowded, cramped appearance. Don't try to cram in too much text. Leave white space and use large type to catch attention.

Specify everything you can—border, size of print, desired location.

Proofread everything (including galley proofs) three times. Don't count on the newspaper to catch spelling or typographical errors.

9.14.3 Advertising

Advertising is promotion you pay for. It attracts publicity that you can largely control. But you may never have to buy advertising space if you have a good promotional program that includes effective public service announcements, in-house promotional brochures, and good contacts with local media representatives and people who regularly communicate with your public. Advertising in a daily newspaper or on any radio or television station is very expensive, even with an institutional discount. Unless you pay top rates, a paid ad does not guarantee that your message will appear when and where you want it to. Furthermore, once you start

Exercise

COMMUNICATING WITH USERS

Think of a specific situation in which you need to communicate with your users (or nonusers). How would you go about it? What forms of communication would be most (or least) appropriate and effective?

Exercise

PROMOTIONAL BROCHURES

Look at the prize-winning promotional brochures in the John Cotton Dana awards. What common characteristics do they have?

Exercise

CREATING HANDOUTS

Write the copy and prepare a layout for: (a) a bookmark to announce new library hours for the library; or (b) an announcement of a new service of a corporate library to senior engineering staff; or (c) a brochure describing a story hour program for toddlers. Exchange your work with another staff member. Together, revise the handout using the best ideas from each draft.

paying for advertising, you may give the impression that you're able and willing to pay for what should be public service time.

However, there are occasions when a paid advertisement is the only effective way to get a message across. Such occasions include political messages (bond issues, for example), high profile ads in special editions of newspaper supplements, and advertising outside the regular media channels (special publications, calendars, or shopping bags.) Use your advertising budget for these items. To make the most of paid advertising, consult Rummel and Perica's *Persuasive Public Relations for Libraries* or other books that give you specific guidelines.

9.14.4 Newsletters for the public

If you're considering a regular newsletter for your public, do your homework: this includes a market survey and long-term plan for production and distribution as well as learning about writing, layout, and printing. A newsletter is a long-term commitment that involves more staff time and expense than you might imagine—if it's going to be effective. Like any other printed material, a good newsletter has to catch people's attention, contain useful information, and be easily available.

Public libraries are not the only ones that need the promotional and informational channels that a newsletter can provide. But a newsletter is generally a bigger undertaking for a public library than for a special or academic library where the "public" is more specifically defined and where distribution channels are usually already in place. In any type of library, it's essential to involve staff, management, and probably board members in preliminary discussions. (Remember that your newsletter may be a formal public relations vehicle, but the proof of the public relations pudding lies in individual responses to your public. You can say wonderful things about your organization in the newsletter, but if your staff are not informed or not responsive, you've done more harm than good. The reality must match the image you create.) Having said that, we recommend that you consult some of the excellent books available on writing newsletters, desktop publishing (see 4.9), and general promotion for libraries.

9.14.5 Handouts: fliers, brochures

The cheapest, fastest way of promoting library services is to produce a handout—fliers, brochures, pathfinders, bookmarks, and booklists are some examples. The main advantage of a handout is its portability and durability (unlike a poster or a public service announcement). That is, people can take it away and use it as a reminder or read it at leisure.

Handouts may be primarily instructional (pathfinders) or primarily promotional (program announcements), but they always have a promotional element in that they make readers aware of a service, policy, or event and encourage them to use it. Every handout that a library distributes is a promotional piece that should communicate a positive image of the library.

SOME QUICK TIPS FOR HANDOUTS

Handouts should never look homemade, no matter how casual an image you wish to convey. If you don't have the resources to do a professional looking job, get it done by a company or freelancer who specializes. If you can't do that, don't do it at all.

Always include your logo or at least the library's name, address, and telephone number in a prominent place.

Don't try to say too much in one handout. Consider instead a series of one-page handouts in the same format, using different colors.

Say it in different ways. Reinforce your message with brochures, bookmarks, posters, public service announcements.

Keep it readable. Don't use dark colored paper for anything that requires close reading (no matter how pretty "raspberry" is.)

Proofread. Doublecheck for spelling, grammar and typos. If you aren't very good at spelling yourself, enlist the help of a colleague who can spell.

For tips on particular kinds of handouts, see Booklists (9.11) and Newsletters for the public (9.14.4)

9.15 CONTRIBUTING TO THE PROFESSIONAL LITERATURE

Librarians have always been concerned with controlling and making available other people's professional literature. Increasingly now they are contributing articles and books to their own professional literature. If you want to publish, you will find much of the information you need to get started in *Librarian/Author: A practical guide on how to get published*, edited by Betty-Carol Sellen. One contributor, Art Plotnik, editor of *American Libraries*, holds out the encouragement that "although a so-so article has only a 10 percent chance of being published, an original and readable article smashes like a comet through the curve of probability and has virtually a 100 percent chance of seeing print" (p. 82).

In addition to articles on how to write articles and books, how to approach a publisher, and what to look for as you sign contracts, *Librarian/Author* surveys the publishers for library and information science books and articles and provides an excellent annotated bibliography for librarians on "Writing for Publication."

9.16 PROPOSALS

Proposals are, above all, rhetorical: that is, their main function is to persuade. You want to get the reader to do something: to approve a project, to approve the purchase of equipment, to give you money to carry out research, etc. Your proposal is competing for scarce resources against other proposals. Therefore, to be successful, your proposal must convince readers that:

—you have a do-able project that is manageable and realistic.
—your project is worth doing (where "worth doing" is defined in terms of the goals of the assessors of the proposal).
—you are capable of doing it.

Here are some suggestions for writing a winning proposal.

BEFORE YOU START WRITING

Analyze your audience (see 4.1). Ask these questions about the assessors of your proposal: What types of projects does this group of reviewers (or this funding agency) want to encourage? Does your proposed project fit its criteria? How can you make clear the relevance of your project to the funding agency's goals?

Assess the project that you are proposing. Has this project already been done before by someone else? (If so, you may not need to do it at all. Or perhaps you can build on this work for your own project.) Before you can convince others of the value of the project, you must be clear in your own mind about the following points:

QUICK TIPS ON WRITING PROPOSALS

If you don't have any experience or publications in the field of your proposed project, it is better to start with a small project. It's like applying for credit: you have to establish your credit rating by being successful in paying back a small loan before you're entrusted with a large loan.

Break up a large project into smaller stages, each of which is self-contained and results in a usable product. Toward the end of stage 1 (to allow for continuous funding), you write another proposal for stage 2, and so on.

Be realistic in what you say you will do, how soon you can do it, and how much it will cost. Remember that everything always takes longer than you think it will and take this into account in your timetable. Don't be extravagant in your cost estimates, but don't be unrealistically penny-pinching either.

DID YOU KNOW?

The four most common reasons cited by the National Institutes of Health for rejecting proposals are (in order of greatest frequency): "The overall design is unsound or some techniques are unrealistic"; "Proposal is not explicit enough, lacks detail, or is too vague or general"; "Investigator does not have adequate experience for this research"; and "Investigator's knowledge or judgment of literature is poor." (Cited in Ronald R. Powell, *Basic Research Methods for Librarians*, pp. 54-5)

DID YOU KNOW?

Most universities have a research office that will help identify sources of funds and provide other support. If you work in a university library, check out the help available in the research office.

Why is this project worth doing? *What* difference will it make? Who, specifically, will benefit from its completion? *How* will they benefit?

You should aim to provide a statement about your project such that nobody, after hearing it, can say "So what?" [Here's a statement that doesn't pass the So-what test: "This project will result in a bibliography of over 2,000 entries." "So what?"]

Think through your methodology carefully. Be detailed and concrete. What, specifically, do you want to do? How do you plan to do it? It's not enough to say that your research project involves surveying public library users to find out their information needs. You have to know specific answers to such questions as these: How do you define "library users" and "information needs"? What research questions are you trying to answer? How will you choose your sample and how many people do you need in the sample? What survey method will you use (self-administered questionnaire? structured interview? unstructured interview?) When will the survey be conducted? Who will conduct the survey (if you plan to hire surveyers, how will you train them?) What specific questions will you put on your questionnaire or interview schedule? How do you plan to pretest your survey instrument? How do you plan to tabulate and analyze the answers? How will the responses given by your subjects help you answer your original research questions? How much will the project cost? In what form will you report your findings?

You have to very clear about the what's, the how's, and the when's of your project in order to persuade assessors of your competence. Vagueness about details is taken as a sign that you don't know what you're doing. A carefully worked out project of limited scope is more impressive than a grandiose project that skimps on concrete detail.

Look, if possible, at other people's successful proposals to see how they did it. Examine published work that has dealt with similar problems or issues.

WHEN YOU WRITE

Having clarified for yourself the proposal's precise objectives and expected benefits, you have to write a proposal that communicates these points to others. Your writing style should be clear and precise (see 4.2 and 4.3). Use active verbs. Your tone should be confident but not inflated or grandiose. Whenever possible, avoid jargon and technical language. Make your proposal understandable to the nonspecialist by beginning with a general statement explaining the overall point of the project before getting into specific details.

The organization to which you are applying may provide a printed proposal form or guidelines to follow. If no format is suggested, set up your proposal to include the following elements:

Project title. This should be a short descriptive title that accurately conveys the nature and scope of the proposed project.

Nontechnical summary. This is like the executive summary in a report—a short, intelligible, nontechnical statement of what you plan to do and why. Write the summary last.

Statement of area in which you are working and the problem (broadly defined). In the case of a research project, the problem is the research question that your project is designed to answer. In the case of a nonresearch project, it is the situation that the project is designed to address.

Context. Put your project in a framework. Describe how the proposal fits into the field. What historical background led up to it? What will happen, as a result of the project, when the work is over? Don't assume that assessors will already know the context. Spell it out. If you are doing a research project, the context should include a discussion of the related literature (which you can put into a separate section, labeled Review of Related Research, although it's often better not to).

Specific objectives. Explain clearly what you are proposing to do. In the case of a research proposal, state your hypothesis to be tested or the questions you are trying to answer.

Procedure. Explain, in precise terms, the who's, what's, how's and when's of your project. In a research proposal, this methodology section is written for the specialist and may use specialized technical language. You would talk about the assumptions underlying the research, the research design, methods of data collection, and the treatment of the data. If you are using subjects or participants, you should discuss ethical issues including how you will ensure confidentiality.

Institutional resources. Mention institutional resources that are available to support the proposed project: office space, computer facilities, library resources, release time for personnel, etc.

Budget. Provide detailed and justified estimates of costs: personnel (including employee benefits), space, travel (justify the travel;

don't just list), office supplies, project materials, support services such as photocopying, equipment.

Significance. You have to demonstrate that your project has social or scholarly benefits sufficient to justify the cost. Again, don't assume that the project's significance is self-evident to everybody just because it is obvious to you. Spell it out.

Qualifications of personnel. In the case of a research proposal, you append a Curriculum Vitae, reworked to highlight your credentials that qualify you to undertake the project. If you don't have all the necessary qualifications yourself, you may want to pool strengths by working with another colleague or a group of colleagues.

AFTER YOU HAVE WRITTEN THE FIRST DRAFT

Proofread for spelling mistakes and grammatical errors.

Ask colleagues to read your proposal with a view to identifying vague statements, inflated statements, obscurities, omissions. Ask the most critical people and tell them that you really do want negative as well as positive feedback. If the colleague gives it back with nothing written on it, saying "It's great," don't ask him or her again. At least one of your readers should be someone who is not particularly familiar with the area: if this nonexpert can understand the proposal, then it will probably be clear to the assessors.

Evaluate your own proposal by asking:

Does the proposal conform to the guidelines of the funding or approving agency?

Is the proposal complete?

Has the need for the project been clearly stated and convincingly documented?

Has the project been placed in a framework or context?

Are the objectives clear?

Is the methodology clear? Is it appropriate?

Is the budget realistic? Are expenditures justified?

Have you been concise? Have you stayed within the suggested guidelines for length?

Have you made it hard for a reviewer to dismiss your proposal with a "So-what?"

9.17 WRITTEN COMMUNICATIONS FOR GROUPS

One of the reasons that people work in groups is to communicate with each other more directly than they could through writing to each other. But written communication can often support or enhance group activities. Some of the purposes of written communication for groups are: to save time, to provide structure to a discussion, and to record the group's actions or decisions. Some examples include:

—to give direction or advance notice (agendas, notices of motions)
—to create a permanent record of group activity (minutes)
—to save the time of the group (background papers, handouts)
—to communicate with people who did not attend the group (minutes, background papers)
—to structure the group's activities (outlines, agendas, handouts).

Use written communication to perform functions that cannot or should not be performed by individuals speaking to each other. For example, background papers and written committee reports save the time of group members, who would waste valuable time were they to read the report during the meeting or listen to someone present the report verbatim. Written communications for groups should follow the general rule that writing be clear, concise, and addressed to the needs of the reader. The following tips relate to additional considerations for writing the documents commonly used in groups. Read these tips in conjuction with Chapter 7 on working in groups.

TO WRITE A RECORD OF A MEETING
See 7.4.3 on the formal meeting for the section: Keeping a record. Consult a standard meeting manual for taking formal minutes.

Exercises

KEEPING A RECORD

1. Examine the minutes of a library board or management committee meeting. What information about this group's activities seems to be missing? What was included that seems unnecessary?

2. Listen to a tape recording of a short problem-solving meeting. Take notes and prepare a record of the meeting.

EXERCISE
Right to write?

Glenn Trimble has been working for just over two weeks in the Collection Development Department of Smalltown University Library (SUL). During this time he has become familiar with the

QUICK TIPS FOR WRITING AGENDAS

In the first lines, include the name of the group or committee, then the date and time (in **bold** or CAPITAL LETTERS), and the location of the meeting.

Consult a standard guide to conducting meetings for the order of business (see also 7.4.3 on the formal meeting).

Old business should include a brief list of items.

New business should include the category "other business."

If a notice of motion was made at the last meeting, include the wording of the motion.

Estimate the time of adjournment to let participants plan their day.

Provide the name and telephone number of a person to contact about attendance at the meeting.

Don't forget to enclose or attach the background material.

collection development policies and procedures and has already started to make contact with some of the user groups. Since Glenn's main area of responsibility is natural science, he has scheduled meetings with a number of faculty in the natural sciences departments.

Today a student came to Glenn's office to suggest that the library buy a major reference work in the area of organic chemistry. The student had used this encyclopedia in a nearby research library and felt it would make a valuable addition to SUL's collection. Following the visit, Glenn found out that the library did not have the encyclopedia, that it was still in print, and that it cost $2,200. Since buying this work would use up much of the book budget for Chemistry, Glenn felt he needed the advice of faculty in the Chemistry Department before he could make a decision to purchase. Glenn realized that at least three options were open:

He could write a memo to the Chair of the Chemistry Department, describing the situation and asking for an opinion.

He could arrange a face-to-face meeting with the Chair of the Chemistry Department.

He could discuss the purchase of the encyclopedia during the meetings with faculty already scheduled.

QUESTIONS FOR DISCUSSION

1. How might the importance of obtaining a quick response affect Glenn's choice of approach? Suppose the encyclopedia were available at a special prepublication price for a limited time?
2. How important is an audit trail? In the case of a major purchase such as this one, should Glenn get in writing the response from the Chemistry department in case anyone questions his decision in the future?
3. First impressions are important. How might the Chair of Chemistry feel about a formal, written first contact as opposed to a less formal, personal contact?
4. All things considered, how should Glenn go about getting advice on buying the encyclopedia? Why?

(Case developed by Bryce Allen, © 1987)

EXERCISE
Effective letters

QUICK TIPS FOR RECORDERS

Sit where you can see everyone.

Have a list of participants' names.

Make yourself a "seating diagram."

Don't be afraid to ask someone to repeat the wording of a motion or to restate the decision as they wish it recorded.

Don't attempt to record everything that goes on. Report the essential accomplishments of the meeting, not all the process and every pro and con. Keep the report brief.

Don't use judgmental or emotional words. Summarize two hours of bitter argument in neutral terms: "After lengthy discussion, the group decided to disband."

Edit or transcribe your notes immediately, before you forget what you meant by "nxt Jn."

Write a letter that would be suitable in the following situations:

1. You are the coordinator of an all-day workshop that will be put on for local librarians from both public libaries and academic libraries. You expect to have about 80 registrants. You will need three rooms, one big enough to accommodate up to 50 people seated around tables, and two that would be suitable for small seminar discussions of 20 people. Your speakers will need blackboards, an overhead projector and screen, lecterns, and sound equipment. You also want to order a buffet style lunch and refreshments for two coffee breaks.

   Write to the reservation manager of the The Wild Goose Motel. Ask for the information you'll need to decide whether or not this motel will be a suitable place in which to hold your workshop.

2. Martha Lorenz, an alumna from your University, has written to your Academic Library to ask for a custom-made bibliography on the topic of reader-response criticism for a project that she is doing. You haven't got the staff time to prepare the bibliography that she wants. However, you can photocopy pertinent pages from the Modern Language Association *International Bibliography* and refer her to an excellent annotated bibliography in a book by Jane Tompkins called *Reader-Response Criticism: From Formalism to Post-Structuralism.*

3. Sajavit Rao, a longtime registered borrower at your public library, has written to complain of the treatment he received at the circulation desk when he tried to take out books. The circulation assistant had explained that he would be unable to charge out the books until he paid $15.00 in charges for fines and a lost book. Mr. Rao says that he refused to pay this $15.00 charge because he doesn't remember even taking out the so-called lost book. However, he's upset at what happened. He wants an apology and he also wants to be able to take out books in future without paying the charge. You are going to have to turn down his request, but you want to keep his goodwill as a longtime patron of the library. (For some help with what you might say, see Handling complaints, 6.3.3.)

FOR FURTHER HELP

9.3 to 9.5 Memos, letters, and reports

Blicq, Ron S. *Guidelines for Report Writing*. Scarborough, ON: Prentice-Hall Canada, 1982. Contains sections on the trip report, progress report, and investigative report.

Fielden, John S. and Ronald E. Dulek. *Bottom-Line Business Writing*. Englewood Cliffs, NJ: Prentice-Hall, 1983.

Lesikar, Raymond V. *Business Communication: Theory and Application*. 5th ed. Homewood, IL: Richard D. Irwin, 1984. Concrete examples illustrate the detailed discussion of how to write direct letters and indirect letters.

Lesikar, Raymond V. and Mary P. Lyons. *Report Writing for Business*. 7th ed. Homewood, IL: Richard D. Irwin, 1986.

Norton, Alice. "What Every Library Needs (and Why)—an Annual Report," in Kathleen Kelly Rummel and Esther Pericia, eds. *Persuasive Public Relations for Libraries*. Chicago: American Library Association, 1983.

Oliu, Walter E. et al. *Writing That Works: How to Write Effectively on the Job*. 2nd ed. New York: St. Martin's Press, 1984.

Paxson, William C. *Write It Now! A Timesaving Guide to Writing Better*. Reading, MA: Addison-Wesley, 1985. Section 2 called "How to Prepare Ten Typical Documents" discusses Major Reports, Trip Reports, and Progress Reports and provides very helpful model outlines which we have drawn upon here for our own discussion of such reports.

Wilkinson, C.W. et al. *Communicating Through Letters and Reports*. 8th ed. Homewood, IL: Richard D. Irwin, 1983.

9.6 Signs

Dreyfuss, Henry, ed. *Symbol Sourcebook: An Authoritative Guide to International Graphic Symbols*. New York: McGraw Hill, 1972. Dreyfuss has selected from a world data bank those symbols that give instructions, directions, or warnings.

Kepes, Gyorgy, ed. *Sign, Image, Symbol*. New York: George Brazaller, 1960. Twenty-two authors from different backgrounds (psychologist, designer, biologist, anthropologist, art historian, painter, philosopher, museum director) discuss signs and symbols. See especially the two contributions by Rudolph Modley and Henry Dreyfyus.

Mallery, Mary S. and David L. Perkins. *A Sign System for Libraries*. Chicago: American Library Association, 1982.

Modley, Rudolf assisted by William R. Myers. *Handbook of Pictorial Symbols: 3,250 Examples from International Sources*. New York: Dover Books, 1976. All but 250 of symbols are copyright free.

Pollet, Dorothy. "You Can Get There from Here," *Wilson Library Bulletin*, 50

(February 1976): 456-462. David Pesanelli, a Washington, DC consultant, answers Dorothy Pollet's questions on aspects of library signage.

Pollet, Dorothy and Peter C. Haskell, eds. *Sign Systems for Libraries: Solving the Wayfinding Problem.* London: R.R. Bowker, 1979. A collection of 20 articles by specialists on various aspects of signage. Includes a helpful annotated bibliography.

Reynolds, Linda and Stephen Barrett. *Signs and Guiding for Libraries.* London: Clive Bingley, 1981. A practical handbook covering the details of how to create an effective system of signs for libraries.

Spencer, Herbert and Linda Reynolds. *Directional Signing and Labelling in Libraries and Museums: A Review of Current Theory and Practice.* London: Royal College of Art: 1977. A good overview of research with suggestions for further reading.

Tinker, Miles A. *The Legibility of Print.* Ames, IA: Iowa State University Press, 1963. An excellent summary of research on the factors that make print legible: the kind of type used, type size, leading, line length, color of print and background.

9.7 Instructions

Carliner, Saul. "Lists: The Ultimate Organizer for Engineering Writing," *IEEE Transactions on Professional Communication,* PC-30, 4 (December 1987): 218-221. Presents guidelines for using lists when writing technical material. Distinguishes among numbered lists for items arranged in order, bulleted lists for items of equal importance, and checklists with boxes that readers check off.

Dobrin, David. "Do Not Grind Armadillo Armor in this Mill," *IEEE Transactions on Professional Communication,* PC-28, 4 (December 1985): 30-37. Uses J.R. Searle's Speech Act theory as a basis for arguing that written instructions should respect the reader's common sense.

Hartley, James. "Eighty Ways of Improving Instructional Text," *IEEE Transactions on Professional Communication,* PC-24, 1 (March 1981): 17-27. An excellent set of suggestions on three aspects of improving instructional texts: the written text, the graphics, and the layout and typography. Includes a bibliography of 80 items. For more detail, see James Hartley, *Designing Instructional Text.* 2nd ed. New York: Nichols Pub., 1985.

9.8 Policy and procedure manuals

For examples (some good and some not so good), look at the ARL Spec Kits. These are collections of actual policies and procedures from various libraries on a particular topic. Topics vary from copyright policies to collective bargaining, binding operations, and fees for service. For a list of topics, write to the Systems and Procedures Exchange Center, Office of Management Studies, Association of Research Libraries, 1527 New Hampshire Avenue N.W., Washington, DC 20036. The ALA will provide sample policy statements on request.

Harmon, Robert E. *Improving Administrative Manuals*. New York: Research and Information Service, American Management Association, 1982. An excellent introduction to policy, procedure and organization manuals.

Stueart, Robert D. and Barbara B. Moran. *Library Management*. 3rd ed. Littleton, CO: Libraries Unlimited, 1987. Provides examples of well-written policy and procedure manuals.

Travis, A.B. *The Handbook Handbook: The Complete How-to Guide to Publishing Policies and Procedures*. New York: R.R. Bowker, 1984. Includes many helpful hints and examples. Chapter 5, "Formatting Techniques," illustrates several different numbering systems.

9.9 Staff newsletters

Arth, Marvin and Helen Ashmore. *The Newsletter Editor's Desk Book*. 3rd ed. Shawnee Mission, KA: Parkway Press, 1984. Contains useful sections on headlines, formats, makeup, and production. Includes guidelines for writing some basic kinds of stories: personnel items, meetings, speeches, reports, notices, and controversies.

Beach, Mark. *Editing Your Newsletter: A Guide to Writing, Design, and Production*. 2nd ed. Portland, OR: Coast to Coast Books, 1982. An excellent guide. Contains 2 useful forms: "Newsletter Production Schedule" and "Newsletter Budget Form."

Levine, Mindy and Susan Frank. *In Print: A Concise Guide to Graphic Arts and Printing for Small Business and Nonprofit Organizations*. Englewood Cliffs, NJ: Prentice-Hall, 1984. Written for small businesses and nonprofit organizations, this concise book offer help on producing short items like brochures and advertisements.

Sutter, Jan. *Slinging Ink: A Practical Guide to Producing Booklets, Newspapers, and Ephemeral Publications*. Los Altos, CA: William Kaufmann, 1982. Offers tips on writing copy and doing layout for inexpensively produced newsletters.

White, Jan V. *Editing by Design: A Guide to Effective Word-and-Picture Communication for Editors and Designers*. 2nd ed. New York: R.R. Bowker, 1982. Full of excellent advice on layout and design.

Wales, LaRae H. *A Practical Guide to Newsletter Editing and Design*. 2nd ed. Ames, IA: Iowa State University Press, 1976. Takes the inexperienced editor through the stages of producing newsletters by either mimeographing or offset printing.

9.11 Booklists

Dixon, John, ed. *Fiction in Libraries*. London: The Library Association, 1986. Pages 174-177 deal with booklists, but the whole book is useful background on types of fiction material and the selection, organization and promotion of fiction in libraries.

9.13 Reviews

Haines, Helen E. *Living with Books: The Art of Book Selection.* 2nd ed. New York: Columbia University Press, 1950. Chapters 6 and 7 deal with reviewing and its place in book selection.

Kamerman, Sylvia, ed. *Book Reviewing: A Guide to Writing Book Reviews for Newspapers, Magazines, Radio and Television.* Boston: The Writer, Inc., 1978.

Meek, Margaret. "Questions of Response," *Signal,* 31 (January 1980): 29-35. A very perceptive reviewer of children's books discusses the questions that she asks about a children's book when she reads it for the first time.

Walford, A.J., ed. *Reviews and Reviewing: A Guide.* Phoenix, AZ: Oryx Press, 1986. A collection of essays aiming to "provide guidelines for the reviewing of books and audiovisual materials in a variety of disciplines." Contains a useful annotated bibliography on reviewing.

9.14 PR, publicity, and promotion

Baeckler, Virginia. *PR For Pennies.* Hopewell, NJ: Sources, 1978. Good tips on graphics, layout and printing.

Kohn, Rita and Krysta Tepper. *You Can Do It: A PR Skills Manual for Librarians.* Metuchen, NY: Scarecrow Press, 1981. Takes a workbook approach to the teaching of PR skills of all kinds.

Moran, Irene E. *The Library Public Relations Recipe Book.* Chicago: ALA, 1978. Includes guidelines for producing newsletters, PSA's, annual reports, etc.

Rummel, Kathleen Kelly and Esther Perica, eds. *Persuasive Public Relations for Libraries.* Chicago: ALA, 1983. A collection of articles on the aims of public relations, planning and marketing, promotional techniques, special resources, and staff training. See especially "A P.R. checklist for Project Coordinators" by Diana C. Proeschel (pp. 35-40) and the bibliography prepared by John D. Hales, Jr., organized by type of library (pp. 189-199). See also "Public service announcements" by Joan Erwin andj Sue Fontaine (pp. 134-145). This excellent article tells you how to write public service announcements on television and radio; how to use "canned" spots; how to work with the station; when to buy advertising.

Sherman, Steve. *ABC's of Library Promotion.* 2nd ed. Metuchen, NJ: Scarecrow Press, 1980. Contains chapters on designing publicity for newspapers and for radio and television.

9.15 Contributing to the professional literature

Alley, Brian and Jennifer Cargill. *Librarian in Search of a Publisher.* Phoenix, AZ: Oryx Press, 1986. Useful as a consciousness raiser to get librarians thinking about writing and publishing.

Chicago Manual of Style: for Authors, Editors, and Copywriters. 13th ed.

Chicago: University of Chicago Press, 1982. A basic guide emphasizing bibliographic form but covering many other aspects of preparing manuscripts.

Sellen, Betty-Carol. *Librarian/Author: A Practical Guide on How to Get Published*. New York: Neal-Schuman, 1985.

Skillin, Marjorie E. and R. Gay. *Words Into Type*. 3rd ed. Englewood Cliffs, NJ: Prentice-Hall, 1974. This guide for writers, editors, and publishers includes sections on preparing the manuscript, copy-editing, grammar, and the choice of words.

Stevens, Norman D. and Nora B. Stevens, eds. *Author's Guide to Journals in Library and Information Science*. New York: Haworth Press, 1981. Lists over 200 journals and contains an introduction on writing for publication.

9.16 Proposals

Boss, Richard. *Grant Money and How to Get It: A Handbook for Librarians*. New York: R.R. Bowker, 1980.

Corry, Emmett. *Grants for Libraries: A Guide to Public and Private Funding Programs and Proposal Writing Techniques*. 2nd ed. Littleton, CO: Libraries Unlimited, 1982.

Hall, Mary. *Developing Skills in Proposal Writing*. 2nd ed. Portland, OR: Continuing Education Publications, 1977. A practical and thorough guide containing useful models and examples. Contains an excellent 13-page "Proposal Development Checklist."

Killingsworth, M. Jimmie. "A Bibliography on Proposal Writing," *IEEE Transactions on Professional Communication*, PC-26, 2 (June 1983): 79-83. An annotated bibliography of 80 selected books and articles on writing proposals.

Powell, Ronald R. "Writing the Research Proposal" in *Basic Research Methods for Librarians*. Norwood, NJ: Ablex, 1985.

10 TRAINING OTHERS

Allen E. Ivey, who developed the microcounseling model for interpersonal skills training, identified four levels of skill mastery: 1) identification, where the learner can recognize both the skill and its effect; 2) basic mastery, where the learner is able to use the skill in a training setting; 3) active mastery, where the learner is able to use the skill on the job, and 4) teaching mastery, where the learner is able to teach the skill to others. This chapter is for those who have reached the fourth level and are beginning to train others. How you use this book as a training resource depends on the type of training program you're planning, the needs of participants, and your own level of expertise as a trainer.

10.1 HOW TO USE THIS BOOK FOR TRAINING

What do we mean by the term training? Although the terms training and education are sometimes used interchangeably, education usually refers to a more broadly based process that includes general principles; training is more narrowly focused on specific skills appropriate for a particular situation or a particular job. The teaching of communication skills is appropriate at all stages of the education/training spectrum: preprofessional education; continuing education; inservice training; conferences and workshops; and informal learning opportunities that occur on the job. We cannot assume that most people naturally pick up these skills on their own without a systematic program, any more than we would assume that most people naturally pick up how to play the piano. Library schools and paraprofessional programs should certainly teach communication skills as part of the preparation for library and information work. But since learning is a lifelong process, practitioners on the job will also benefit from opportunities to update or enhance their basic education.

How do you know when people need training in communication skills? In the area of continuing education, the need for training in communication skills often appears as an interest in conference sessions on, for example, "Handling problem patrons" or "How to present your budget." In libraries and information centers, training needs often arise as a result of changes, small or large—for example, the arrival of a new staff member, the introduction of a new telephone system, or major organizational change such as the

DID YOU KNOW?

Researchers have discovered the following about how people learn:

1. People learn when they are ready to learn.
2. Learning is active, not passive.
3. Learning occurs through trial and error and through association.
4. Learning is multisensory.
5. People usually learn one thing at a time.
6. Learning occurs from practice.
7. Positive feedback is necessary for learning.
8. The rate of forgetting tends to be rapid immediately after learning.

(Selected and adapted from Sheila D. Creth's *Effective On-the-Job Training*, pp. 14-15.)

development of a new public service or the restructuring of the lines of authority. Sometimes inservice training programs are designed in response to problems such as complaints from the public or evidence of poor staff morale. In fact, the first clue to unmet training needs is usually a gap between expected and actual performance of an employee.

For all of these settings, the first step in training is to *assess the need* for training. Before launching into a training program to resolve some problem, you should ask, Is this problem really one that can be solved with training or is it some other kind of problem altogether? If training is needed, you should strive to understand how the need arose, how your staff or students perceive the need, and how training can help meet it. Wherever possible, trainees should be fully involved in the needs assessment and planning process. The next steps in planning training are:

—identification of the focus: the skills that should be taught
—selection of appropriate training methods
—development of the training programs or formats
—development of the means of evaluation of the success of the training.

These steps are not described in detail here because there are already many excellent publications on the training process. Anyone involved at any level in planning staff training programs should certainly consult the *Public Library Development Program Manual for Trainers*. Written by Peggy O'Donnell for public libraries, it is applicable in many more settings and contains checklists, case studies, and workforms in addition to much wise advice. The rest of this chapter focuses instead on how to use *Communicating Professionally* as a training resource.

If you are experienced trainers looking for new approaches, exercises, or suggestions for reading, you will already know how best to incorporate the ideas in this book into your own programs. Some of you will be planning training sessions for the first time and may be looking for a recipe. We have no magic answers or guaranteed formats for training, but there's no reason why you can't begin simply by reading this book and using selected sections almost verbatim with your trainees. The one proviso is that you practice active listening and solicit feedback so that you can adapt these materials to the needs of your participants. Some other suggestions:

1. Ask trainees to read and discuss specific sections. The discussion might include sharing opinions about the applicability of specific skills to the job or ways for adapting these skills to unique situations that arise in your library. Use the tips provided in Sections 7.4 and 7.5 on discussion techniques in order to generate a productive exchange of ideas and reactions. You can use this approach in the classroom or in regular staff meetings when the last half hour is reserved for discussion.

2. Follow the procedure for teaching one microskill at a time. For a more formal training program, select the microskills that will be most useful to your trainees. Follow the sequence that occurs within each section on individual skills: explanation of the skill and how it functions; recognition of examples; demonstration through exercises; and practice with suggestions for followup. Use the applications chapters (6 through 9) to provide examples and exercises.

3. Or begin with problem situations. Sometimes, it's more appropriate to begin with a discussion of the situation that has generated communication problems (for example, the reference interview, book talks, or dealing with awkward customers) and then proceed to teaching single skills that will help trainees deal with these situations. Use the applications sections of this book (Chapters 6 through 9) as an outline that you can expand by introducing individual skills from Chapters 1 through 4 at the appropriate points.

4. Teach at the point of need. Sometimes an impromptu training session can help to resolve an employee's communication accident. It takes only a few minutes to teach a skill such as acknowledgment by following the microskills principle: describe the skill and its function; give an example; model the skill; ask the trainee to demonstrate it; and then ask the trainee to use it on the job and let you know what happened.

5. Train for improved performance. Individual training sessions can also be useful after performance evaluations. You may have used the DESC technique to let the employee know that some of her communication skills need improvement, let's say attentiveness to library users. But people find it easier to accept requests for improvement if they have some concrete idea of how to bring about the improvement. Therefore it may help the employee to work through the sections of this book on acknowledgment or eye contact, sections that provide manageable steps for changing the dysfunctional behavior.

6. Use this book to heighten awareness. Orientation of new employees provides another opportunity for individual or group

training in communication skills. Some sections of this book—the reference interview, writing reports, and handling complaints—may be especially useful in sensitizing new employees to the range of situations that they'll encounter on the job and to help them understand that it's not only necessary but also possible to achieve high standards of personal performance. An important message for employees is that there are many ways to interact with others, that some ways tend to be more effective than others, and that skills training provides more opportunities for choosing effective ways of working with others.

10.2 TEACHING ADULTS

Adults learn differently from the way in which children learn. Therefore staff trainers and college faculty should know something about andragogy, the study of how adults learn. Andragogy takes into account the learner's maturity and how life experience affects learning patterns. Adults learn best when they are involved in planning, implementing, and evaluating their own learning experiences. Bringing a wealth of complex experiences, attitudes, and beliefs to the learning process, adults can readily see when training programs are irrelevant or inappropriate to their needs. They want to be able to apply what they have learned immediately. Dugan Laird summarizes characteristics of learning situations that suit the way adults learn.

—they are problem-centered rather than content-centered
—they permit and encourage the learner's active participation
—they encourage the learner to introduce past experiences as a way of reexamining that experience
—they foster a collaborative learning climate rather than one that is based on authority
—they emphasize experiential activities
—planning is a mutual activity between learner and instructor
—evaluation is a mutual activity between learner and instructor
—evaluation is a way of identifying new learning needs and interests

Dugan Laird, *Approaches to Training and Development.*

SOME QUICK TIPS FOR PLANNING TRAINING PROGRAMS

Use checklists to make sure everything runs smoothly. For extensive programs, you should have separate checklists for budget, arrangements for equipment and accommodation, resource people, materials, and other things you need to keep track of.

Use training handouts, demonstration tapes, and transparencies of high quality. Materials should not look home-made (see 8.6.6). Prepare the materials well in advance.

Keep your training materials in a loose-leaf binder, with lots of divider tabs separating the different sections: objectives, agendas, audiovisual aids, notes, handouts, and the list of participants. The file helps you to know where everything is.

10.3 PLANNING THE TRAINING PROGRAM

10.3.1 Setting training objectives

To ensure that your training program is systematic and not hit-and-miss, you will want to set objectives. Your objectives should be:

—concrete
—realistic
—time bound
—measurable

Some examples of manageable program objectives for communication skills training are:

To conduct a two-hour orientation session for each new staff member in the circulation department within that person's first month of service.

To provide each permanent staff member on the information desk with three hours of continuing education annually.

To conduct a session on telephone answering procedures for switchboard staff before a fixed date.

Then, for each program, write specific learning objectives. An example:

By the end of this program on effective questioning, participants will be able to:

1. Recognize the difference between an open and closed question.
2. Demonstrate use of open questions in a role-played interview.
3. Use open questions on the job.
4. Teach another staff member how to use open questions.

For the example above, you might be able to measure the extent to which the objectives were met through an exercise, through observation, or through self-report. Although objectives should be measurable, it is more important for them to be specific and realistic. In *The Training Wheel*, Rogoff points out that training designed to teach skills should be based on explicit, measurable objectives, but that training designed to change attitudes or improve motivation should not be objective-based.

10.3.2 Formats for training

Training should vary in format, according to the needs of participants and according to program objectives. Even within one session, you can use several training formats. You might want to start with a short lecture to explain a skill, go on to role-playing and or a demonstration, follow with a group discussion, and finally recommend some reading for independent study. Such variation in format provides a change of pace for participants and is compatible with training objectives. The lecture on its own doesn't usually work very well for teaching people new communication skills. Consider alternatives to the lecture. For two excellent summaries of the major formats for training, see Peggy O'Donnell's *Public Library Development Program Manual for Trainers* and "What Methods Shall We Use?"—Chapter 10 in Dugan Laird's *Approaches to Training and Development*. Some examples of formats are:

—lectures or mini-lectures
—demonstrations, modeling
—role-plays
—simulation exercises
—field trips
—programmed instruction
—panel discussions
—small group discussions
—case studies
—group exercises such as fishbowls, buzz groups, games
—readings

10.3.3 Checklists for planning and other aids

Sections 8.6 and 8.7 provide an overview of planning principles and procedures that are basic to all presentations, including training programs. When you're the trainer, it is all the more important to demonstrate your skill at program planning and implementation, because trainees are learning from your performance, good or bad.

10.4 USING THE MICROSKILLS TRAINING MODEL

The best introduction for trainers to the microskills teaching model is provided by Chapter 12 of Ivey's *Intentional Interviewing and Counseling*. This chapter is specifically directed to new trainers. It includes a section on the basic teaching model and specific suggestions on the teaching of interviewing skills. We highly recommend that you read this book!

The microskills hierarchy, illustrated in section 6.2.3, consists of a series of single skills that are progressively more complex, beginning with the basic listening sequence and moving towards the most difficult part of training and learning: skill integration. With the exception of teaching skill integration, a cardinal rule in microteaching is to *teach one skill at a time*. Although good and bad examples of other skills may occur during the training session, focus only on the skill being taught.

For each of these single skills, the basic microskills teaching model involves five steps: definition, recognition, reading, practice, and feedback. You have probably noticed that, for the most part, Chapters 1 through 4 of this book work through these same five steps in the presentation of the speaking and writing skills needed in library settings.

Here are the five steps that you can use in your own training sessions for teaching microskills.

1. Warmup and definition of the skill. Discuss the value of the skill with examples of library situations in which it could be used, define the skill, and explain how it functions.
2. Recognition: examples and modeling. Ivey recommends video, audio, or live demonstrations of the skill. The modeling might involve two trainers role-playing the skill. Alternately, you could ask two volunteers to read the transcript of a conversation between a librarian and a user, following which other trainees identify the skill modeled and discuss its effect. Anoth-

er suggestion is to make a pair of prepared tapes or transcripts in which the first example is an exaggerated model of the failure to use the skill well and the second example involves a clearly effective use of the skill. Model only one skill at a time.

3. Reading. Ask trainees to read the relevant sections in this book or some other reading that summarizes and provides examples of the skill. Putting relevant readings on handouts to be read either before or after the training session can be effective (see section 9.1). The handouts give the trainee time to think about the skill and work as aids to the memory.

4. Practice. The key component in microskills training is practice—the "do" part of "Learn, do, and teach." Trainees should be given an opportunity to demonstrate use of the skill in the training session through supervised exercises or role-plays. (The acknowledgment exercise in Chapter 3.2 is a good example of role-plays used to provide supervised practice.)

5. Self-assessment, feedback and generalization. Using the tips for practice (5.5), encourage trainees to practice one skill outside the training session, preferably on the job. Trainees can demonstrate mastery through practice in teaching the skill to someone else. Group discussion or exercises will help the trainee assess the level to which the skill has been mastered. Feedback of what worked and what didn't will help you assess the need for further training.

10.5 MODELING GOOD BEHAVIOR

One way in which trainees learn communication skills is by watching the trainer's behavior and consciously or unconsciously imitating it. Therefore the trainer must model the effective use of communication skills in a consistent, intentional, and spontaneous way. Trainees notice how the trainer talks, moves, looks, and behaves in informal contacts as well as in formal training sessions. If there is a discrepancy between the way the trainer communicates and the way the skills are taught ("Do as I say, not as I do"), a credibility gap occurs. This incongruity reduces the trainees' confidence in the training sessions and affects their ability to integrate the skills into their own behavior.

QUICK TIPS FOR MODELING GOOD BEHAVIOR

Examine your own communication behavior. How well are you able to integrate the skills that you are teaching into your communication with trainees? When you're having lunch with trainees, how does your communication behavior differ from when you're leading a session? How often do you use open questions in small talk?

Consciously practice your skills, especially those skills that are hardest or newest for you. You can overcome your own awkwardness by making this explicit: "Now I'm going to ask an open question!" Don't be afraid of communication accidents, but do let trainees see your efforts to repair them: "I just interrupted you, which means I wasn't listening—exactly what I said not to do—so tell me again."

Ask your colleagues for feedback. Other trainers can practice giving feedback by telling you how you're doing. The structured criticism exercise (8.10) is a good way to learn from each other. Make sure you get positive feedback as well as negative feedback.

CHECKLIST FOR TRAINERS: MODELING NONVERBAL SKILLS

What is my *posture* saying to trainees? Am I showing interest and encouragement? Or am I showing boredom or irritation? Do my crossed arms indicate resistance to what trainees are telling me? Am I controlling my nervous gestures?

What are my good (or bad) *speech habits*? Can people hear me? Am I speaking slowly (or quickly) enough? When I give instructions, do I make my voice stronger and lean forward?

Do I periodically make *eye contact* with everyone in my group? How often do I catch myself talking to the floor or the blackboard?

Am I considering *cultural differences* between myself and my trainees and taking these differences into account?

CHECKLIST FOR TRAINERS: MODELING SPEAKING SKILLS

How often am I using *open questions* to encourage trainees to talk? For example: "What problems do you think you might have in using this skill?" NOT, "Do you think you might have problems with this?"

When I want to structure discussion around situations, how often am I asking *neutral questions*? For example: "Tell me what happened when you practiced this skill" NOT, "Did you have trouble practicing this skill?"

How well am I *giving instructions*? Do I give explicit instructions and check to make sure they're understood? For example: "Turn to the person beside you and describe one recent situation in which you had trouble understanding a user. . . . Now, just so the exercise is clear, tell me what you are going to do." NOT, "In pairs, discuss typical problems of this type."

What *communication accidents* am I having? How often do I interrupt trainees unnecessarily? What assumptions am I making about trainees? What am I doing (or not doing) when trainees misunderstand something?

To what extent do I *reflect content* or paraphrase trainee's remarks? When a trainee says, "I wrote a report about online services," am I showing my attentiveness by repeating some of these words?

How accurately am I *reflecting feeling?* When a trainee says, "I don't think I'm ever going to be able to do this," how do I respond? "You feel it's going to be hard to change your behavior" or "Nonsense, everyone can learn this."

How well do I *model feedback?* Am I asking for feedback regularly? Am I listening actively to verbal and nonverbal feedback? How helpful is the feedback I'm getting? What am I doing about it?

**CHECKLIST FOR TRAINERS:
MODELING WRITING SKILLS**

When do I communicate with my trainees in writing? Is the written communication necessary? Would personal contact be more effective? Do I use a written description of the training program to supplement the personal contact?

How effective are my training materials—handouts, reading lists, and transparencies? Am I trying to cram too much on one page? Is the type easy to read? Are key concepts highlighted? Are my transparencies readable from every seat in the room, not just from the front row?

When I send a memo or letter to trainees, is it clear? Brief? Written in a style appropriate to the situation and the reader?

How good are my written instructions? Are they clear? Are the sentences short and simple? Are the instructions put in a logical order and numbered?

What spelling, grammar, or punctuation errors do I need to guard against? Am I proofreading my written material carefully?

10.6 USING TAPES FOR TRAINING

10.6.1 Making the tapes

An essential feature of microskills training is the opportunity for trainees to observe and evaluate their own behavior. In order to provide a record of this behavior that is both objective (not just based on self-reports) and durable (so the trainee can use it at leisure), trainees often find it useful to make audiotapes or videotapes of themselves role-playing a skill or reacting to a simulated situation. The exercise of making a tape should be productive and not endanger the trainee's self-esteem and motivation. You can avoid some common pitfalls by following these basic procedures.

1. Respect the privacy and integrity of the trainee.

   Communicate the purpose and value of taping clearly to each individual trainee and to the library administration. State the

QUICK TIPS FOR MAKING AUDIOTAPES

Use a neck or lapel microphone so that the trainee doesn't have to worry about speaking into the unit microphone built in to the recorder. In fact, with a neck mike, you can shove the recorder into a drawer or under the table to reduce its obtrusiveness.

Teach trainees to test the recorder and identify tapes before they actually start recording. Test the volume and clarity by recording and playing back an identification statement such as, "This is the role-play for XPL training program, November 24, 1991." This also ensures that the first part of the role-play is in fact recorded, not spoken before the magnetic part of the tape begins to wind.

Always have extra blank tapes on hand, as well as an extension cord and batteries.

Label the tape to identify the content and date.

ways in which the tape will *not* be used. Trainees often are afraid that tapes provide evidence for performance appraisal.

Taping must be voluntary. No one should be forced to tape or be taped. Those not wanting to be taped should not be required to give a reason or be treated differently in any way. Provide an alternate activity.

Instruct trainees who are taping their interviews with others—friends, family, or other trainees—always to ask for permission. The simple question "Do you mind if I tape this?" or "Are you willing to be taped?" is sufficient but must always be asked.

Never tape real library users or staff members without written permission from the library administration and formal consent, preferably written, from those who are to be taped.

Tell trainees that they have the right to request erasure of all or part of their tape at any time. If they do ask for erasure, erase the tape in view of the trainee.

Specify in advance the uses—both present and future—to be made of the tapes. Within the training group, provide assurance that no one other than the trainee will hear or see the tape without the trainee's permission. The trainee should be in control of playing the tape and selecting the portions to be played. "Would you mind playing your tape for us?" should always be asked, and trainees must feel free to refuse if they wish. State clearly who owns the tape and what will happen to it after training—a good rule of thumb is to give ownership to the person taped and to arrange to erase all tapes after the course.

2. Ensure effective technical production. If possible, enlist the aid of an audiovisual technician who is not part of the training program. If you want your trainees to learn how to operate the equipment, separate the two goals of learning communication skills and learning how to operate equipment. Provide a brief training session or instructions for operating the equipment, followed by a rehearsal that focuses on learning how to set up the room, run the recorder, and so on. Each trainee should participate in the rehearsal. A good exercise that serves two purposes is to have trainees practice giving instructions by writing up an instruction sheet for the recording equipment.

Ensure that the equipment is in good working order and available when needed. Have equipment checked after every use.

Provide a comfortable, secure, and private room for the taping.

Demonstrate the equipment in advance.

Provide a foolproof instruction sheet.

10.6.2 Working with tapes

Trainees are often anxious about working with their own tapes and they almost always need guidance in using the tapes effectively to improve their performance. Here are some suggestions.

Before the tapes are made, you've explained the purpose of taping. Restate the purpose and then specify the immediate use of the tapes.

Say, for example, "your tape is your own property. We're going to ask you to listen to it privately and then fill out a checklist (or whatever the task is). Bring the tape with you to the next session and we will ask for volunteers to share the tapes with the group; if you don't want others to hear your tape, that's OK."

Tell trainees what to expect when they first see or hear themselves on tape. Trainees are often initially alarmed by their appearance or sound of their voice and the trainer must take time to overcome this reaction.

Say, for example, "when you first listen to yourself, you might think, 'Hey, that can't be me. How awful! I sound weird (childish, gruff).' This is a normal reaction. Just listen to the tape all the way through and then play it again. The second time around, you'll start hearing or seeing the things you do well and you'll be able to analyze the tape more objectively. So even if you're horrified at first, promise that you'll play it at least one more time. The more you play it, the more you'll get out of it."

In individual or group feedback, focus on what the trainee is doing well, not on what they're doing poorly or not doing. Reinforce the positive; the negative is all too apparent to the trainee and to others. When a tape is made as an exercise in a particular skill, comment only on that skill, not on other skills or behaviors no matter how good, interesting, or unusual they are. Use closure (3.10) to discourage discussion that doesn't focus on the particular exercise.

Focus on behavioral units, not on personality or on general impressions. Help participants look for the smallest, most concrete evidence of skills. Model good feedback behavior (see 3.14) and teach the trainees how to give good feedback to each other.

TIPS FOR DISCUSSING BEHAVIOR ON THE TAPES
Say
What helpful questions did the librarian ask? What questions did not seem to help? What did the user do or say that communicates his feelings about the service?

She had no eye contact with the user.

She asked four open questions.

The user did not answer his question and went away without saying if the book was useful.

What could you have done to get more information?

Instead of saying
How would you rate that interview?

She doesn't look interested.

She found out what he wanted to know immediately.

He didn't get much information.

You shouldn't have asked an open question there.

Reduce trainees' anxiety. Some trainees are visibly anxious about their performance as seen or heard on tape. Even those who seem quite confident, motivated to learn, and objective may be inwardly anxious. Do some general discussion and problem-solving as the need occurs. Encourage trainees to express their fears, no matter how trivial. Ask, "What is your worst fear about this taping?" Then listen, and take anxieties seriously. Don't say, "Oh, nonsense, you'll love it." Because taping involves risk-taking on the part of the trainees, and because the methodology is somewhat intrusive, you need to be especially careful. Build trust by focusing on positive, not negative, performance.

THINGS TO TELL TRAINEES TO REDUCE ANXIETY
1. Nothing that happens inside this room is going outside. Peter, our audiovisual technician, is sworn to secrecy. [Make sure he is!]
2. We'd like you to try to tape yourself because it's a proven training technique and we know you will learn something from it. But if you don't want to do it, you don't have to. And you don't even have to give a reason.
3. Listening to (viewing) yourself the first time is always a shock. Promise to listen (view) at least twice.
4. The technical quality of this tape isn't important. This isn't the Barbara Walters Show. What is important is what you can see (hear) about yourself.
5. This is your tape, and you get to say how we can use it. If you want to erase it, you can.
6. If you think the taping didn't work out, do it again.
7. Take a dry run through your interview to make sure the equipment is working and you're not distracted by it.
8. Sometimes we can learn more from looking at mistakes than by looking at a perfectly executed interview.
9. Wear clothes that you like. It's not necessary to get dressed up, but be comfortable.

10.7 WHEN TRAINEES ARE RESISTANT

If everyone in your training group is enthusiastic, open, and happy to be there, you are unusually lucky. This ideal scenario hardly ever happens: people are often required to go to training sessions against their own desires; it may turn out that the training session is being held on a day when they'd rather be doing something else; some people are skeptical about the effectiveness of any kind of training. In a required credit course on communication skills, there are usually some students who are reluctant or even openly hostile.

Some typical comments from trainees with misgivings are:

This will never work. We're far too busy to smile at everybody.

You can't learn these skills. You're either born a good communicator or you're not.

I feel silly doing this stuff. If I go, "Uh-huh" or "You seem frustrated," people will really wonder about me.

Aren't you trying to change people's personalities by teaching these skills?

I know all this. I took psychology.

I have been doing all these things for years anyway.

Are we librarians or social workers?

Be prepared to deal with this resistance. Here are some suggestions:

Consider the extent to which these remarks are expressions of real concerns. If staff are indeed overworked in unsatisfactory conditions, smiling at every user can't be a priority and may indeed seem ridiculous, even to the user.

Acknowledge the legitimacy of trainees' comments. Then ask for a chance to provide a different perspective. For example: "You're right. Some people seem to be naturally good communicators. But we have pretty good evidence that the rest of us can improve our skills, so could you reserve your judgment until the end of the session? Let's see what we can do here."

Show that you have attended to their anxieties by reflecting feelings: "Many people feel awkward using this skill for the first time" or "I understand your concern that these skills could be manipulative."

Handle the "know-it-all" according to the procedures outlined in section 7.5.2. Acknowledge that this person may have been a perfect communicator for years, but suggest that everyone can learn something new. Asking this person to share his or her expertise with the group sometimes works; but it can backfire when the know-it-all is also a monopoliser.

The "librarian/social worker" argument appears in every training session sooner or later. An answer along these lines seems to satisfy concerns:

It's true that social workers get training in basic communication skills to do their jobs as counselors. But other helping professions need some of these same skills, such as listening accurately and asking productive questions. That doesn't make us all into social workers. The skills are much the same, but the applications are different. We're not trained as counselors or therapists, and nobody is suggesting that we perform those functions.

Don't ignore resistance: failure to deal with it promptly will make the group less productive. With a group of people who know each other fairly well and have come to trust you as a leader, you may be able to deal together with the problem by using the skill of confrontation.

When trainees become hostile in a training session, Ivey advises responding without defensiveness: "That's an interesting point" and not attempting to persuade or argue but looking away from the resistant trainee towards the rest of the group. Do not make eye contact with persistent critics. You might invite the critic to discuss the problem with you privately after the session.

Group anxieties and resistance are reduced as you, the trainer, develop a reputation for fairness, nonjudgmental behavior, and what psychologists call unconditional positive regard. This means that you like your trainees anyway, no matter what they do or don't do. If you don't like and respect your trainees, don't train. Outside the group, never discuss a trainee's performance with other trainees, their supervisors, or anyone else.

10.8 EVALUATION AND FOLLOWUP

When we first began to give our workshops on interview skills, the director of a large public library asked us: "How do we know that our staff have learned anything from your workshop?" At that time, we were using a brief evaluation form that asked participants to rate the workshop as excellent, good, fair, or poor on two dimensions: content and presentation. We pointed out that the workshop had been highly rated. "That's all very well," said the director, "but we still don't know if they learned anything or if they're doing a better job as a result of the workshop." Of course he was absolutely right. From an administrative viewpoint, performance changes as a result of training are a prime concern.

10.8.1 Evaluation

Until recently, little attention has been paid to developing practical methods of evaluating the outcome of training for library workers. Recently, however, several good guides have appeared, and we refer you directly to these for detailed accounts of evaluation methods and tools.

Some basic ideas are summarized here.

What's the difference between measurement and evaluation? Measurement is the process of gathering data; evaluation is the process of making judgments about those data. It's not necessary to measure in order to evaluate, but measurement provides concrete evidence (usually in the form of numbers) to reduce disagreement about judgments and to enable pretraining and posttraining comparisons. (See Laird's *Approaches to Training and Development,* pp. 241-243.)

What do you want to measure or evaluate: Knowledge? Skills? Ability? Job performance? Attitudes? Beliefs? Are you measuring change or are you assessing the extent to which training objectives have been met? Be clear about your goal. A trainee who fills out a form and says she is highly satisfied with a workshop may or may not have changed in any fundamental respect. The Library Association's pamphlet *The Evaluation of Staff Training* provides a clear guide to five different levels of evaluation: reactions, learning, job behavior, organizational value, and ultimate value.

What are the methods of measuring? Depending on what you want to evaluate, there are usually two basic methods of measuring: observation and questioning. Direct observation techniques include activity sampling and watching a trainee's performance at specified times. Indirect observation techniques include self-reports, usually through a diary kept by the trainee or through a record of events related to the employee's behavior such as the number of complaints about an employee or the number of revisions required in the employee's written work. Questioning includes questionnaires completed by the trainee and interviews either with the trainee or with people who observe the trainee's behavior, including library users. Numerous sample questionnaires, logs, and interview schedules are reproduced in the books by Conyers and O'Donnell.

Why evaluate? Evaluation benefits the trainer, the trainee, and, in the case of inservice training, the library administration. Evaluation helps to place in context the training program as a long-term rather than a hit-and-miss project. For a successful evaluation, it is important for the trainee to have a full understanding of the

QUICK TIPS FOR FOLLOWUP

Explain to trainees the importance of practicing immediately.

Ask trainees to report on results of practicing the new skills and to collect specific examples of their efforts.

Encourage trainees to share these examples with the group at a followup session or clinic.

Make handouts that trainees can tape to their desks to remind themselves to practice.

Provide time in staff meetings or subsequent training sessions to review the skills previously learned.

Announce followup clinics at the three-week, eight-week, and six-month point. Review skills, analyze examples, and set new objectives.

Distribute evaluation forms after trainees have had a chance to practice their skills, not at the training session itself.

Encourage trainees to teach others. Create opportunities for practice teaching of one skill to two or three other people.

Be available for problem-solving and trouble-shooting and to reinforce successful practice attempts.

Route relevant articles, clippings, or reports to trainees. You might, for example, circulate a news photo that illustrates bad or good nonverbal behavior.

reasons for evaluation and to participate fully in designing and implementing the evaluation process.

10.8.2 Followup

The evaluation process may be conducted immediately after training or at later intervals. Because most evaluation of skills training occurs immediately after training, usually without any measurement of pretraining or baseline performance levels, we know very little about the longterm effects of training. Research into the effects of training counselors suggests that training effects are very short-lived—that skills can be lost within 24 hours of the training session—but that trainees are more likely to maintain their new skills if they are able to integrate these skills immediately into their everyday communication behavior. What this means is that the trainer must help trainees follow up on their training experience.

10.9 WHERE TO GET HELP

Help in planning and carrying out the training program is available from many sources. We have found the following types of sources particularly helpful:

Barbara Conroy's *Library Staff Development and Continuing Education* (Littleton, CO: Libraries Unlimited, 1978) is an example of a good basic guide to articles, books, and organizations. Other resource lists and bibliographies on training are constantly appearing.

ALA's Clenexchange (Continuing Library Education Network and Exchange Round Table) puts you in touch with other trainers and issues a newsletter full of practical advice, reviews and short articles that are well worth the membership fee. Smaller library associations sometimes have special interest groups, such as the Staff Training and Development Guild of the Ontario Library Association.

Many library association newsletters and journals have regular columns devoted to library education and staff development. See, for example, the Continuing Education column in the *Journal of the Association for Library and Information Science Education*, and "Keep on Learning," which appears regularly in *Public Libraries*.

Monitor specialized periodicals that focus on certain aspects of interpersonal communication. For example, the *Journal of Business Communication* is geared largely to the business community but almost always has articles about new techniques for training people to write and speak more effectively.

Local organizations that focus on training are often helpful. In your community there may be an association of personnel managers or a council of continuing education agencies. They can help you a great deal, even if (or maybe because) they're not library oriented.

Watch for noncredit courses in leadership skills, group dynamics, public speaking and other communication topics. Take the course yourself, or, if the leader has a good reputation, recommend it to others. For college and university instructors, programs for improving teaching techniques are sometimes offered. Colleges of education often have good resource people.

Finally, and perhaps most important, get help from the people you work with, including other trainers, administrators, staff, and students. Solicit their ideas and feedback. And listen!

FOR FURTHER HELP

Casteleyn, Mary. *Planning Library Training Programmes*. London: Andre Deutsch, 1981. Includes procedures for planning inservice training, field placement supervision, and continuing education. Also provides useful outlines of programs for paraprofessionals.

Conyers, A. *Guidelines for Training in Libraries*. 2nd ed. Volume 2: *The Evaluation of Staff Training*. London: The Library Association, 1986. An excellent, detailed approach. Provides examples of evaluation instruments.

Creth, Sheila D. *Effective On-the-Job Training*. Chicago: American Library Association, 1986. Deals with the following topics: training objectives (knowledge, skill, attitudes); overcoming resistance to training; learning principles; and public service attitudes. Provides good, practical examples.

Ivey, Allen E. *Intentional Interviewing and Counseling*. Monterey, CA: Brooks/Cole, 1983. See Chapter 12 on Teaching Interviewing Skills. You can also write to Microtraining Associates, Box 641, North Amherst, MA 01059 and ask to receive notification of microtraining materials, including handbooks and videotapes. Most of these materials are geared to counselors, but some are sufficiently general to be used with librarians.

Jennerich, E.Z. and Jennerich, E.J. *The Reference Interview as a Creative Art*. Littleton, CO: Libraries Unlimited, 1987. The authors offer training tips and practical checklists.

Knowles, Malcolm S. *The Modern Practice of Adult Education: From Andragogy to Pedagogy.* Revised 2nd ed. New York: Cambridge Book Co., 1980. A classic, fairly scholarly work for background reading.

Knowles, Malcolm S. *The Adult Learner: A Neglected Species.* 3rd ed. Houston: Gulf Publishing, 1984.

Larson, Dale. "Giving Psychology Away: The Skills Training Paradigm" in *Teaching Psychological Skills*, edited by Dale Larson. Monterey, CA: Brooks/Cole, 1984, pp. 1-14.

Laird, Dugan. *Approaches to Training and Development.* 2nd ed. Reading, MA: Addison-Wesley, 1985. A wonderful resource book for the trainer, with clear explanations of the relationship between learning theory and training practice. Includes practical sections on the training environment, training formats, and audiovisual aids.

Library Video Network. *On the Job Training: You've Been Doing It All Along.* Baltimore, MD, 1987. VHS, Beta, 3/4" formats. 21 minutes. Distributed by ALA Video, Chicago. This excellent video shows you how to give instructions on a one-to-one basis.

McLaughlin, W. Keith and Evelyn Piush. "Planning Checklist for Seminars or Workshops," *Canadian Library Journal*, 37, 3 (June 1980): 175-177. A real checklist that you can use with minor modifications.

O'Donnell, Peggy. *Public Library Development Program Manual for Trainers.* Chicago and London: American Library Association, 1988. An excellent planning tool with checklists, exercises and training materials that you can duplicate. A must for public library trainers.

Prytherch, Ray. *Handbook of Library Training Practice.* Aldershot, Hampshire and Brookfield, VT: Gower Publishing, 1986. An excellent guide to inservice training. See especially Casteleyn's section on evaluating training (pp. 90-128) and Jordan's practical tips for training staff to interact with library users (pp. 167-190).

Renner, Peter Franz. *The Instructor's Survival Kit: A Handbook for Teachers of Adults.* 2nd ed. Vancouver, BC: Training Associates, 2665 West 42nd Street, Vancouver BC, Canada V6N 3G4. 1983. Describes a variety of learning techniques and gives practical hints on audiovisual aids. Focuses on teaching planning and interpersonal skills.

Rogoff, Rosalind. *The Training Wheel: A Simple Model for Instructional Design.* New York: John Wiley, 1987. This book expands on an article in the April 1984 issue of *Training magazine.* Chapter 5 is a plain language guide to setting and evaluating goals and objectives.

Simerly, Robert G. and Associates. *Strategic Planning and Leadership in Continuing Education.* San Francisco: Jossey-Bass, 1987. Gives the big picture; not a handbook.

Spaid, Ora. *The Consummate Trainer.* Englewood Cliffs, NJ: Prentice-Hall, 1986. An introduction to the theory and practice of adult learning that deals with designing, developing, and delivering training.

Warncke, Ruth. *Planning Library Workshops and Institutes.* Chicago: American Library Association, 1976. A classic guide.

Feedback

We'd like to know how this book has helped you.

What specific ideas or tips have you used? How did they work? What didn't work for you? What suggestions do you have for the next edition of this book? Do you have new material that you'd like to see included?

Please drop us a note:

Catherine Ross or Patricia Dewdney
School of Library and Information Science
University of Western Ontario
London, Ontario, Canada N6G 1Hl

We promise to answer every letter!

BIBLIOGRAPHY

Alley, Brian and Jennifer Cargill. *Librarian in Search of a Publisher: How to Get Published*. Phoenix, AZ: Oryx Press, 1986.

Alred, Gerald J. et al. *Business and Technical Writing: An Annotated Bibliography of Books 1880-1980*. Metuchen, NJ: Scarecrow Press, 1981.

American Library Association. *ALA Library Clip Art*. Chicago: American Library Association, 1983.

American Library Association Video. *A Library Survival Guide: Managing the Problem Situation*. Chicago, 1987.

Anderson, Ronald H. *Selecting and Developing Media for Instruction*. 2nd ed. New York: Van Nostrand Reinhold, 1983.

Anderson, Virgil A. *Training the Speaking Voice*. 3rd ed. New York: Oxford University Press, 1977.

Arth, Marvin and Helen Ashmore. *The Newsletter Editor's Desk Book*. 3rd ed. Shawnee Mission, KS: Parkway Press, 1984.

Association of Research Libraries, Office of Management Studies. SPEC Kit 54. *Internal Communication: Policies and Procedures*. May 1979.

Association of Research Libraries, Office of Management Studies. SPEC Kit 55. *Internal Communication: Staff and Supervisory Roles*. June 1979.

Association of Research Libraries, Office of Management Studies. SPEC Kit 56. *External Communication*. July/August 1979.

Atwater, Eastwood. *"I Hear You": Listening Skills to Make You a Better Manager*. Englewood Cliffs, NJ: Prentice-Hall, 1982.

Auster, Ethel, ed. *Managing Online Reference Services*. New York: Neal-Schuman, 1986.

Auster, Ethel and Stephen B. Lawton. "Search Interview Techniques and Information Gain as antecedents of user satisfaction with online bibliographic retrieval," *JASIS*, 35, 2 (1984): 90-103

Baeckler, Virginia. *PR for Pennies: Low-cost Library Public Relations*. Hopewell, NJ: Sources, 1978.

Baeckler, Virginia. *Sparkle! PR for Library Staff*. Hopewell, NJ: Sources, 1980.

Baird, Lloyd S., Craig Eric Schneier, and Dugan Laird, eds. *The Training and Development Source Book*. Amherst, MA: Human Resource Development Press, 1983.

Bales, Robert F. *Interaction Process Analysis*. Reading, MA: Addison-Wesley, 1950.

Bareham, S. "Improve Your Public Speaking," *Emergency Librarian*, 16, 1 (September/October 1988): 21-25.

Bateson, Gregory. *Steps to an Ecology of Mind*. San Francisco: Chandler Publishing Co., 1972.

Beach, Mark. *Editing Your Newsletter: A Guide to Writing, Design, and Production*. 2nd ed. Portland, OR: Coast to Coast Books, 1982

Berger, Patricia. "An Investigation of the Relationship Between Public Relations Activities and Budget Allocation in Public Libraries," *Information Processing and Management*, 15, 4 (1979): 179-193.

Berger, Peter L. and Thomas Luckmann. *The Social Construction of Reality: A Treatise in the Sociology of Knowledge*. New York: Doubleday, 1966.

Bernstein, Richard J. *The Restructuring of Social and Political Theory*. Oxford: Basil Blackwell, 1976.

Berry, Cicely. *Voice and the Actor*. London: Harrap, 1973.

Berry, Cicely. *Your Voice and How to Use It Successfully*. London: Harrap, 1975.

Bianchi, Sue and Jan Butler. *Warm Ups for Meeting Leaders*. Ventura, CA: Quality Groups Publishing, 1984.

Birdwhistell, R. *Kinesics and Context: Essays on Body Motion Communication*. Philadelphia, PA: University of Pennsylvania Press, 1970.

Blicq, Ron S. *Guidelines for Report Writing*. Scarborough, ON: Prentice-Hall, Canada, 1982.

Bligh, Donald A. *What's the Use of Lectures?* 2nd rev. ed. Exeter, UK: Briarhouse, n.d.

Bodart, Joni. *Booktalk! 2: Booktalking for All Ages and Audiences*. 2nd ed. New York: H.W. Wilson Co., 1985.

Borden, Richard C. *Public Speaking as Listeners Like It*. New York: Harper and Row, 1935.

Boss, Richard. *Grant Money and How to Get It: A Handbook for Librarians*. New York: R.R. Bowker, 1980.

Bower, Gordon and Sharon Bower. *Asserting Yourself: A Practical Guide for Positive Change*. Reading, MA: Addison-Wesley, 1976.

Bowman, Mary Ann and Joan D. Stamas. *Written Communication in Business: A Selective Bibliography 1967 to 1977*. Champaign, IL: American Business Communication Association, 1980.

Breivik, Patricia. *Planning the Library Instruction Program*. Chicago: American Library Association, 1982

Brilhart, John K. *Effective Group Discussion*. 5th ed. Dubuque, IA: William. C. Brown, 1986.

Brown, Richard H. *A Poetic for Sociology: Toward a Logic of Discovery for the Human Sciences*. Cambridge: Cambridge University Press, 1977.

Capek, May Ellen S., ed. *A Woman's Thesaurus: An Index of Language Used to Describe and Locate Information by and about Women*. New York: Harper and Row, 1987.

Caputo, Janette S. *The Assertive Librarian*. Phoenix, AZ: Oryx Press, 1984.

Carliner, Saul. "Lists: The Ultimate Organizer for Engineering Writing," *IEEE Transactions on Professional Communication*, PC-30, 4 (Dec. 1987): 218-221.

Carnes, William T. *Effective Meetings for Busy People: Let's Decide It and Go Home*. New York: McGraw-Hill, 1983.

Carparelli, Felicia. "Public Library or Psychiatric Ward?" *American Libraries* (April 1984): 212.

Cassata, Mary B. and Roger C. Palmer, eds. *Reader in Library Communication*. Englewood, CO: Information Handling Services, 1976.

Casteleyn, Mary. *Planning Library Training Programmes*. London: Andre Deutsch, 1981.

Cawelti, John. *Adventure, Mystery and Romance: Formula Stories as Art and Popular Culture*. Chicago: University of Chicago Press, 1976.

Chambers, Aidan. *Booktalk: Occasional Writing on Literature and Children.* London: The Bodley Head, 1985.

Chelton, Mary K. "Booktalking: You Can Do It," *School Library Journal,* 22 (April 1976): 39-43.

Chicago Manual of Style: for Authors, Editors, and Copywriters, 13th ed. Chicago: University of Chicago Press, 1982

Clark, Alice S. and Kay F. Jones, eds. *Teaching Librarians to Teach: On the Job Training for Bibliographic Instruction Librarians.* Metuchen, NJ: Scarecrow Press, 1986.

Cole, John Y. and Carol S. Gold, eds. *Reading in America: Selected Findings of the Book Industry Study Groups 1978 Study.* Washington, DC: Library of Congress, 1979.

Conroy, Barbara and Barbara Schindler-Jones. *Improving Communication in the Library.* Phoenix, AZ: Oryx Press, 1986.

Conroy, Barbara. *Learning Packaged To Go: A Directory and Guide to Staff Development and Training Packages.* Phoenix, AZ: Oryx Press, 1984.

Conroy, Barbara. *Library Staff Development and Continuing Education: Principles and Practices.* Littleton, CO: Libraries Unlimited, 1978.

Conyers, A. *Guidelines for Training in Libraries.* 2nd ed. *The Evaluation of Staff Training, Vol. 1.* London: The Library Association, 1986.

Corbett, Edward P. *Classical Rhetoric for the Modern Student.* 2nd ed. New York: Oxford University Press, 1971.

Corry, Emmett. *Grants for Libraries: A Guide to Public and Private Funding Programs and Proposal Writing Techniques.* Littleton, CO: Libraries Unlimited, 1982.

Craig, Robert L., ed. *The Training and Development Handbook.* 2nd ed. New York: McGraw-Hill, 1976.

Creth, Sheila D. *Effective On-the-Job Training.* Chicago: American Library Association, 1986.

Dair, Carl. *Design with Type.* Toronto: University of Toronto Press, 1967.

Dalton, Phyllis I. *Library Service to the Deaf and Hearing Impaired.* Phoenix, AZ: Oryx Press, 1985.

Dance, James C. *Public Relations for the Smaller Library.* Small Libraries Publication no. 4. Chicago: LAMA, ALA, 1979.

Delberg, Andre L. et al. *Group Techniques for Program Planning: A Guide to Nominal Group and Delphi Processes.* Middleton, WI: Green Briar Press, 1986.

Dervin, Brenda. "Useful Theory for Librarianship: Communication Not Information," *Drexel Library Quarterly,* 13, 3 (July 1977): 16-32.

Dervin, Brenda and Kathleen Clark. *ASQ: Asking Significant Questions. Alternate Tools for Information Need and Accountability Assessments by Libraries.* Sacramento, CA: Peninsula Library System, July 1987.

Dervin, Brenda and Patricia Dewdney. "Neutral Questioning: A New Approach to the Reference Interview," *RQ,* 25, 4 (Summer 1986): 506-513.

Dewdney, Patricia and Catherine S. Ross. "Effective Question-asking in Library Instruction," *RQ* 25, 4 (Summer 1986): 451-454.

Dixon, John, ed. *Fiction in Libraries.* London: The Library Association, 1986.

Dobrin, David. "Do Not Grind Armadillo Armor in this Mill," *IEEE Transactions on Professional Communication,* PC-28, 4 (December 1985): 30-37.

Dowding, Martin. "Problem Patrons: What are they Doing in the Library?" *Quill and Quire* (November 1985): 4-6.

Dreyfuss, Henry, ed. *Symbol Sourcebook: An Authoritative Guide to International Graphic Symbols.* New York: McGraw-Hill, 1972.

Duca, Diane J. and John E. Trapman. *Nonprofit Boards: A Practical Guide to Roles, Responsibilities and Performance.* Phoenix, AZ: Oryx Press, 1986.

Eastman, Ann H. and Roger H. Parent, eds. *Great Library Promotion Ideas: JCD Library Public Relations Award Winners and Notables.* Chicago: American Library Association, 1984.

Edwards, Margaret A. *The Fair Garden and the Swarm of Beasts: The Library and the Young Adult.* New York: Hawthorn, 1969.

Ehninger, Douglas et al. *Principles and Types of Speech Communication.* 10th ed. Grenview, IL: Scott, Foresman, 1986.

Eichman, T.L. "The Complex Nature of Opening Reference Questions," *RQ,* 17, 4 (Spring 1978): 212-222.

Emery, Richard. *Staff Communication in Libraries.* London: Clive Bingley, 1975.

Euster, Joanne R. *Changing Patterns in Communication in Large Academic Libraries.* Occasional Paper no. 6. Washington, DC: Association of Research Libraries, Office of Management Studies. 1981.

Evans, David R. et. al. *Essential Interviewing: A Programmed Approach to Effective Communication.* 2nd ed. Monterey, CA: Brooks/Cole, 1983.

Farace, Richard V. et al. *Communicating and Organizing.* Reading, MA: Addison-Wesley, 1977.

Fearing, Bertie E. and Thomas M. Sawyer. "Speech for Technical Communicators: A Bibliography," *IEEE Transactions on Professional Communication,* PC-23, 1 (March 1980): 53-61.

Ferguson, Douglas. "Marketing Online Services in the University" in Blaise Cronin, ed. *The Marketing of Library and Information Services.* London: ASLIB, 1981.

Fielden, John S. and Ronald E. Dulek. *Bottom-Line Business Writing.* Englewood Cliffs, NJ: Prentice-Hall, 1983.

Fisher, Hilda B. *Improving Voice and Articulation.* 2nd ed. Boston: Houghton Mifflin, 1975.

Flexner, Jennie. *A Readers' Advisory Service.* New York: American Association for Adult Education, 1934.

Franklin, Linda Campbell. *Display and Publicity Ideas for Libraries.* Jefferson, NC: McFarland and Co., 1985.

Geertz, Clifford. *Local Knowledge: Further Essays in Interpretive Anthropology.* New York: Basic Books, 1983.

Gers, Ralph and Lillie J. Seward. "Improving Reference Performance: Results of a Statewide Study," *Library Journal* (November 1985): 32-35.

Goodale, James G. *The Fine Art of Interviewing.* Englewood Cliffs, NJ: Prentice-Hall, 1980.

Gordon, Thomas with Ruth Gordon Sands. *P.E.T. in Action*. New York: Bantam Books, 1987.

Gordon, Thomas. *P.E.T.: Parent Effectiveness Training*. New York: New American Library, 1975.

Gothberg, Helen M. "Managing Difficult People: Patrons (and Others)," *Reference Librarian*, 19 (1987): 269-282.

Gray, Bill. *Tips on Type*. New York: Van Nostrand Reinhold, 1983.

Gunning, Robert. "The Fog Index After Twenty Years," *The Journal of Business Communication*, 6, 2 (Winter 1968): 3-13.

Hackett, Alice Payne. *80 Years of Bestsellers, 1895-1975*. New York: R.R. Bowker, 1977.

Haines, Helen E. *Living with Books: The Art of Book Selection*. 2nd ed. New York: Columbia University Press, 1950.

Hall, Edward T. *The Silent Language*. Garden City, NY: Doubleday, 1959.

Hall, Mary. *Developing Skills in Proposal Writing*. 2nd ed. Portland, OR: Continuing Education Publications, 1977.

Harmon, Robert E. *Improving Administrative Manuals*. New York: Research and Information Service, American Management Associations, 1982.

Harnack, R. Victor et al. *Group Discussion: Theory and Technique*. 2nd ed. Englewood Cliffs, NJ: Prentice-Hall, 1977.

Hart, Lois B. and J. Gordon Scheicher. *A Conference and Workshop Planner's Manual*. New York: AMACOM, 1979.

Hartley, James. "Eighty Ways of Improving Instructional Text," *IEEE Transactions on Professional Communication*, PC-24, 1 (March 1981): 17-27.

Hartley, James. *Designing Instructional Text*. 2nd ed. New York: Nichols Pub., 1985.

Hernon, P. and C.R. McClure. "Unobtrusive Reference Testing: the 55% rule," *Library Journal*, 111 (April 15, 1986): 37-41.

Hoffman, Irene and Opritsa Popa. "Library Orientation and Instruction for International Students: the University of California-Davis Experience," *RQ*, 25, 3 (Spring 1986): 356-360.

Hunt, Gary T. *Effective Communication*. Englewood Cliffs, NJ: Prentice-Hall, 1985.

Ivey, Allen E. *Intentional Interviewing and Counseling*. Monterey, CA: Brooks/ Cole, 1983

Ivey, Allen E. and Jerry Authier. *Microcounseling: Innovations in Interviewing, Counseling, Psychotherapy and Psychoeducation*. 2nd ed. Springfield, IL: C.C.Thomas, 1978.

Ivey, Allen E. *Counseling and Psychotherapy: Skills, Theories, and Practices*. Englewood Cliffs, NJ: Prentice-Hall, 1980.

Janis, Irving L. *Victims of Groupthink*. Boston: Houghton Mifflin, 1973.

Janke, Richard V. "Presearch Counselling for Client Searchers (End-users)," *Online*, 9, 5 (1975):13-26.

Jennerich, E.Z. and E.J. Jennerich. *The Reference Interview as a Creative Art*. Littleton, CO: Libraries Unlimited, 1987.

Johnson, David W. and Frank P. Johnson. *Joining Together: Group Theory and Group Skills*. 3rd ed. Englewood Cliffs, NJ: Prentice-Hall, 1987.

Jones, Barbara S. *Written Communication for Today's Manager.* New York: Lebhar-Friedman Books, 1980.

Kamerman, Sylvia, ed. *Book Reviewing: A Guide to Writing Book Reviews for Newspapers, Magazines, Radio, and Television.* Boston: The Writer, Inc., 1978.

Kepes, Gyorgy, ed. *Sign, Image, Symbol.* New York: George Brazaller, 1960.

Kies, Cosette. *Marketing and Public Relations for Libraries.* (The Library Administration Series, no. 10). Metuchen, NJ: Scarecrow Press, 1987.

Killingsworth, M. Jimmie. "A Bibliography on Proposal Writing," *IEEE Transactions on Professional Communication,* PC-26, 2 (June 1983): 79-83.

King, Geraldine. "Open and Closed Questions: The Reference Interview," *RQ,* 12, 2 (Winter 1972): 157-160.

Klauss, Rudi and Bernard Bass, eds. *Interpersonal Communication in Organizations.* New York: Academic Press, 1982.

Kleper, Michael L. *The Illustrated Handbook of Desktop Publishing and Typesetting.* Blue Ridge Summit, PA: Tab Books, 1987.

Knowles, Malcolm S. *The Adult Learner: A Neglected Species.* 3rd ed. Houston: Gulf Publishing, 1984.

Knowles, Malcolm S. *The Modern Practice of Adult Education: From Pedagogy to Andragogy.* Rev. ed. New York: Cambridge Book Co., 1980.

Kohn, Rita and Krysta Tepper. *You Can Do It: A PR Skills Manual for Librarians.* Metuchen, NJ: Scarecrow Press, 1981.

Laird, Dugan. *Approaches to Training and Development.* 2nd ed. Reading, MA: Addison-Wesley, 1985.

Laird, Dugan. *Writing for Results: Principles and Practices.* Reading, MA: Addison-Wesley, 1978.

Lam, Errol R. "The Reference Interview: Some Intercultural Considerations," *RQ,* 27, 3 (Spring 1988): 390-393.

Larson, Dale, ed. *Teaching Psychological Skills: Models for Giving Psychology Away.* Monterey, CA: Brooks/Cole, 1984.

Leech, Thomas. *How to Prepare, Stage and Deliver Winning Presentations.* New York: AMACOM, 1982.

Lesikar, Raymond V. *Business Communication: Theory and Application.* 5th ed. Homewood, IL: Richard D. Irwin, 1984.

Lesikar, Raymond V. and Mary P. Lyons. *Report Writing for Business.* 7th ed. Homewood, IL: Richard D. Irwin, 1986.

Levine, Mindy, and Susan Frank. *In Print: A Concise Guide to Graphic Arts and Printing for Small Business and Nonprofit Organizations.* Englewood Cliffs, NJ: Prentice-Hall, 1984.

Library Video Network. *A Library Survival Guide: Managing the Problem Situation.* Chicago: American Library Association, 1986. *Coaching: Practice Makes Perfect.* Chicago: American Library Association, 1986. *Does This Answer Your Question?* Chicago: American Library Association, 1985. *The Difficult Reference Question.* Chicago: American Library Association, 1986. *Who's First . . .You're Next.* Chicago: American Library Association, 1980.

Lieberman, J. Ben. *Type and Type Faces*. 2nd ed. New Rochelle, NY: The Myriade Press, 1978.

Lindsey, Jonathan A., ed. *Performance Evaluation: A Management Basic for Librarians*. Phoenix, AZ: Oryx Press, 1986.

Lubans, John Jr., ed. *Progress in Educating the Library User*. New York: R.R. Bowker, 1978.

Lynch, M.J. "Reference Interviews in Public Libraries," *The Library Quarterly,* 48 (April 1978): 119-142.

Maggio, Rosalie. *Nonsexist Wordfinder: A Dictionary of Gender-Free Usage*. Phoenix, AZ: Oryx Press, 1987.

Mallery, Mary S. and David L. Perkins. *A Sign System for Libraries*. Chicago: American Library Association, 1982.

Marsh, Patrick O. *Messages That Work: A Guide to Communication Design*. Englewood Cliffs, NJ: Educational Technology Publications, 1983.

Marshall, Joan K., comp. *On Equal Terms: A Thesaurus for Nonsexist Indexing and Cataloging*. New York: Neal-Schuman, 1977.

Materka, Pat R. *Workshops and Seminars: Planning, Promoting, Producing, Profiting*. Englewood Cliffs, NJ: Prentice-Hall, 1985.

Mathews, A.J. *Communicate! A Librarian's Guide to Interpersonal Relations*. Chicago: American Library Association, 1983.

McGarry, Kevin. *Communication, Knowledge and the Librarian*. London: Clive Bingley, 1975.

McLaughlin, W. Keith and Evelyn Piush. "Planning Checklist for Seminars or Workshops," *Canadian Library Journal* (June 1980): 175-177.

Meek, Margaret."Questions of Response," *Signal,* 31 (January 1980): 29-35.

Mehrabian, Albert. *Public Places and Private Spaces: The Psychology of Work, Play and Living Environments*. New York: Basic Books, 1980.

Mendelson, Michael. "Business Prose and the Nature of the Plain Style," *The Journal of Business Communication,* 24, 2 (Spring 1987): 3-18.

Michell, Gillian and Roma Harris. "Evaluating the Competence of Information Providers," *RQ,* 27, 1 (Fall 1987): 95-105.

Miller, Casey and Kate Swift. *The Handbook of Nonsexist Writing For Writers, Editors, and Speakers*. New York: Barnes and Noble, 1980.

Modley, Rudolf assisted by William R. Myers. *Handbook of Pictorial Symbols: 3,250 Examples from International Sources*. New York: Dover Books, 1976.

Moran, Irene E. *The Library Public Relations Recipe Book*. Chicago: American Library Association, 1978.

Moran, Michael and Debra Journet, eds. *Research on Technical Communication: A Bibliographic Sourcebook*. Westport, CT: Greenwood Press, 1985.

Munce, Howard. *Graphics Handbook: A Beginner's Guide to Design, Copy Fitting and Printing Procedures*. Cincinnati: North Light Publishers, 1982.

Munter, Mary. *Guide to Managerial Communication*. 2nd ed. Englewood Cliffs, NJ: Prentice-Hall, 1987.

Nadsiejka, David. "Can They Read When You Speak?" *Bulletin of the American Society for Information Science,* 13 (April/May 1987): 22-23.

Nichols, Ralph G. and Leonard A. Stevens. *Are You Listening?* New York: McGraw-Hill, 1957.

Nilsen, Alleen Pace and Kenneth L. Donelson. *Literature for Today's Young Adults.* 2nd ed. Glenview, IL: Scott-Foresman, 1985.

Northey, Margot. *Impact: A Guide to Business Communication.* Scarborough, ON: Prentice-Hall Canada, 1986.

O'Donnell, Peggy. *Public Library Development Program: Manual for Trainers.* Chicago and London: American Library Association, 1988.

Ogilvy, James. *Many Dimensional Man: Decentralizing Self, Society, and the Sacred.* New York: Oxford University Press, 1977.

Oliu, Walter E. et al. *Writing That Works: How to Write Effectively on the Job.* 2nd ed. New York: St. Martin's Press, 1984.

Page, William T. "Helping the Nervous Presenter: Research and Prescriptions," *The Journal of Business Communication,* 22, 2 (Spring 1985): 9-19.

Parr, Jim. *Any Other Business: How to be a Good Committee Person.* Toronto: Clarke, Irwin, 1977.

Paxson, William C. *Write It Now! A Timesaving Guide to Writing Better.* Reading, MA: Addison-Wesley, 1985.

Pejtersen, Annelise and Jutta Austin. "Fiction Retrieval: Experimental Design and Evaluation of a search system based on users' value criteria," *Journal of Documentation,* 39, 4 (December 1983): 230-246; part 2, 40, 1 (March 1984): 25-35.

Penland, Patrick R. *Communication for Librarians.* Pittsburgh, PA: University of Pittsburgh Bookstore, 1971.

Pfeiffer, J. William and John E. Jones, eds. *Small Group Training Theory and Practice: Selected Readings.* La Jolla, CA: University Associates, 1977.

Pfeiffer, J. William and John E. Jones. *A Handbook of Structured Experiences for Human Relations Training.* Vols. 1-8. LaJolla, CA: University Associates, 1973-1981.

Pocket Pal: A Graphic Arts Production Handbook, 13th ed. New York: International Paper Company.

Pollet, Dorothy and Peter C. Haskell, eds. *Sign Systems for Libraries: Solving the Wayfinding Problem.* London: R.R. Bowker, 1979.

Pollet, Dorothy. "You Can Get There from Here," *Wilson Library Bulletin,* 50 (February 1976): 456-62.

Powell, Judith W. and Robert B. LeLieuvre. *Peoplework: Communications Dynamics for Librarians.* Chicago: American Library Association, 1979.

Powell, Ronald R. "Writing the Research Proposal" in *Basic Research Methods for Librarians.* Norwood, NJ: Ablex, 1985.

Prytherch, Ray. *Handbook of Library Training Practice.* Aldershot, Hampshire: Gower Publishing Co., 1986.

Prytherch, Ray, ed. *Staff Training in Libraries: The British Experience.* Brookfield, VT: Gower Publishing Co., 1986.

Rader, Hannelore B. "Library Orientation and Instruction," *Reference Services Review,* 15, 2 (Summer 1987): 65-76.

Read, Nat B. Jr. "How to Prepare for the TV Interview," *IEEE Transactions on Professional Communication,* PC-23 (March 1980): 45-47.

Rehnberg, Marilyn, ed. *Self-Assessment Guide for Staff Communication.* St. Paul, MN: Office of Public Library & Interlibrary Cooperation, 1984.

Renner, Peter Franz. *The Lecturer's Survival Kit: A Handbook for Teachers of Adults.* 2nd ed. Vancouver, BC: Training Associates, 1983.

Reynolds, Linda and Stephen Barett. *Signs and Guiding for Libraries.* London: Clive Bingley, 1981.

Robert, Gen. Henry M. *The Scott Foresman Robert's Rules of Order, Newly Revised.* Glenview, IL: Scott, Foresman, 1981.

Robertson, Carolyn, comp. *Bibliography: The Reference Interview* (pamphlet). Ottawa: Library Documentation Centre, National Library of Canada, 1985.

Rochman, Hazel. *Tales of Love and Terror: Booktalking the Classics, Old and New.* Chicago and London: American Library Association, 1987.

Rogers, Carl and Richard Farson. "Active Listening" in Richard Huseman et al, eds. *Readings in Interpersonal and Organizational Communication.* 2nd ed. Boston: Holbrook Press, 1973.

Rogers, Carl. *On Becoming A Person.* Boston: Houghton Mifflin, 1961.

Rogers, Everett M. and D. Lawrence Kincaid. *Communication Networks: Towards a New Paradigm for Research.* New York: The Free Press, 1981

Rogers, Everett M. and F. Floyd Shoemaker. *Communication of Innovations: A Cross-Cultural Approach.* New York: The Free Press, 1971.

Rogoff, Rosalind. *The Training Wheel: A Simple Model for Instructional Design.* New York: John Wiley, 1987.

Rosenberg, Betty. *Genreflecting: A Guide to Reading Interests in Genre Fiction.* 2nd ed. Littleton, CO: Libraries Unlimited, 1987.

Ross, Catherine Sheldrick and Patricia Dewdney. "Reference Interviewing Skills: Twelve Common Questions," *Public Libraries* (Spring 1986): 7-9.

Ross, Catherine Sheldrick. "How to Find Out What People Really Want to Know," *Reference Librarian,* 16 (Winter 1986): 19-30.

Rummel, Kathleen Kelly and Esther Perica, eds. *Persuasive Public Relations for Libraries.* Chicago: American Library Association, 1983.

Salter, Charles A. and Jeffrey L. *On the Frontlines: Coping with the Library's Problem Patrons.* Englewood, CO: Libraries Unlimited, 1988.

Sellen, Betty-C., ed. *Librarian/Author: A Practical Guide on How to Get Published.* New York: Neal-Schuman, 1985.

Selzer, Jack. "Readability is a Four-Letter Word," *The Journal of Business Communication,* 18, 4 (Fall 1981): 22-30.

Seybold, John W. "The Desktop Publishing Phenomenon," *Byte* (May 1987): 149-154.

Seybold, John W. and Fritz Dressler. *Publishing from the Desktop.* New York: Bantam Books, 1987.

Shannon, Claude C. and Warren Weaver. *The Mathematical Theory of Communication.* Urbana: University of Illinois Press, 1949.

Shelby, Annette N. "The Theoretical Bases of Persuasion," *The Journal of Business Communication,* 23, 1 (Winter 1986): 5-29.

Sherman, Steve. *ABC's of Library Promotion*. 2nd ed. Metuchen, NJ: Scarecrow Press, 1980.

Shuman, Bruce A. *The River Bend Casebook: Problems in Public Library Service*. Phoenix, AZ: Oryx Press, 1981.

Shuman, Bruce A. *River Bend Revisited: The Problem Patron in the Library*. Phoenix, AZ: Oryx Press, 1984.

Shuman, Bruce A. *River Bend in Transition: Managing Change in Public Libraries*. Phoenix, AZ: Oryx Press, 1987.

Simerly, Robert G. and Associates. *Strategic Planning and Leadership in Continuing Education*. San Francisco, CA: Jossey-Bass, 1987.

Skillin, Marjorie E. and R. Gay. *Words into Type*. 3rd ed. Englewood Cliffs, NJ: Prentice-Hall, 1974.

Skopec, Eric W. "A Problem-solving Approach to Preparing Professional Presentations," *IEEE Transactions of Professional Communication*, PC-26, 1 (March 1983): 30-35.

SLA/Fashion Institute. *Image Builders* (60-minute audio cassette). Special Libraries Association, 1987.

Somerville, Aileen N. "The Presearch Reference Interview: A Step-by-step Guide," *Database*, 33 (February 1982): 32-38.

Spaid, Ora. *The Consummate Trainer*. Englewood Cliffs, NJ: Prentice-Hall, 1986.

Spencer, Herbert and Linda Reynolds. *Directional Signing and Labelling in Libraries and Museums: A Review of Current Theory and Practice*. London: Royal College of Art, 1977.

Spradley, James P. *The Ethnographic Interview*. New York: Holt, Rinehart and Winston, 1979.

Stephan, Sandy et al. "Reference Breakthrough in Maryland," *Public Libraries*, 27, 4 (Winter 1988): 178-181.

Stevens, Norman D. and Nora B. Stevens, eds. *Author's Guide to Journals in Library and Information Science*. New York: Haworth Press, 1981.

Stevens, Peter S. *A Handbook of Regular Patterns: An Introduction to Symmetry in Two Dimensions*. Cambridge, MA: The MIT Press, 1981.

Stewart, Charles J. and William B. Cash. *Interviewing: Principles and Practices*. 5th ed. Dubuque, IA: William C. Brown, 1987.

Stone, Janet and Jane Bachner. *Speaking Up: A Book for Every Woman Who Wants to Speak Effectively*. New York: McGraw-Hill, 1977.

Strunk, William, Jr. and E.B. White. *The Elements of Style*. 3rd ed. New York: Macmillan, 1979.

Stueart, Robert D. and Barbara B. Moran. *Library Management*. 3rd ed. Littleton, CO: Libraries Unlimited, 1987.

Sutter, Jan. *Slinging Ink: A Practical Guide to Producing Booklets, Newspapers, and Ephemeral Publications*. Los Altos, CA: William Kaufman, 1982.

"Ten Tips for Preparing Guest Speakers: Good Advice from the Connecticut Friends," *The U*n*a*b*a*s*h*e*d Librarian*, 59 (1987): 9.

The 3M Meeting Management Team. *How to Run Better Business Meetings*. New York: McGraw-Hill, 1987.

Thomas, Carol H. and James L. Thomas, eds. *Meeting the Needs of the Handicapped: A Resource for Teachers and Librarians.* Phoenix, AZ: Oryx Press, 1985.

Timm, Paul R. *Functional Business Presentations: Getting Across.* Englewood Cliffs, NJ: Prentice-Hall, 1981.

Tinker, Miles A. *The Legibility of Print.* Ames, IA: Iowa State University Press, 1963.

Tompkins, Jane P. *Reader-Response Criticism: From Formalism to Post-Structuralism.* Baltimore and London: Johns Hopkins University Press, 1986.

Travis, A.B. *The Handbook Handbook: The Complete How-To Guide to Publishing Policies and Procedures.* New York: R.R. Bowker, 1984

Tufte, Edward R. *The Visual Display of Quantitative Information.* Cheshire, CT: Graphics Press, 1983.

Turnbull, Arthur T. and Russell N. Baird. *The Graphics of Communication: Typography, Layout, Design, Production.* 4th ed. New York: Holt, Rinehart and Winston, 1980.

Turner, Bonnie L. and Rondi Downs. *Patron Relations: A Survival Manual.* Yakima Valley Regional Library, WA: ED 254255 MF01, 1983.

Uris, Dorothy. *To Sing in English: A Guide to Improved Diction.* New York: Boosey and Hawkes, 1971.

Waite Group. *Desktop Publishing Bible.* Indianapolis, IN: Howard W. Sams & Co., 1987.

Wales, LaRae H. *A Practical Guide to Newsletter Editing and Design.* 2nd ed. Ames, IA: Iowa State University Press, 1976.

Walford, A.J., ed. *Reviews and Reviewing: A Guide.* Phoenix, AZ: Oryx Press, 1986.

Warncke, Ruth. *Planning Library Workshops and Institutes.* Chicago: American Library Association, 1976.

White, Jan V. *Editing by Design: A Guide to Effective Word-and-Picture Communication for Editors and Designers.* 2nd ed. New York: R.R. Bowker, 1982

White, Jan V. *Mastering Graphics: Design and Production Made Easy.* New York: R.R. Bowker, 1983.

White, Marilyn Domas. "The Dimensions of the Reference Interview," *RQ* 20, 4 (Summer 1981): 373-381.

Wilkinson, C.W. et al. *Communicating Through Letters and Reports.* 8th ed. Homewood, IL: Richard D. Irwin, 1983.

Willis, Jerry. *Desktop Publishing with your IBM PC and Compatible.* Tucson, AZ: Knight Ridder Press, 1987.

Woelfle, Robert, ed. *A Guide to Better Technical Presentations.* New York: IEEE Press, 1975.

Wolff, F.I. et al. *Perceptive Listening.* New York: Holt, Rinehart and Winston, 1983.

Xicom-Video Arts. *Awkward Customers* (16mm film or videocassette, color, 24 min.) *It's All Right, It's Only a Customer* (16mm film or videocassette, color, 29 min). 1973. *Meetings, Bloody Meetings* (16mm film or videocassette, color, 30 min). 1976.

Yates, Rochelle. *A Librarian's Guide to Telephone Reference Service.* Hamden, CT: Shoe String Press, 1986.

Zelko, Harold P. and Marjorie E. Zelko. *How to Make Speeches for All Occasions.* New York: Doubleday, 1979.

Zinsser, William. *Writing with a Word Processor.* New York: Harper and Row, 1983.

Zinsser, William. *On Writing Well: An Informal Guide to Writing Nonfiction.* 3rd ed. New York: Harper and Row, 1988.

Zweizig, Douglas. "The Informing Function of Adult Services in Public Libraries," *RQ,* 18, 3 (Spring 1979): 240-244.

INDEX

Dr. Catherine Sheldrick Ross is Associate Professor, and Dr. Patricia Dewdney is Assistant Professor at the School of Library and Information Science, University of Western Ontario, London, Ontario, Canada.

Dr. Bill Katz is Professor at the School of Library and Information Science, State University of New York at Albany. He is the author of many distinguished works in library science.

Book design: Gloria Brown
Cover design: Gregory Apicella
Typography: Roberts/Churcher